"Readers will hear a united shout   's riveting collection of stories, *When Go*   *ys*, the tales in this book remind us to have courage. In sad moments, the stories bring the promise of joy. And on ordinary days, the stories encourage us to pay attention and listen to the voice of God in our own lives. Doyle has given us a great gift in this book—the opportunity to hear God speak and act in the lives of real people."

—Rev. Rochelle Y. Melander,
Write Now! coach and author of *A Generous Presence*

"I loved *When God Spoke to Me*! I've now added it to my library of resources for developing sermons. These fantastic stories are powerful illustrations of the Truth principles of love, compassion, and forgiveness that I teach."

—Rev. Lane Williams, Unity of Vermont

"In *When God Spoke to Me,* DavidPaul Doyle reveals intimate stories of God speaking to ordinary people every day. And through these inspiring examples and accounts, readers learn that when we listen to God and follow His voice, we experience more than an ordinary existence; we begin to take hold of the extraordinary life God wants for us every day."

—Ed Young, senior pastor, Fellowship Church

"This book has perfect timing. Never before has the world been more ready and open to receive the message that *When God Spoke To Me* brings. If you would like to learn how to open to divine guidance and healing, this is the book for you. Pick up two copies; one for you, and one for someone you really care about."

—Keith Leon,
"The Singing Trainer," and best-selling author
of *Who Do You Think You Are?*

"I have been reading your book daily and I can't put it down. It has enlivened my life and touched my soul. I find my self in almost every story. I highly recommend this book to anyone who wants to understand the many ways God speaks to us."

—Ken D. Foster, author of *Ask and You Will Succeed*

"Each and every story included in this book speaks to me, and of my experience. When we hear what we believe to be the voice of the God of our understanding, our hearts are forever changed. Your heart will never be the same after you read these stories, told by those who have heard and understood what a loving and merciful God has spoken directly to them."

—Lama K. T. ("Thubten") Shedrup Gyatso, Portland, Oregon

"This book reeks of hope. These raw stories of genuine people and their encounters with God have a compelling way to help us re-member hope, restoration, and goodness. It gives us living, breathing examples of how God scoops us up when all is lost."

—Daniel McIntosh, pastor, Believer's Church, Tulsa, Oklahoma

"I loved this book! I told all the ministers who graduated from seminary with me to read it! These heartwarming stories brought me to tears, not tears of sadness, but tears of joy knowing that the tangible love and presence of God is with us always."

—Rev. Brad Langdon, Unity Church of Anderson, Indiana

"It seems that God does not check on either one's green card, photo ID, or denominational membership before He speaks! Nothing seems cooked up or even unlikely about these testimonies from a range of people. As for the rest of us: are we really listening?"

—Harvey Cox, Harvard Professor of Divinity,
author of *The Future of Faith*

"You'll weep as you read contributors' experiences with cancer, paralysis, drug addiction, depression, the 9/11 tragedy, and the deaths of loved ones…and you'll rejoice as they describe the contentment, love, freedom, and faith that touched their hearts…as promised in Proverbs 3:6: "In all your ways acknowledge Him, and He shall direct your paths." *When God Spoke to Me* is 256 uplifting pages of proof that if you listen for His voice everywhere you go, He will keep you on track!"

—Loree Lough, best-selling Christian author of
nearly 80 award-winning books

"DavidPaul Doyle's *When God Spoke to Me* is an inspirational, heart-warming, and uplifting collection of stories that demonstrate how God's guidance is always there for us to heal and support our lives."

—Dr. Joe Rubino, founder, CenterForPersonalReinvention.com

"I've always loved stories about miracles. And I really do believe God is capable of doing above and beyond what we can imagine. The stories in *When God Spoke to Me* are no exception. Both moving and inspirational, I challenge you to "just read one" and see if you don't feel a genuine rush of joy. What a great reminder that God is good and gracious and kind!"

—Melody Carlson, author of more than 150 books

"As you read the real-life stories of ordinary people who heard the Voice of God, your hope will be renewed. You will learn that God is ever present and desires to interact with you on a personal level, giving divine guidance, courage, assurance, love, mercy, and grace to those who take the time to listen with obedient hearts and minds."

—Germaine Copeland, founder of Word Ministries, Inc. and
author of the *Prayers That Avail Much* book series

"Is God silent? Does He still speak? Thankfully DavidPaul Doyle has sought the answers. The resulting stories of those who have listened to God's voice and obeyed are profoundly moving—even for a skeptic like me."

——Phil Callaway, author and speaker

WHEN GOD SPOKE TO ME

*The Inspiring Stories of
Ordinary People Who Have
Received Divine Guidance
and Wisdom*

DavidPaul Doyle

New Page Books
A Division of The Career Press, Inc.
Franklin Lakes, N.J.

WHEN GOD SPOKE TO ME
EDITED AND TYPESET BY KARA KUMPEL
Cover design by Wes Youssi/Tweedfiero
Printed in the U.S.A. by Courier

To order this title, please call toll-free 1-800-CAREER-1 (NJ and Canada: 201-848-0310) to order using VISA or MasterCard, or for further information on books from Career Press.

The Career Press, Inc., 3 Tice Road, PO Box 687,
Franklin Lakes, NJ 07417
www.careerpress.com
www.newpagebooks.com

Library of Congress Cataloging-in-Publication Data

Doyle, DavidPaul
    When God Spole to me : the inspiring stories of ordinary people who have received divine guidance and wisdom . by DavidPaul Doyle.
        p. cm.
    Includes index.
    ISBN 978-1-60163-106-0
    ISBN 978-1-60163-737-6
        1. Spiritual life--Anecdotes. I. Title.

BL624.D695 2010
204'.40922--dc22

2009050342

ACKNOWLEDGMENTS

I would like to thank everyone who courageously submitted their personal accounts of hearing God's Voice for this book. Their bravery, vulnerability, and willingness to share such intimate life-changing experiences is a tremendous gift to us all. I also want to thank my wife, Candace, and my daughter, Hannah, for always supporting me in pursuing my dreams; my literary agent, Cathy Hemming, and her assistant, Rajul Punjabi, for believing in this project and never giving up; and my editor, Anita Grimm, for her generosity, dedication, and skill, without which this book might never have happened.

CONTENTS

Introduction...13

She Is Mine...15

The Subway Train That Saved My Life.................19

The Whisper in My Dreams.................................23

The Lesson From the Tattooed Angel.......................25

A Prisoner's Experience.......................................28

Goose Bumps From Heaven.................................30

Lord, Stay With Me...34

The Buick That Changed My Life.........................36

Throw-Up Yellow Just Like Me............................40

The Man Who Hears the Voice.............................43

The Day the Twin Towers Fell.............................48

A Surrogate Sermon...50

Tiny Prayers...54

The Gift of Grace...57

Remembering Oneness...60

Lukie's Love...62

From Monster to Emissary.................................66

The Listener...70

Initiation..74

New Beginning...76

The Shade...79

Drive South...81

On Loan..85

Through the Mouth of a Stranger...........................89

Four Glorious Days..91

Three Words..95

Succumbing to an Unlikely Death..........................98

Now Is the Time, This Is the Place........................102

In My Own Backyard...104

My Angel..107

The Day I Got a New Name.................................108

Just in Time...111

Free at Last...116

Finding a Personal God.......................................119

Clarity...122

The Simplest Thing...123

Brothers and Sisters...125

Healing With God..129

Mom and the Birdhouse......................................132

Cutting Through the Fog of Uncertainty.................134

Journeying to God's Voice...................................137

One Breath at a Time..140

Expressing God's Voice.......................................144

A New Sensation..149

Twist of Faith..152

Falling in Love...156

Love in its Purest Form.......................................159

Don't Judge a Book by its Cover..........................162

God's Whispers...166

Simple Synchronicity...169

Overcoming My "Autism" 174

Tap, Tap, Tap.. 178
A Homeless Man... 181
Awakening...184
Ugly Teddy... 188
God Speaks Up..192
Eggs, Farm Smells, and Hidden Gifts.......................194
Alone but Not Alone..196
Becoming the Change... 200
Follow Me Home.. 203
I Do it for You.. 207
Healing for a Wounded Heart................................209
The Auction.. 212
Finding Peace Amidst Despair................................216
Fall in Love With Yourself.................................... 219
Third Time's the Charm....................................... 222
Coins From the Heart..225
Advice From a Dear Friend................................... 228
Life-Changing Birthday Gift..................................230
He Was There All Along.......................................234
In Conclusion..237
Submit Your Story...243
Index...245
About the Author...251

INTRODUCTION

Have you ever questioned whether your inspiration, insight, or sudden shift in experience was the result of receiving divine guidance or communication? Have you ever thought you received a sign or message from God only to afterward second-guess yourself? How do you know if you are hearing God's Voice or not?

When God Spoke to Me is a collection of inspiring stories from ordinary people that shares the many ways God speaks to all of us in our lives. God speaks to everyone. All it takes to hear His Voice is the desire and willingness to do so.

As these touching accounts from around the world demonstrate, hearing God's Voice has the power to heal our wounds, mend our relationships, provide life-changing guidance and direction when we need it, and instill within us a profound experience of peace, love, and awareness of our union with God.

It is my hope that these heartfelt and moving accounts of hearing God's Voice will help you receive these benefits in your own life, help you recognize how you may already hear God's Voice without knowing it, and inspire you to receive guidance, healing, and communication from God in new and life-changing ways.

Thank you for joining the millions of people around the world who desire to experience God's Voice in their lives. May you find yourself in these stories over and over and over again.

With love and gratitude,

DavidPaul Doyle
Ashland, Oregon
June 2009

She Is Mine

I was terrified—crying out to Him with all of my heart. I couldn't believe God was speaking to me, nor could I believe He would say this...ask this. Not now.

I grew up in a non-religious or spiritual home. We neither read the Bible nor attended church, except for Easter Sunday. I began talking to God at age 13 when I discovered my parents were not my biological parents. It didn't matter that I never heard a response from Him. He was my "imaginary friend."

At 26 I married, and we had our only child 18 months later. Our daughter was hospitalized twice in her first 90 days with different forms of RSV pneumonia. We struggled financially. While I worked two jobs, my husband ran his own resume business so he could stay with our child during the day and prevent another bout of RSV. The new business produced income but took all that it made to continue. We had no health insurance and no way to obtain any for a child who was hospitalized so early in life.

Eight months after her birth, I was involved in a car accident and unable to work for months. I remember thinking, my God, what's next? Why are you punishing me? The stress was unbearable. Times were excruciatingly difficult, and we were approaching financial disaster. For the first time I truly felt helpless, and real depression set in.

One Sunday afternoon, our child suddenly became very ill. Within 15 minutes, she changed from an active two-year-old playing with her toys to a lifeless form lying on our living room floor, unable to keep any food down. Her temperature was 102 degrees and climbing. My mom, who lived right behind me, told me to bring her over. We bathed her in cool water and swabbed her down with alcohol to reduce her fever, but still it soared. We gave her Tylenol, but

15

the medicine wouldn't stay down. Repeated messages we left with her pediatrician's answering service brought no replies.

As she lay on Mom's floor, I suddenly remembered a lady at work who was an evangelical holy roller. At their church, they laid hands on each other and people were healed. The lady never explained how they did it, but I thought it was worth a try. Crying and praying, I kneeled over my child, laid my hands upon her tiny back, and begged God to heal her. I promised God all kinds of things. I begged for forgiveness. I even begged for her illness to be put upon me. My mother watched in amazement.

The doctor finally returned my calls at 6:45 p.m. saying he had called in a prescription to a local pharmacy. It closed at 7:00 p.m. on Sunday and was at least 15 minutes away.

Driving down the road past the church where outdoor sermons were preached from a grounded boat each Sunday, I began to cry hysterically. It hit me that my child could suffer brain damage or die from the high fever. I hated to leave her, but I had to get the medicine. Again I begged God to heal her tiny, innocent body, but this time, I was screaming it out loud in the car through the tears and mucus streaming down my face.

It was then that I heard a firm but loving male voice. The loudness of it seemed to fill the van, but it also seemed to be just in my head. I stopped breathing.

"Will you give her to me?" the voice asked.

"What?!" I screamed. I gulped my first breath in seconds, wiping my eyes and nose on the sleeve of my shirt, and glanced around my van to see if someone had somehow slipped inside.

Again, the voice spoke, louder yet softer somehow. It asked again, "Will you give her to me?"

My mind spun in circles. Had I somehow slipped off of the edge of reality? This was a real possibility considering the stress I'd been under for the past few months. I began a series of small "systems checks." Am I driving? Yes. Is it evening? Yes. Is today Sunday? Yes. I even pinched myself on the arm to be sure I wasn't dreaming or hallucinating. That hurt! The voice waited patiently for me to process what was happening.

"Will you give her to me?" He asked.

"How can you ask me that question?" I screamed. "Are you trying to tell me it's already too late? Have you already taken her and are preparing me so when I get to my mom's house and find she's dead, I can cope with it? Why would you ask this of me?"

I felt so angry and scared that I had actually pulled over into a grocery store parking lot and wondered if I should just go back home. I couldn't stop shaking. If God was taking my child and I headed back home right now, maybe I could spend the last few moments with her in my arms as she left this world and returned to Him.

As this last terrible thought crossed my mind, I realized that, in truth, she was already His. She was "on loan" to us from God. I cried so hard I nearly choked. As this reality sank in, I whispered the answer through my tears.

"Yes, I will give her back to You, if I must."

It was the single most profound moment of my life. My heart was breaking, yet at the same time I was relieved because the fear had gone. I couldn't lose what I didn't possess. This was the first time since her birth that I fully realized my little girl belonged not to me, but to her Creator.

As if He were right there listening to my thoughts, He said, "I created her. I breathed life into her. She is mine."

"I understand," I responded, sobbing. "I don't want to lose her, Father, but I will give her back to you."

"Well done, my good and faithful servant," He said quietly in the most loving voice I'd ever heard.

This startled me almost more than actually hearing the voice. How could I be a good and faithful servant when I don't even attend church regularly?

The pharmacy was now closed, and I arrived back at Mom's house within 20 minutes. Climbing the stairs, an indescribable, surreal peace filled me. I knew I would open that door to find my mother hunched over my daughter's lifeless body. I didn't know how I would handle it.

"Ma-ma," my daughter said, as she greeted me at the door, "I feel all better now."

She had a big cup of juice in one hand and a cherry popsicle in the other as she hugged my leg, turned around, and ran off to play. It was as if she had never been sick at all. The fever was gone, and her appetite had returned as if nothing had happened.

I glanced at my mom who was sitting in her chair munching a popsicle as well.

"What happened to her, Mom?"

"I don't know," Mom replied. "Her temperature shot up to 104 degrees right after you left and I couldn't get her to wake up. I got up to call an ambulance, and when I came back she was sitting up asking for something to drink. It happened about 20 minutes ago."

What I learned that day changed me forever. God is real. I never needed to know that more than in the moment He spoke to me. What I thought was mine, never was; she is His. And I was "enough" for God, just the way I was.

Rita Carlson is a 45-year-old Tampa native who explores her creative side making and selling jewelry. She and her daughter volunteer their time for the homeless and support other local nonprofit organizations.

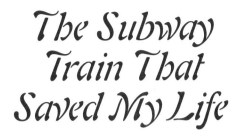

The Subway Train That Saved My Life

My life took a turn down a dark path sometime after my eighth birthday. I was diagnosed with Sydenham's Chorea and St. Vitus' Dance. It was thought that my subsequent development of epilepsy may have grown out of that. In any case, epilepsy remains misunderstood by many people even today, but when I was a child, it caused shame and unbearable pain in my life. Not only did school children make my life miserable on account of my seizures, even certain adults who should have protected me turned away.

I reacted to this pain and humiliation with anger. Anger began to rule my life as I grew older. School became just another public place to experience humiliation that grew out of general ignorance and an apparent lack of compassion, and I had no use for teachers or the classroom. Any authority figure in my life became a focal point for my rage, a challenge I ached to conquer by rebellion and force. Even my poor mother couldn't handle me.

By age 14, I stood up to life with both fists doubled. My attitude was that everyone in my life was dead wrong. I was the only person who knew anything, and I was ready to fight the world to prove it. Constant run-ins with authority figures and frequent truancy from school finally landed me in the Branon Lake Institute for Boys.

This did nothing to help my out-of-control anger. I did my four months in the institute and got out shortly after turning 15, but my problems continued. A few weeks after my release, I broke into a home and stole a full bottle of rye whiskey. Drinking was probably just another way to numb myself against my unrelenting pain and anger, but I didn't recognize that at the time. I just smuggled the bottle home and swallowed every drop.

At that point I had only an hour before I was to report for my job at a drugstore, and I got on my bike to start the trip. Try as I might, the bike just wouldn't stay upright with me on it. Looking back, I know if I had arrived for work weaving around in a cloud of whiskey fumes, my employer would have fired me on the spot. But I never made it. After pushing my bike a few blocks, I passed out cold on the street. Back I went to the Institute for Boys—this time for a whole year.

Life continued to be dark and rough. By 1971, at age 23, I had sneaked across the border from Canada to Philadelphia. The turning point in my life occurred sometime after 7 p.m. on December 10th that year as I walked through a turnstile to catch the subway. Two police officers surveyed the station but failed to notice as I began to suffer a petite mal seizure. Such a seizure is often not recognized by other people, but it can leave the epileptic in a dazed, confused state.

In my confusion, I approached the platform to look for the train, and, not seeing one, jumped down onto the tracks and began to walk south. The police officers should have immediately pulled the red flag that would have alerted a coming train to halt and avoid danger on the track. But they didn't; I walked more than a block before I heard a horn and saw a white light coming straight for me. In my dazed state, I just stood there and put up my fists, ready to fight. The train struck me with full force, knocking me 150 feet down the track. All four cars rolled over me. One of my hands landed on the rail, and all four fingers were neatly sliced off, but I was not killed. God must have been watching me, even then.

I awoke briefly four hours later, lying on a gurney in the hallway of an emergency hospital. My body was battered and broken, and there was nothing more that could be done for me there. I don't remember being transferred to another hospital, but I'll never forget my next moments of awareness.

Floating. I was hovering up near the ceiling of an operating theater, gazing down at nurses and doctors operating on somebody's thigh. My thigh. They suddenly stopped the operation and began a series of furious attempts to resuscitate the body lying below me, but I was no longer in there. I was only a detached observer. My mind became overwhelmed by the sight and I struggled to understand what was happening. The next instant, I found myself flying through the night sky. The stars were clear and bright, and I felt no fear. I came to a stop in front of a tunnel. It was black and round, about 10 feet high and 8 feet wide, and stretched a long way. At the end I saw what appeared to be a bright light bulb. Curiosity compelled me to enter the tunnel and find out what the light bulb was all about. As I made my way, a pervasive, soothing calmness surrounded me. By now, my death had become clear to me, but that didn't matter. There was no pain here in the tunnel, and the closer I walked toward the light bulb, the happier I felt.

As I approached the light, it became obvious that this was no light bulb. I walked toward it until I was surrounded by a glorious brightness that soothed my core. I felt energized, buoyant with joy, immersed in a welcoming brilliance that filled my heart with great love and infused me with the warmth and calmness of perfect Peace. It was then I heard the Voice.

It was a male voice; calm, loving, soothing, but strong. It seemed to be coming from everywhere—surrounding me just as the light did. It spoke words I *could* hear and words I could not, saying, "Go back. We are not ready for you yet."

No! I didn't want to go back! I was happy here, and wanted to stay where I was more than I had ever wanted anything in my life. Going back to the pain, the anger, the darkness that defined my existence was the last thing I wanted. But the choice was not mine to make.

Three months later, I emerged from a coma in the same hospital where I had hovered over my body, confused, stuck between two worlds. I looked down, staring at my mangled self. My right elbow had become separated at the joint during the train's impact and was still in a cast. The two bones in my lower right leg had suffered a compound fracture. My left leg was broken above and below the knee, and the muscles around my thigh had been shredded. Part of my femur had to be surgically removed before it was set, and both legs were encased in white plaster casts. The doctors said I had died on the operating table, and had been dead nearly five minutes before they were able to restart my heart. It was a miracle, they said, that I had survived being run over by the subway train.

It was a year before I was well enough to leave the hospital, but by then I was not the same man who had entered it on the brink of death. The angry, rebellious man who'd been ready to fight the world had died between the subway tracks. What had changed me were not the words God had spoken to my ears, but the subliminal words He had spoken to my heart—the message that I wasn't done here on earth yet. I hadn't managed my life very well before I walked through the subway's turnstile. Now I had a second chance— borrowed time to learn the lessons of Love.

The memory of the tunnel and beautiful white light of Peace has been vivid and foremost in my mind ever since I emerged from my coma. For the last 37 years I have been using my time on earth to help other people, to think about others' needs, and to demonstrate compassion to friends and strangers alike. I would never have guessed so many years ago as that angry young man, that God could turn my life around and show me the path to rid my heart of self-pity and anger. I had to nearly kill myself in order to let God wake me up and point me in a new direction. I thank Him every day.

Leonard Robertson was born and raised in Vancouver, British Columbia. He worked on Vancouver tugboats in the harbor until a seizure cost him his job. He enjoys spending time with his two sons, plays the piano, accordion, and organ professionally, and as a member of the Polar Bear Club, takes a dip in a 33-degree Ontario lake every January 1.

The Whisper in My Dreams

The doctor's voice was a wooden bell. Her words had no resonance, no import. "I'll meet you there," she said. "Don't let Bill drive."

By the time I put the phone down I was empty-headed. I had lost my memory, even of the dream that had been with me every day all those months. The dream had poked and nudged at me to dance every dance with him, to put the top down on the car and play "Mustang Sally" as loudly as possible. The dream had insisted I stand with him on the cliffs just those few extra moments that allowed us to see pelicans fly in formation against the curl of a wave.

The dream: His vivid whispering, "I hate to put you through this." My assurances, "It's okay. I'm supposed to be with you when you die." All the ominous symbols were present—black clouds, sinister wind, shimmering clear light on the horizon. And in the midst of all that, a sense of privilege; a significant and inexplicable sense of the gift of being there in that moment.

There was nothing so significant that day in December as my empty head and I rode up and down in the hospital elevator. I wanted to be somewhere without molded plastic chairs and earnest, practiced voices. I wanted to be somewhere I wasn't.

When I got back to his room, Bill was sitting on the edge of the bed in that silly gown, his bare legs dangling in space. Without his red tie or his camel's hair sports coat, he was unrecognizable. Maybe someone else's husband. A stranger with something growing in his head.

He told me he had been trying to write letters to the kids. Telling them what they already knew: how much he loved them, how proud he was, and how he forgave them for losing every piece of camping equipment we ever owned, and for the marijuana farm on the garage roof.

"But," he said, "I can't do it. I can't figure out how to say goodbye." Then he looked up at me and whispered, "I hate to put you through this."

And I remembered the dream. The memory came like a sudden rain that leaves the air so clear everything seems freshly drawn, the edges almost too sharp. I prayed for the courage not to look away, the courage to be fully present. I understood the terror. What I wanted to understand was the gift.

"It's okay," I said, "I'm supposed to be with you when you die." Those were the very words in my dream, and there I was standing in that harsh fluorescent light saying them again. That's when I knew. I had been lovingly prepared so that I might understand the tumor wasn't just some random horror. It was simply part of a picture too big to see. A purpose too great. What I'd thought was a nightmare had been the Voice of God.

Doctors imaged Bill's brain while he silently read words flashing on the ceiling of the MRI. They were making a map of his language centers for the surgery.

He asked if I might consider having the same test. "I'd just like to get a look at those language centers of yours. I've been wondering about them for 30 years."

I cautioned him that being a smartass wasn't recommended during high-tech procedures. Keeping up the banter was something I knew how to do. I was just the right person to be with him. I was chosen, and I was honored. I was fully present. I knew him.

I knew his goodness. In those long last days, even when I wasn't sure if he could hear me, I relived for him the stories of our life. I reminded him how often he had sat beside me and pointed out the flowers that were growing right at my feet. I remembered an afternoon in crosshatched sunlight on the patio when, with the tips of his square fingers, he had broken pieces from soft toast and fed them to the baby. He never took his eyes off her while she chewed with those four new teeth. I told him how I had fallen in love with his eyelashes in that moment, something about them in that specific light, a dark fringe for his amber eyes.

I was conscious of them again. His eyes were closed. They'd been closed for days, his thick lashes quiet on his cheeks. It is what I will always see when I think of him.

My peaceful memory of him is a gift. But my greater gift is the knowledge that I will always be where I am supposed to be, and that God's Voice doesn't have to ride a bolt of lightning out of a cloud. It can whisper in my dreams. It can take on the song of a seabird to make sure I notice the ocean slapping against the shore and that I don't look away and miss the miracle when the water retreats and reveals the life of those thousands of tiny creatures that burrow in the sand.

Janice Uebersetzig recently retired from a busy law practice. To make sure she hadn't left her brain in one of those storage boxes under her desk, she's been writing, mostly on a reading curriculum project with her daughter.

The Lesson From the Tattooed Angel

Christmas morning in our home was a celebration of love, blessings, and family. We prayed, opened presents, enjoyed each other's company, and savored a delicious breakfast feast. All was well in our home, until my 13-year-old, usually a mild-mannered son, began ranting and raving. He was furious. I had forgotten to buy several items he needed to prepare his famous pound cake recipe so he could serve his masterpiece at

Christmas dinner. His anger escalated when he remembered that every store was closed for the holiday.

My crisis-management skills kicked into high gear. I remembered that our local Walgreen's never, ever closed. I hopped into the car thinking I would run into the store quickly, get what I needed, and head home. Little did I know that God had a profound lesson waiting for me.

As I gathered the sugar, eggs, and butter, I noticed a young man of 16 or 17 whose body was completely covered in tattoos and multiple piercings. Although his appearance attracted my attention, what was most evident was the level of pain and sadness on this young man's face. It was a look of utter despair, deep loneliness, and mournful suffering.

My heart expanded with compassion, thinking this was someone's child in the deepest state of despair. I began to pray for him, asking God to surround him in comfort. Each aisle I walked down, there he was—not following me, but there for me to notice and to continue praying for.

Knowing the power of prayer and trusting God would take care of this child, I thought the whole experience was over. I paid for my items and walked out of the store. As I left, I was once again confronted with this precious child of God. The young man sat on a bench with his face buried in his hands. His hard tattooed exterior trembled with overwhelming sadness. Each tear showed his deep vulnerability. I could no longer ignore the depth of this child's anguish and began to feel this young man's pain. Here it was, Christmas morning, when most families are together, and this teenager was alone, in utter despair.

In my mind I called out to God: Please show me how to uplift this young man. Do I need to sit with him? Do I need to call Mental Health Services? Do I need to bring him home with me?

Then, as it often happens, the still, small voice spoke to my heart—a voice familiar yet so different from my own inner thoughts. As the Creator spoke to my soul these tender and loving words reverberated through my entire being: "Buy him a present. Show him that someone notices him and cares that he is here."

I quickly ran back into the store and bought him a small gift. As I exited the store, I approached this young man. I handed him the present and wished him a Merry Christmas. He looked completely shocked. I began to speak, telling him that I noticed how sad he looked and wanted to do something to cheer him up.

As he listened, he burst into tears. Through his crying he kept saying over and over again, "God bless you! Thank you! You do not know how much this means to me."

I said, "You're welcome," and asked him if he needed anything else and if he was going to be alright. Within moments his entire presence changed. He lifted his head, his tear-filled eyes began to sparkle, and for the first time I saw his beautiful smile. He said now he would be okay. I said goodbye, wishing him a Merry Christmas and God's blessing.

As I got into my car, a flood of tears flowed down my face. Could a simple act of noticing a teenager's pain change his life? Could a small gift to acknowledge another human being's suffering uplift him? I will never know how this encounter changed this young man's life. All I know is that my life will never be the same. This young man was an angel, bringing me so many profound lessons. I was able to see how blessed my family was to have each other. I was able to see how life affirming it is to perform intentional acts of kindness. Finally, I was able to understand how every teen needs to be loved, noticed, acknowledged, and connected to others.

Debbie Milam enjoys the natural beauty of South Florida where she lives with her husband and two children. A former occupational therapist, she now donates her time to charitable organizations that help families in need.

A Prisoner's Experience

Sometimes, in our darkest hours, God turns on a light that changes the whole trajectory of how we view the world. My darkest hours came while serving a 10-year prison sentence, when I made the potentially fatal mistake of engaging in a hot verbal confrontation with another convict. He was the leader of one of the largest and most dangerous street gangs in the Chicago area, and he wielded as much power inside the prison walls as he had on the street.

I don't fully recall what the argument had been about, but it had been serious enough that the order came down from the gang leader that on the following morning I was to be killed. There would be no escape from that fate. Alone in my cell that night, I paced nervously and smoked the last of my cigarettes. I experienced the darkest moments of dread and fear I had ever suffered in this lifetime. Visions of a horrible physical struggle followed by my inevitable death filled my thoughts. A major life-threatening confrontation was about to explode, and I was afraid—more afraid than ever before.

For the first time in many years I turned to God. I got down on that concrete cell floor and prayed. Long ago I'd given up on the God thing. To me, God had become nothing more than a fairy tale—something only the gullible believed in. Until that moment, God had all but been forgotten except for those moments when He took the predominant blame for all my sorrows and circumstances.

I prayed for hours, begging, pleading, promising, asking God for a way out. Soon I had the thought to write out a note for help and give it to the next guard who would pass by my cell. In the note, I described my predicament and the impending danger.

After many more hours on the floor of my cell, my prayers were answered. I'd passed the note to a guard who returned much later, just before dawn, and led me away. That same morning I was transferred from that maximum-security prison to another facility, a minimum-security confinement prison miles away.

The moment I was delivered to that new environment and heard the door of my cell locked behind me, I got down on my knees and thanked God for what I considered to be divine intervention. I thanked Him for a long time, remaining on my knees in grateful prayer, convinced beyond all doubt that my rescue had been nothing less than God answering my pleas for help. After hours of thankful prayer I became weary of kneeling. I laid down on my new bed, and the instant my head rested on the pillow it happened. A vibrant sensation of comforting lightness, gentle but all powerful, engulfed my body. It saturated me and seemed at first to lift me away. Musical sounds filled my being—the sounds of a gradual progression up the musical scale. I heard three notes in all—do, re, mi. All the instruments of every band and orchestra in all the world and in heaven saturated that tiny cell in perfect harmony.

Then something else began to occur. I felt an expansion. Slowly I became aware of a distinct new connection with everything around me. It felt as if new life had been breathed into the walls of that cell, into the air, the floor and the ceiling, and the tree outside my barred window. I heard the rustle of every leaf on the tree; I felt the warmth of the sunlight, and I smelled the grass in a new way, as if for the very first time. I was becoming the floor, the ceiling, and the walls of my cell. I felt at one with the air, the trees and grass outside that window, with the rustle of the leaves and the sunlight.

I wanted to go farther, but as quickly as the power began to flow, it subsided and very gently returned my awareness to my body. I was dumbfounded. What was this strange feeling? Although it seemed oddly familiar and comforting, it remained like something out of science fiction or religion. Religion had never held my interest. In fact, until that precarious previous night, when I begged for help and prayed for the first time in years, I'd long since given up any belief in spiritual subjects or in God. This had to be something bigger than all of it—bigger than anything I'd ever been told about or taught.

I was convinced that the feeling I'd just experienced had *something* to do with God-stuff, or maybe there was some scientific explanation, but without knowledge or a reference of any sort I could only wonder in awe. But something else stayed with me. There was the unmistakable conviction that God had acknowledged my prayers; God had answered me with a glimpse of an experience that would remain with me from that day on. God had blessed me with a brief but all-comforting assurance that real Love is unshakable, all-prevailing, all-powerful and forever devoted. It is the sort of compassion that a Father has for His Child.

What was it? Where did it come from? How could I feel it again? I couldn't answer those questions, but I have since spent the past 30 years asking them over and over before finally coming to understand that God is always with me, has never left, and never will.

After losing his wife and family and serving a 10-year prison sentence, Joseph Wolfe now lives in Sedona, Arizona. He wrote and published *Letter to a Prisoner* to help convicts everywhere understand that there are greater powers beyond what their eyes can see.

Goose Bumps From Heaven

A strange sensation came over me 15 years ago during an excruciating funeral I would never forget. A warm feeling surrounded my whole body, and a bright glowing light with beaming rays pierced my eyes. I felt goose bumps all over. I had lost someone dear to me, but was comforted by a long-time Friend with whom I had become reacquainted. This death was unbearable, but this Friend would be unforgettable.

Our family of four sisters had an infinite and everlasting love for each other. We lived a great distance from friends and extended family members, and social events of any kind were rare. My dad traveled with his business five to six days a week, so it was a treat to have him home on weekends. My mother stayed home with us and was a loving soul. My sisters and I did everything together, from bike rides to riding our pony, Peanuts, to playing hopscotch and sharing chores. We even prayed together at night, hand-in-hand.

Then one cold evening when we were grown, my sister Karen was taken away from us in an automobile accident. She was killed instantly by a drunk driver. The death of my sister tore a large hole in my heart, and in the hearts of all my family. I had to hold on tight to what faith I had, and the strong love of my two other sisters. I dropped to my knees and cried until there were no more tears. I yelled at the top of my lungs, "Where are you, oh Lord?"

There was silence. I heard no answers. I was so alone and afraid that even my sisters' love couldn't fill that void. Totally and utterly lost, I couldn't know my life was about to be changed forever, that soon I would come face to face with a powerful Presence—my Holy Father, King of Kings, my Jesus Christ.

The day of Karen's funeral was a day of total shock. I remembered that when Karen was still with us, she and I had always joked about doing each other's eulogies. She and I wanted everyone to know how special we were while on earth. I couldn't let Karen down, so I told the minister and my family that I would give this special gift. Why had I promised this to Karen? She would never know if I didn't do this favor—or would she?

I battled with this promise for three days and nights. The minister put even more pressure on me by stating that the eulogy was to be testimonies of the Lord, not so much of Karen. I thought this was to be Karen's day!

I was a wreck on the day of Karen's funeral—so confused and exhausted that I had written only a page of what Karen meant to me and her loved ones, but no real testimonies of the Lord. I just sat there in the church pew with my family, the piece of paper in my hands, and started to cry profusely. Was this a dream?

I never blamed my Lord, Jesus Christ, for this event in my life. I just didn't know why Karen had to die so young and leave her loved ones. She had so much faith and love for others, especially her family and sisters. I wanted to hear answers, but I was deaf to the world. Sitting on the church pew, I looked around me and saw so many loved ones who needed my comfort and love. I wanted so badly to stretch my arms out to them, but I was frozen where I sat. "Oh, sweet Jesus," I prayed silently, "please help me get through this crisis. I need You, oh Lord, so much!"

When it was time for me to walk up to the altar and present Karen's eulogy, I slowly stood, with my husband's help. I put my glasses on, not so that I could read any better, but to hide my red, sore eyes. I could barely see to walk with the tears streaming from my eyes.

When I had made it to the altar with my husband at my side, I took one quick glance at all the people crowding the church, and then at my one piece of paper. My hands trembled so badly I couldn't hold the paper straight. Finally my husband whispered to me, "Let me read this for you."

I looked him in the eyes, trying to express the great love I felt for him, and said, "No, I will try to do this."

Though it felt like hours, only seconds had passed when suddenly something came over me. My journey with Jesus Christ was about to bloom right in front of my eyes and deep in my soul! I stood at the altar not knowing if I could deliver my gift to Karen, when a warm sensation spread over me. I felt at total peace, with an inner calmness I could not explain. I felt so far away from my family and all the people in the church, isolated in this warm bubble of calm, but I wasn't alone. Someone was holding my left hand. It wasn't my husband, because he was holding my right hand.

The weakness I had experienced before was replaced with a strength of security, the way a child feels cradled in its mother's arms. Then a glorious bright light radiated from one end of the church to the other. It beamed through the stained glass windows and shone with magnificence! This shining light blinded all my fears, erased my emptiness, and dried my tears. It gave me instead a sense of hope and extreme joy. I could speak to all Karen's loved ones so clearly. I wanted to speak all day! Please, I thought, let this go on and on and never end!

This was the greatest feeling I had ever had in my life. For the first time I honestly felt God's presence! This was my long-time friend, my Father of Heaven, my Jesus Christ! He let me know that not only would He comfort me and Karen's loved ones, but that Karen would live a happy life eternally with Him. I truly felt goose bumps all over me—goose bumps straight from Heaven!

After the funeral, many people came up to me and said that my words had given them comfort, more than they could express. I seriously didn't remember all the words I had spoken in the eulogy. All I had was one piece of paper in front of me, and the rest came from Jesus. I told each of them that those words weren't mine, but the Lord's. It finally dawned on me that the Lord had surrounded me with His love and gave me hope to continue my journey on earth without Karen. Now I would travel the rest of my days with Him, my Jesus Christ.

My sisters and I are still together, forever—one in Heaven, as our personal Angel watching over us each day. Yes, The Lord, Jesus Christ, is with me always. I am profoundly honored to have had this special inspiration of the Lord's presence, an experience that will never be forgotten. This was a gift from Heaven, and I pray I will have more to come. I listen to the Voice of Love each day and that Voice is my Lord. The Lord gave me a promise that He would never forsake me, so when goose bumps come my way, for any reason, I know in my heart I'm feeling Heaven!

A graduate of Williamson County Medical Center's nursing school in 1980, Terri Nelson serves as a nurse anesthetist for an oral surgeon. She and her family live in Franklin, Tennessee, and devote their lives to Jesus Christ.

Lord, Stay With Me

After seven happy years in our retirement dream home on a lake, my husband of 34 years suffered a debilitating stroke. Therapy and prayers eventually restored some mobility, but life grew more complicated when my dear mother contracted Alzheimer's and also needed my care. With so many continual demands on my time, we weren't able to attend Sunday church services anymore.

One of the church ladies telephoned to ask if we were alright. When I explained the situation, she told me her four special words that would give me daily strength: "Lord stay with me." Eventually, I had no choice but to place Mother in a nearby nursing home.

Every morning, I set a small breakfast on the bedside table for my husband before going across the hall to my utility room to play Nintendo. We could still communicate with each other. One morning, halfway through my game, I suddenly heard the most beautiful music. I sat motionless, wondering where this unique sound was coming from. After a few moments, I looked up to see the top half of my utility room filled with cloud-like formations of angels in blues, pinks, and white. They were tightly clustered together, but I could see their wings—such a beautiful, peaceful scene. I tilted my head back, gazing and listening, realizing they were singing to me.

After a few awe-filled moments, I managed to get up from my chair and returned to our bedroom where my husband sat on the side of our bed. I asked him if he'd heard any music, and when he shook his head, I described what I had just seen and heard. That was when their message was revealed to me. I told my beloved husband their message was simply not to worry, because everything was going to be alright. My dear husband looked down at me and smiled so sweetly. We sat there for a few minutes without speaking a word.

The following morning at 4 a.m., my dear husband died in my arms from a massive stroke. I drew strength from the beautiful angels and knew he was alright and in God's loving arms.

A year later I had to sell our dream home. Mom and I moved to Florida where I met a wonderful Christian gentleman, Tom, vacationing from Indiana. He persuaded me to come live in Indiana and place my mom in the same home where his mother stayed. Tom found me an apartment near his home and close to our mothers.

Tom suffered from severe arthritis throughout his body, so every morning I would drive the short distance to his home where we spent our days together. One morning, I stopped to pick up some items Tom needed, then found myself driving through rush hour traffic. I thought this was a good time to say my four special words. Out loud I said, "Lord, please forgive me for anything I might be doing wrong, and Lord stay with me." As I said the last word I heard the most beautiful, peaceful, monotone voice say very slowly to me, "Gayle, I am always with you." His Voice was like none I had ever heard.

It was as if the Voice was preparing me. The next day my only child suffered a heart attack. As awful as that was, I experienced great peace and a profound "knowing" that God would not take him before taking me.

Three years later, while returning to my apartment after visiting Tom, I suffered congestive heart failure. I managed to grab my cordless phone and call for help. Minutes later, emergency people were breaking down my door to gain entry. I had lost consciousness. The doctors later told me that I died three times the first two days in the hospital. They put me in an induced coma for six weeks in an attempt to stabilize my vital organs and installed several stents in my arteries, removed the main artery from my right leg, and implanted a pig's valve in my heart. I slowly returned to life, but had to re-learn how to sit, stand, and walk. I kept saying my four special words for strength.

One month later, my pig's valve became infected. Another six weeks of hospitalization was required. Every Thursday morning I'd be taken to radiology, given a slight anesthetic, and a camera inserted down my throat saw if the infection was healing. After the fourth week, I stood at my bedroom window looking up at the moon and the stars and prayed with all my heart for God to please heal me so that I could go home. Immediately, I felt a warm, peaceful feeling envelop me, and a tingling sensation shot through my body from my head to my feet. I knew God had answered my prayer.

The next morning when my scheduled camera procedure was performed, there was no infection. I was released from the hospital. That was three and a half years ago. Three out of five people who go through what I did die. My doctors call me their "miracle lady."

Lord stay with me...

Gayle Lelekatch and her husband, Tom, spread their message of hope by visiting and feeding the homeless. Known to those suffering such hardships as Grandma and Grandpa, they feed both the bodies and spirits of those down and out, and inspire them to never give up hope and trust in God.

The Buick That Changed My Life

It was a breathtaking Florida Saturday when the driver of that car changed everything in my life. I had been flying high from another successful week at my new job, having become a shining star in just five months in this new position. It seemed I could do no wrong, and I had already earned a corner office with windows looking out on the park. Sitting at my mahogany desk in a plush chair, I felt proud and satisfied with myself and my life. My talents had served me well, and being fearless in sales had made me cocky. It seemed I had it all: a good job, a nice house and car, and a great husband. Even my mirror confirmed I was young, beautiful, and healthy.

Despite all this success, I felt somehow disconnected from my life. This unease had kept me awake many nights, like an itch I could not scratch. Nothing I tried to fill this void was working. I talked to God in conversational tones about it because actual praying, the way I had been taught, felt uncomfortable. I asked Him how to feel real peace and happiness in my life. Sadly, I only complained to God and never talked to Him when things were going well. In truth, I wasn't even sure that God was real.

They say to get a stubborn mule to pay attention you have to use a two-by-four. That two-by-four for me was a car accident, which soon made my life resemble a jigsaw puzzle whose pieces lay scattered on the ground.

The driver of an older-model Buick ran a stop sign and plowed into the side of my friend's Triumph Spitfire. The tiny two-seater sports car was no match for the Buick. I had a second to react before impact and made the mistake of bracing my right arm and leg against the dashboard and floorboard.

The beat-up Buick had definitely seen better days, and its driver looked about 13 years old. She kept saying she was sorry. Her baby screamed from its car seat and I urged her to check on the child. The young woman pulled the screaming infant out of the car seat, begging us not to call the police because she had no driver's license or car insurance. When I stepped out of the car and tried to stand up, my legs buckled and my head swam. I couldn't walk. We had no choice but to call the police and an ambulance.

Going to an understaffed emergency room on a weekend was a nightmare. Bracing myself on impact had made my injuries more severe. Some vertebrae had moved from their original positions and my right shoulder was frozen. I'd suffered torn tendons and my hips had twisted out of position.

After a week in the hospital, I was sent home with painkillers and talk of surgery when all the swelling had gone down. I could walk only with great difficulty, and soon my new job was gone. The doctors told me it would be at least a few months before I could return to work. The painkillers made me groggy and cranky, and months of tests and doctor visits took their toll on my marriage. My husband left, saying he couldn't take it, and I was alone with two little dogs, starved for attention, that I could neither walk nor play with. My bills were piling up.

A year passed slowly and painfully. My bitterness and anger caused me to blame everyone and everything for my sad state of affairs, and sapped any spiritual comfort I so desperately needed.

On one of those dark panic-filled days I decided to visit a large bookstore. I loved to read and that was something I could still do. Reading had become my refuge, and I spent hours there drinking coffee and blazing through the books. I became inexorably drawn to books on spirituality. One book recommended keeping a journal as a way of recording the spiritual journey. I realized then that I was on such a journey. I purchased a notebook and began meditating.

To get quiet and still and go within was supposed to be a powerful way to know oneself. I also learned that one could receive guidance and messages this way. It was an avenue to make conscious contact with God. I found a place at home and made it my meditation room as suggested, establishing an altar of things precious to me. It wasn't easy at first, but with every attempt it got easier. Before long I was meditating every chance I got, soaking in the powerful peace and opening the channel to God. I started practicing gratitude, which was suggested by my books as a way to know God. As long as I held gratitude in my heart and mind there was no room for negative thinking. I was grateful for what I had and felt calmer. Immense change was taking place.

My pain gradually subsided and I stopped taking medication. I chose acupuncture, massage, and herbal remedies instead. Yoga strengthened me and I started feeling better. The surgeries suggested by the doctors became unnecessary.

What I learned felt intoxicating. Color and joy streamed back into my life. I started painting and writing again, producing my finest work. The anxiety and depression that had clouded my life for so many months disappeared.

Then on one of those bad stormy days for which Florida is so famous, my journey to grow closer to God was completed. Lightning crackled across the sky, and the rain, tossed by fierce winds, fell sideways in driving sheets. I was enthralled by the beauty of it.

With a CD of violin concertos playing, I watched the storm. The music was so hauntingly beautiful that I started to weep. I mouthed the words, "Thank You." That's when I heard it. The words were startling clear.

"You're welcome!"

It was at once loud and soft. It was thousands of voices and yet it was one voice. It vibrated through my entire body and froze me in place. I knew instantly that the voice I heard was the powerful force of God speaking to me. I had never felt so complete, or so immersed in happiness, joy, and such overwhelming love.

I made a decision that day to communicate with God every day because it was clear that God was with me all the time. I sat in quiet expectation and listened to God talk to me through my hungry heart. I used all my senses to communicate with Him, coming to understand that I should not discount anything because God could speak to me through the beauty of a flower or the words of a song.

When I wrote and allowed His energy to flow through me, He communicated to me in written form through my heart and being. Everything was precious because I absolutely knew God was there, expressing His presence through me and everyone. There were no coincidences. God answered my pleas to know him. I had only to pay attention.

Diannia Baty lives in the Salisbury, North Carolina, area with her little Chihuahua Hector. She is passionate about writing, art, photography, nature, and being of service to others.

Throw-Up Yellow Just Like Me

It was depressing staring at my half-painted bedroom wall—another project still unfinished. Deep, dark blue and throw-up yellow, just like me: Half the time I was dark and blue, and the other half I felt like throw-up yellow with nausea and stomach pain. How did I ever get in this situation? I was scarcely 19 with a tiny baby and a husband who regularly used my body as a punching bag to release his pent-up tension.

How did I blunder into this life of violence with no phone and no car, cut off from my friends? I couldn't eat without pills to calm my stomach. I couldn't sleep without pills to induce sleep. Roy Orbison's haunting song voiced my feelings: "Only the Lonely."

I lay in bed mindlessly, trying to put myself to sleep with the drone of the TV. Nuts! The shows were preempted by some crusade...this Billy Graham thing was even on the billboards. I left it on, too lazy to get up and change the channel. Man, there sure were a lot of people packed into that stadium. The men, looking well-pressed in their suits and "Christian clean," paraded up to the microphone one by one, talking about God while the choir sang about God. Yeah, yeah, God.

I had declared myself an agnostic. I would have liked to believe in God, but I really wasn't sure He even existed. It all sounded good on TV and in songs, but I figured talk was cheap and it was all a bunch of hype. All of these thoughts swarmed in my head, yet I was compelled to keep watching and listening.

After a time the big guy himself, Billy Graham, came to the microphone. His eyes looked clear and direct, rather intense in a "what you see is what you get" kind of way. I liked his strong chin that belied his soft southern drawl lilting into my bedroom. Something about him drew me in and I listened as he asked people to come forward and accept Jesus. I really didn't get that part for myself because I wasn't too sure about what I believed. The song "Just as I Am" blended into the background like wallpaper, setting the stage as Billy's soothing words kept flowing like honey about how God loves me and accepts me just as I am. Billy even spoke to those of us watching TV and said we could accept Jesus and God in our hearts right then.

I had begun to ponder how that could possibly happen when tears began streaming down my face. I didn't hear Billy Graham or the TV anymore. All of it was muted by the strong sense of a presence right in my bedroom, a presence so all-pervasive I felt nothing but smoothness and peace where a moment ago there had been nothing but roughness and pain. My whole body seemed to melt as if thawing from an ice age. I felt alive and—can it be—actually hopeful for the first time since I could remember. A misty fog wafted into my bedroom, absorbing the dark blue and vomit yellow that was coloring my world. In its place shone gold and violet. I felt love in every part of my being, and my tears kept pouring. So powerful was this feeling of gold and violet, of all that is sweet and calm, that I felt totally wrapped in peace. I sobbed from the depths of my being with relief and, surprisingly, acceptance that God really *does* exist. I was not lost and was *definitely not alone*. The Presence, which I knew without a doubt to be God, was with me and in me. I felt this loving mist, this color and smoothness, in every part of me. Truly, nothing existed but me and the Presence, soft and strong and gentle all at once. Time stopped as I experienced a profound communication that penetrated far beyond words or anything known to me. I received a deep understanding that I was loved and accepted no matter what I had done or what had been done to me.

From that instant I was changed. I sent for the free literature offered by Billy. Somehow it was my link to learn more about this God, my God. A place opened in me that was starved for knowledge, a hunger to know all there was about this gentle, powerful presence that somehow had imparted love to me with complete acceptance of exactly who I was.

I have never spoken about this experience to anyone. It was too profound and personal, and I could find no way to share it. I have never been the same but have lived my life with this blessed private experience, secure in the knowledge that I would never be abandoned. No matter how bad things might get, I will always have God's love and acceptance. This awareness has increased my self-worth, making it possible to keep going when I thought I might not be able to take another step. It was from this experience at age 19 that I began my quest for knowledge of God and what life was all about.

I joined a local church and, of all things, was asked to teach Sunday school. A few months later the pastor visited me at home. The church elders had taken a vote and decided to ask me to teach the "difficult" junior high kids in summer Bible School. No one else would agree to teach them. After some reassurance from the pastor, I agreed to take on the group. It turned out to be a very successful class, to no one's amazement but mine. My life became filled with church and social activities as my world expanded into happier times. Even my bedroom got painted.

My husband and I still had our battles, but this time I had a life beyond the depressing times at home. Eventually I left and made a life on my own as a single mother. Though life was difficult at times, I continued to raise my family. Whenever I was running close to empty I would remember the violet and gold reservoir safely tucked in a corner of my heart. The tears would well up and the Presence once again would encompass me, settling love and peace over me like a down comforter. At each crossroad in my life, I continued to return to the memory of that brief experience. I could draw on the loving guidance of that Presence by simply remembering my first encounter. I was surprised to discover that, unlike an old photograph that fades and becomes hazy throughout time, my experience has remained clear and powerful, with every detail imprinted forever on my memory.

Looking back I would never have thought that being too lazy to get up and change the TV channel would result in my receiving the help from God I so desperately needed. Billy Graham has no idea that he was the vehicle that brought me to God. I could have searched the world, yet I found God in my own half-painted bed-room on TV when I wasn't even looking for Him...or so I thought.

Originally from South Florida, Ariadne Romano now lives in Pennsylvania with her two daughters. She enjoys exploring the mountains and hiking trails where she lives, as well as dancing, reading, listening to music, watching movies, and attending live theater performances.

The Man Who Hears the Voice

I was born in 1926 on a farm in the province of Quebec, Canada. When I grew to adulthood, I started my own life on that same farm, raising an old-fashioned French family with eight girls and one boy. I enjoyed a successful and happy life up to the time political tensions made me move my family to the province of Ontario, where I found seasonal work as a carpenter. Because of the long, bitter winters, I worked only four months a year, but the salary proved big enough for my family to live a comfortable life. Through the winter, I worked for a few small customers here and there, picking up enough extra money during the lean months to take care of our needs.

All was well until recession hit the province between 1975 and 1980. My customers suffered and became tight with their money. Work was scarce for everyone. With my girls ready to go to university, I was home, doing nothing but surviving on unemployment insurance and facing financial disaster. I not only had to pay for my family's basic needs, but I also had to pay back the money I had borrowed for the first year of university for my second-oldest daughter.

My worries mounted steadily. If I lost our home, who would rent a house to a family with nine children? The fear of being on the street kept me staring at the ceiling as my family slept. I berated myself for being stupid. Why had I borrowed that money? Why hadn't I saved more when times were good? Now I had no money to pay my bills.

With work so scarce near home, I ventured farther and farther away looking for any job to help my family survive. This was hard on my wife. With me gone so much of the time, she became fed up with being alone and began keeping company with another man. My pain from this was only compounded by the man's bad reputation and the knowledge that he would care nothing for my children. He only used my wife, and once told me he would give her nothing.

I tried my best to be understanding, but my heart and pride were breaking. My poor lady had been seriously affected by giving birth to nine children and could not cope mentally with reality. It affected her judgment and decisions, and, working out of town so much, there seemed little I could do. I could not be in two places at once, and I had to feed my children. I hated knowing that a terrible man was abusing my lovely wife, and I feared for my girls, knowing they were vulnerable with him there. The frustration I felt threatened to tear me apart. If I tried to get my children out of that situation, the chances were great that they would be separated from each other. I paced from one wall of the house to the other, raging like a lion in his cage.

All my life I had been an honest man, been the best that a man can be. I was a hard worker, dependable, and had never hurt anybody. I know there are consequences for making mistakes, but what was happening to me and my children was not my fault. Who had put me in this miserable situation? I shook my fist at the ceiling. "If it is not You, God, then who did this?

I stopped walking abruptly. Enraged, I said, "Jesus, Mary, and all you Catholic Saints people pray to, throw them in a bag and dump it. To me they don't exist. The whole thing with religion feels like nothing but lies! Now there is nobody here but You and me,

God. If You are really there, I will give you not three years, not three months, not three days—I will give you three hours to show up. If You don't show me You are real and You are here by then, You will be dumped with the rest."

At that moment, my wife called me for the evening meal. The table was full of food and the kids were gathered around it, noisy as always. I sat at the table, but before I touched my plate, I heard a friendly Voice speak to me. I knew I had not imagined it, though it didn't belong to my wife or any of the children. It was too loud and clear to mistake, but at the same time, mild and friendly. It said to me, "You tried to write something yesterday. Go get your paper. I have something for you to write down now."

I nearly jumped out of my chair, but no one was there, and the family was so busy passing food and eating that no one at the table seemed to notice anything. Obviously, they had not heard this Voice. Was I losing my mind?

I started to touch my plate again, but the Voice repeated itself as loudly as the first time. "Get some paper and a pencil, I have something for you to write."

I turned around toward the wall. It was impossible for somebody to be behind me. The tone of that Voice was so nice and so friendly, but I couldn't help being somewhat wary. This was something completely new for me.

I went to get several sheets of paper and a pencil that I laid beside my plate. Nobody at the table noticed.

The Voice spoke to me, but only in my head, syllable by syllable; it was impossible for me to know what I was writing. The Voice repeated itself until I had written exactly what it said. I wrote three pages, maybe more, I don't remember. Suddenly, I realized I was alone at the table. One of my daughters, walking by, told me, "Your plate was clean, so I picked it up," and she went away.

I arranged the sheets and I started to read. I can relate only part of it now.

Three days ago you told your friend that your family never missed their three meals a day and that two-thirds of the world eats only one meal a day— sometimes one meal in three days—and still you cried you were a poor man.

You say you don't have a penny left to pay your bills, yet I see money in many envelopes in your drawers. Poor people don't have that.

(I immediately thought to myself, that is a lie, but three days after, I found my collection of old money, in a number of envelopes, in my drawers).

You are deeply hurt about your wife, and that fact is important to you. That is not important. Every day, remember, your children are very happy with you, no matter what your situation. That is important.

Know that love is the key. Everything is attached to that. Learn to love and there is no real problem anymore.

Now, you must know that you will never be alone again. You asked Me to show Myself and I came to you. I am always here.

There was so much more. With every page, the Voice straightened my way of thinking. I had been wrong all along. As I was reading, my wife walked close to me and it felt as if God was coming to me. I was so grateful that she came toward me like that, I didn't say a word in case it would make her afraid. The same feeling of intense love rose in my chest as every child passed my chair. I was so filled with joy and happiness, no words can describe my emotion. I was just happy to *be*, for no reason.

As the days passed, I could feel that intense happiness fading away. I prayed on my knees to keep it, but after three or four days I was a normal fellow, except that there were no longer negative thoughts in my mind. I tried to share my experience with others, but they called me "the man who sees things that we don't see. The man who hears the Voice."

Since that night, strange things have happened to me. I have never borrowed any money since then. Nobody gives me anything. I still have my money collection resting in envelopes in the drawer, and I don't remember how I paid my bills. It wasn't until the following spring that I started to work steadily again, but I never owed anybody money or encountered any financial troubles, though I have no recollection of where the money came from to pay my debts.

One day, I got a call from a hospital. They needed a carpenter for work outside on that windy day when the temperature hovered near a shivering -30 degrees. I dressed for that weather and went.

When I arrived, they sent me to see the person in charge of hiring inside the hospital. After a few jokes, he said, "There is nothing for you to do outside. We need somebody to do the maintenance inside the building as a carpenter, and no matter who applies for the job, you have it. You start tomorrow."

At that time, being Catholic, I belonged to the Knights of Columbus. The people I worked for were Freemasons. These two groups have always been seen as international enemies. It didn't matter. I knew from hearing the Voice that the only thing that matters is love.

For many years I communicated with the Voice with no need to write the messages down. The Voice spoke to me in my head anytime I wanted. Eventually, being happy and satisfied with my life, and to make people forget I was hearing a voice, I stopped the communication and forgot how to do it.

One day I came across a book about how to hear God's Voice called *The Voice for Love*, telling something close to my story, so I bought the book and the companion CDs. When I followed the techniques, the Voice began communicating with me again.

Yesterday the Voice asked me to be specific about my needs so it could help me. I have no need for any help because my life is so happy. The Voice answered, "I would like you to know that I am happy with you."

The author wishes to remain anonymous.

The Day the Twin Towers Fell

On the morning of September 11th in 2001, in my peaceful abode in Adelaide, South Australia, I walked into my youngest son's bedroom to see him watching television, witnessing the horror of the Twin Towers falling in New York City.

"Mum, look! The U.S. is being attacked."

I sat on the bed with him in disbelief. I wasn't sure if this was real or not. Perhaps it was a hoax or just an advert for a movie.

Once I realized that it was absolutely and disturbingly real, I stopped all I was doing, connected to my source, and asked my inner wisdom, "Who am I in conflict with? Who is it that I need to make peace with right now?"

I knew on some level—no matter how small—I had been contributing to the madness. Immediately a woman's name came to me. It was someone I had been quite judgmental about. In that moment I handed it all to God.

"I offer this to you, God," I said. "I totally release this conflict within me and will be aware of my words from this moment on. I offer this to you to be healed." I knew I'd been heard.

That morning was like any other. The boys needed to go to school. My husband was due to catch his plane back to work, and I needed to take him to the airport. We all went about our daily business in an unusually calm manner, partly because we were in a state of shock, but there was also something else at hand—a gentle stillness present.

On the way back from the airport I decided to visit St. Peter's Cathedral. It has an exquisite area at the back of the main altar called The Lady Chapel. I love this beautifully appointed little haven for women just at the edge of the city. The Cathedral is one of Adelaide's finest icons and a place I often visit when I need to make a symbolic connection to The Holy Mother. It's a place I go when I need a little shelter from the harshness of the world.

I walked into the chapel to find only one other person in there: the woman I had been so judgmental about, the one I needed to make peace with. There we were—just she and I—both in the same place, at the same time, doing the same thing. She had her eyes closed so I gently put my hand on her lap and whispered her name.

She looked up and so sweetly said, "I thought you were The Madonna."

How beautiful! She was seeking comfort from the Holy Mother just as I was. My hand on her lap, me saying her name, and her innocent response was all a precious blessing from the divine to heal us both.

Nothing else was said. I quietly smiled, made eye contact, and moved on to enter my silence and be with my God. I knew that what had occurred in that brief moment was a faithful and authentic acknowledgment of each other's sacred presence. I will never forget the gift I was given that day.

I call on this experience often to remind myself how beautiful my life is, how blessed I am in this world, and how precious our connections are. I learned that as a spiritual woman, I make a difference in this world with every word I speak, every breath I take, and every song I sing.

Elizabeth Ellames lives in the beautiful Adelaide Hills of South Australia with her husband and family. Her favorite thing to do each day is to visit her garden first thing in the morning as the sun comes up.

A Surrogate Sermon

"He said he would die if I left him alone," I worriedly explained to the nurse. "I *have* to stay!"

My stepfather, Claude, had been in ICU for several days already. He had been run down by a car in the Houston Astrodome parking lot, and it seemed every part of his body had been shattered. He had died during the initial surgery, but doctors were able to revive him. I imagined he sometimes wished they hadn't.

Day after day, my mother and I sat at his bedside, praying. This particular evening, he became extremely agitated. On several occasions, he hallucinated.

Claude was the minister at a local church, and throughout that day he had fantasized being at a meeting, preparing for a wedding, or asking us to arrange the tables for a banquet. We pretended to comply, not wanting to upset him. At one point, he looked me in the eyes and calmly stated, "If you leave me alone tonight, I will die." There was no way I was leaving!

Even though it was against regulations, the hospital staff agreed I could stay. I sent Mother home, urging her to rest.

"He'll be okay," I promised. "I won't leave him."

I sat at his bedside fidgeting while nurses tended to his various needs. I couldn't contain my sense of betrayal any longer. Looking at his mangled body only reminded me of my own broken life. I had grown up in a home with an abusive parent, leaving me a timid and fearful child. To escape the painful memories, I married young. Nine bitter, lonely years and two children later, my husband revealed a dark secret so repulsive to me that I could barely stomach seeing my own face in the mirror. How could I have been so blind? We divorced, but the emotional trauma had been firmly embedded in me and my children. One of my children suffered with bipolar disorder so severely that three times she tried to commit suicide. I lost track of how many times she had run away. She turned to drugs.

Alcohol became my personal avoidance method, and many nights Jack Daniels helped me temporarily lose my woes in a drunken oblivion. It seemed everyone I knew was looking for a way out. The previous year, my older sister, after suffering through years of depression, had taken her own life. Sometimes, I envied her; she no longer had to struggle with the burden of this life.

Sitting here in the hospital staring at a "man of God" writhing in pain, I had to wonder if he felt like me. Did he also question why a loving God would abandon him? I swallowed the bitter taste of burning indigestion rising in my chest.

Sometime around 3 a.m., I heard Claude stirring in bed. He mumbled and moaned with pain. I reached over to pull the sheet up to his chest. The enormous amount of morphine dripping into his veins was obviously not enough to keep him comfortable. As I slumped back into my chair, he suddenly sat straight up in bed. I was shocked. It usually took two of us to turn him over, and he had not been able to even raise his head alone!

Without a pause, Claude thanked his "audience" and began one of the most amazing sermons I had ever heard. His voice was clear and strong. I frantically glanced around, hoping someone else would come into the room to witness this. No one did. I, alone, was meant to hear.

My stepfather spoke of the importance of using visualization to create a positive state of mind. He urged his invisible audience to use their imaginations to see their circumstances in a better light. He said that seeing things in a positive vein, as if that was the truth, would mirror that perception in reality. Visualization, he went on to say, was a way to bring healing and hopes into expression, because seeing things the way one wished they were would cause them to become one's experience. For 15 minutes, he eloquently described how thoughts and actions become reality.

It was Claude's voice—his body—that delivered that sermon, but the source of those words was *not* of this world. He had never before uttered the word "visualization" to me! He came from a background of traditional practices, and these ideas were foreign to a conservative church like his. Even though he acted as if this were one of his usual Sunday sermons, he would *never* have said these things in his own church.

I chuckled as I imagined the response he would receive if he repeated this sermon to his own congregation. I was also entranced by it. This concept was something I was open to. This sermon, clearly, was meant for me. I perched on the edge of my chair, eagerly listening, barely breathing for fear of missing even one word. Every sentence was relevant for me. Every word was directed at my attitude toward life. My heartbeat thundered in my ears and my breathing grew shallow. A warm fullness filled my chest, expanding into the room. The deepest love I'd ever known exploded all around me. I tearfully whispered through measured gasps, "Oh my God!"

Just as suddenly as it all began, it ended. He fell back on his pillow and was sleeping once again. I sat motionless—stunned. The voice still echoed in my head, interrupted only by the steady beeping of the hospital monitors in the background. I understood why I had needed to stay that night.

After years of endless begging for God to explain the "why" of my life, I had received the answer. Every past experience, whether defined by me as good or bad, held a gift—an answer—if only I chose to recognize it. Until now, I had seen only the bad. I had lived immersed in negativity. Now, I could look back without regret or blame. I could choose to see things differently. All my experiences had benefited, even accelerated, my growth. I had always had the option of choosing forgiveness, love, and joy. In all that asking for answers, I had never listened—until now.

A few days later, the time came for me to return home. Re-entering the troubled environment I had so willingly left behind, I was now a different person. I bent down to tell Claude I had to go. Tears streamed down my cheeks as he reached out and gently wrapped his hands around mine.

"Something good will come from this," he told me.

He was right. Something good *did* come from that experience. I never again took another drink of alcohol. I learned to observe the traumas of my life without becoming absorbed in their drama. I dusted off my Bible and returned to the roots of my spiritual understanding. No longer did I hang on to past resentments and anger. I was a better wife, a better mother, and a better person. God was so much nearer than I had ever realized, and I saw God in everything. Most importantly, however, I went back and rescued the abandoned little girl of my youth. I told her how much I loved her. I promised her I would always be there for her and I would never leave her fate in the hands of others again. I understood that I was the one responsible for taking care of her.

Four months after my stepfather's devastating accident, he returned home. He continues to touch lives with his messages of hope and love, as he shares his miraculous story of survival. A few scars and a slight limp remain the only visible reminders of that fateful day at the Astrodome. The real healing, however, came on a much deeper level—a level unseen to many. I see it, though. I see it every day.

Today, when Reverend Claude McDonald takes the podium to deliver his messages on the power of positive thinking, many people hear his voice. His words inspire and encourage others to see the good in every seeming challenge. He shares that there is a gift in every life experience, if only we are open to it. As I hear his words, I realize how many ways God speaks to me. Sometimes my lessons come from the minister at the podium. Other times, they come individually wrapped in a surrogate sermon.

Jodi McDonald earned her BS in education from Midwestern State University, and has served as a teacher and director in two alternative educational facilities. She and her husband currently own a homebuilding business in New Braunfels, Texas.

Tiny Prayers

As an infant, he had journeyed to Eastern Oregon in 1901 by covered wagon, growing up poor on his family's homestead, never seeing electricity or running water until after he'd finished the 8th grade and left school. But Ernie, now white-haired and slightly bent by the years, had seen things I had not. He enjoyed a special relationship with God, and related stories of inspired guidance in his life and divine rescue from certain disaster that I silently doubted. The God I'd heard about as a child was vengeful and judgmental, much too busy tallying sins to help a simple man invisible to society.

I befriended this shy little man 30 years ago, soon after arriving in Oregon myself, and tamed his bashfulness as one would a wild creature with gifts of food. His silence soon evaporated, and, hunched over a steaming mug of coffee in my kitchen, he'd fill my imagination with tales of capturing wild mustangs, high-spirited escapades in the one-room schoolhouse of his youth, of Indians and "buckaroos" and gun battles on the dusty main street of his town.

Often I'd catch glimpses of Ernie's deep faith in God from his stories, a spiritual place to which I was not yet ready to follow him. I admired him for it, even envied his peace and serenity, but I lacked the clarity and conviction that glowed from Ernie's face like a candle undeterred by the fiercest gale. Instead, I circled with caution my collected conceptions of a confusing God shrouded in paradox. But then, Ernie saw things I didn't see.

One day, after several cups of coffee and tales of his lonely shepherding days, Ernie stood up and clapped his old felt hat back on his head.

"I'll be heading on down to the barn to see how your husband's coming with that new stall," he said. "Maybe I'll even whack in a nail or two while he's away if I get the notion." He turned to leave, then stopped. "You ain't seen my pocketknife lying around by chance, have you?"

I carried the coffee mugs to the kitchen sink. "No, Ernie. I didn't even know you carried one. When did you lose it?"

He lifted his hat briefly to scratch his white hair. "Oh, it's been maybe six or eight months now. Turned over my whole house looking for it, but I must've lost it somewheres else."

"If you lost a knife outside here that long ago, it would have rusted to nothing by now," I told him.

He replaced his hat and grinned at me. "During my morning devotionals this morning, I mentioned it to the Lord. Told Him I was plumb frustrated, and if there was some way He could show me the knife, I'd sure be beholden."

There he went again, thinking God heard millions of tiny prayers about tiny insignificant problems. If God really answered prayers at all, which I seriously doubted, he'd be cherry-picking the ones about cancer or finding missing children, not wasting time with lost pocketknives. I watched Ernie fondly as he turned, shuffled toward the back door, and tottered down the road to the barn. Then I gathered the household trash.

Our burn barrel sat down by the garden, rusted to a burnt coppery brown. A worn dirt path led to it, one I walked every day unless it rained. I lugged the bag of trash along the path, glancing down the road at the barn where Ernie stood fooling with something outside the barn door. At the barrel, I heaved the trash bag over its rusty lip, letting it tumble onto the ashes at the bottom.

As I rummaged in my jacket pocket for matches, a glint of sun sparkled against something lying at the foot of the burn barrel. I leaned over and picked up a pocketknife. I'd walked that path more than a hundred times in the last six months and would have sworn in any court of law there'd been nothing lying there in the dirt before. This knife was not rusted. Neither was it coated with ashes and dirt. It was as shiny and clean as if it had been kept in somebody's pocket until that moment. I knew it didn't belong to my husband, but thought this unblemished knife couldn't possibly be Ernie's.

In spite of that bit of logic, I left the trash unburned and hurried down the road to the barn.

"Look, Ernie! Look what I found!" I exclaimed, holding out the knife for his inspection.

He peered at it and then grinned. "You found my knife!"

Instead of taking it from my hand, however, his grin evaporated and he sank down onto the stump we used as a resting spot. His face grew pale.

"What wrong, Ernie?" I asked, still holding out the knife in my hand.

He blinked at the knife. "I didn't ask God to let me find my pocket-knife," he said slowly. "I only asked Him to *show* it to me."

Now it was my turn to feel weak in the knees. Did God really hear and answer tiny prayers? Had I been used by God to answer Ernie's? Maybe I had been used by God in a loving way to open my heart and eyes to Him. I glanced down at my outstretched hand and felt the knowingness, the warmth of Loving Guidance so familiar to Ernie. God had opened my eyes enough to glimpse what Ernie knew existed all along, and set me on the road to recognizing the Voice of God.

Anita Grimm graduated from Lewis and Clark College with a BA in education. Now semi-retired, she has been a public and private school teacher, a corporation president, a horse trainer and riding instructor, a writer, and an editor.

The Gift of Grace

Just like any other day, I woke up homeless, sleeping in the park, with my clothes in a bus station locker. I was 23 years old and a Baptist minister's kid...how could this have happened to me? I headed to the Arcade bar where the businessmen hung out at lunch. Attractive, witty, and charming, I knew if I paid for my first drink, they would pick up the tab from then on.

I was having a particularly good time and "feeling no pain," as they say, when I experienced a tapping sensation on my head and heard a very firm voice telling me to go call Alcoholics Anonymous. It was a loud voice with a tone of authority. Whether it was truly loud, or if it was just noisy where I was, I'm not sure. It was as if I heard the voice audibly in my mind and wondered if anyone else did too. It seemed to be coming from all around me.

Whether it was the relaxed state I was in or it just seemed familiar, the voice didn't appear strange to me. I didn't think of it as being the Voice of God, I just knew it was interfering with my good time. I argued with it, begging it to leave me to my party, but to no avail. I mean, all I knew about AA was they were a bunch of old people sitting in a cloud of smoke in the church basement where my father was pastor. I certainly couldn't be one of them.

The voice kept repeating itself and wouldn't leave me alone, so I went downstairs to the pay phone and called AA. The woman said I'd missed the meeting for that day, but there would be another in a couple of days. I thanked her and went back to my bar stool and my party.

Five minutes later, there was another knocking sensation on my head. The voice was back, louder than before. It told me to go call again. I angrily argued, "Look, I called, and there's no meeting, so please just let me be."

It persisted, telling me to go call again. Unable to take it anymore and seeing no relief in sight, I went to call again. This time a man on the phone told me if I got on a bus right outside the Arcade, it would take me where the meeting was.

Reluctantly, I followed his instructions. I actually got on the wrong bus and the bus driver put me on the right bus. By divine providence I arrived at the meeting. Someone asked me how long I'd been sober. I was drunk and must have reeked of booze. I couldn't tell them the last time I'd been without a drink. When asked if I was an alcoholic, I just laughed and asked them what an alcoholic was. I didn't even know what I was doing there. They brought it up for the topic of discussion and I just cried and cried. The thought that I could be an alcoholic who could never drink again was overwhelmingly devastating; I lived to drink away my feelings and achieve numbness. I must have had a death wish, as I constantly put myself in dangerous situations in which I felt vulnerable.

The AA members showed me the first of the 12 steps to recovery. It said, "I am powerless over alcohol and my life has become unmanageable." I knew my life was unmanageable—that much was clear—but me? Powerless over a beer? I didn't think so. They told me to have just two drinks a day for the next 30 days and let them know how that worked.

By the third day I awoke in a motel in another state without a dime in my purse or a clue as to how I'd gotten there. I knew the jig was up. I had to get the state police to transport me from one state to the other and get me to my parents' home. My parents had told me long before that if I'd been drinking, I couldn't come home. I told them I was ready to surrender and put down the booze and drugs, so they let me stay. My will had been broken down, though at first I defiantly said, "Well, fine, if that's what you want, God, then fine!" I was stomping my feet in anger, though I was willing to be willing.

Two years before I had sat in my favorite spot in the woods near my parents' house drinking, smoking pot, pondering life, and communing with nature. I used to think if I got high enough, I could reach God. I actually told God I was planning to give my life to Him, but I just wasn't ready yet. I had too much partying left to do! I guess God got tired of waiting for me to come to Him and stepped in to intervene.

Now, one day after returning home from hiking, I found myself back at that favorite spot in the woods. I stood there—sober this time—opened my arms, and said, "Take me, God. I am yours. Do with me as you will."

That was in 1983. It's been a tough road, but God has never left me comfortless. I was such a mess I had to go into rehab. While there, I discovered I was pregnant from a rape. Everyone said to abort the baby, but I had given a daughter up for adoption when I was 16. That had triggered my drinking in the first place, and I didn't know if I could mentally and emotionally survive an abortion. I had no idea what to do.

In the rehab, they taught us how to meditate. One day, sitting on my bunk bed, practicing a deep, quiet meditation, I deliberated on what to do with this tiny growing fetus inside me. I was searching, reaching for some form of guidance. Suddenly, two guys in white gowns appeared before me. It was as if I could see them in my mind.

At first I was startled, but I'd always had a deep faith; having a minister as a father, I had been literally raised in the church. Also, my mother was a Rosicrucian minister, and when I wasn't at church, I was sneaking into her room to read her books on the Mysteries and the Essenes and a very different Jesus from the one I'd learned of in church. I had experienced the presence of angelic beings on occasion since I was young. These two beings looked male, but it was hard to tell. They said I was going to have another girl and she was coming just for me. They explained she was a gift from God, a replacement for the one I'd given away. They even gave me her name and spelled it for me.

From then on, I have never looked back at the past or questioned the method of her conception. I had that baby and she's been the greatest joy and gift in my life. She's a beautiful, sensitive, and caring person with an affinity for the homeless population and is currently getting her master's degree in social work. Brienna has saved my life many times throughout the years and is the best gift of grace I could receive in this world. I thank God for her every day.

With the exception of a four-month "slip" 17 years ago, I have remained sober ever since.

Raena Avalon's lifelong passion is helping animals and people through volunteer organizations ranging from Cerebral Palsy telethons to soup kitchens. A mother of three grown daughters, she shares life in Sedona, Arizona, with two cherished cats and a dog.

Remembering Oneness

You idiot, I thought as I left the 12-Step meeting and cut across the street out front. *Why didn't you speak to him? How is he ever going to get to know you, or you him, when you can't even muster the courage to speak to him?*

Sure, he had heard my story many times before, shared from the floor in a meeting: I was the child of an alcoholic, recovering from a traumatic childhood and had spent many years in addiction. Why was I so afraid to speak to him outside of a meeting? How many times had I played out this same old scenario, asking God to erase my fear yet still feeling too afraid to approach him?

"Why am I so afraid, God?" I asked. "Please show me what to do. I can't go on like this, being petrified by fear itself."

Moments after asking, I felt a sudden strong urge to enter a little bookstore. I asked God to show me what I needed to see. A particular shelf seemed to hold more appeal so I wandered over and noticed a green book with fancy gold writing on its cover that spoke about the teachings of Jesus and the Holy Spirit. I could *feel* that this book was why I was here. I found just enough money in my purse to pay for both the book and my bus fare home. I felt at peace, knowing that all was being arranged in perfect orchestration around me.

For three months, I immersed myself in the book's teachings. Each paragraph boggled my mind. I could only read two or three sections before a strange exhaustion overtook me and I had to lie down. One particular afternoon when the exhaustion hit, I made myself comfortable and lay on my sofa peacefully thinking of Jesus. As I settled into the cushions, I suddenly realized a gentle, loving, male voice was speaking with me in my mind. Amazed, I fell in love instantly. It was clear that the voice was Jesus.

I listened attentively as He explained the book's passages in a form that easily fit with my own spiritual ideas and concepts. He spoke in my own language with a voice so strangely familiar that I easily surrendered to hearing what he was teaching. I fell asleep listening to Love speak in the form of Jesus. On waking, I couldn't contain the love and gratitude I felt. My smile far exceeded the dimensions of my face. I was amazed at the clarity and insight his voice had brought me.

I continued to hear Jesus, though the communication was sporadic. I did not yet realize He was always with me and I could call on Him at any time. I sometimes awoke in the night, amazed at being taught in my sleep. I started handing myself over to the Holy Spirit's care each night for this purpose. I found that the Holy Spirit could wash away my anxiety, discontentment, anger, sadness, and guilt, replacing it with an indescribable feeling of peace, love, and joy.

When I prayed for guidance, inviting the Holy Spirit to be my eyes and ears, desiring only to see and hear what He would have me hear, often something miraculous happened within me. I was shown that Love was everywhere when the Holy Spirit was looking *with* me.

One night I felt an incredible desire to invite the Holy Spirit and Jesus to have all of me. With a conviction and willingness I had never felt before, I surrendered to the Will of my Father. It was raining outside as I drifted off to sleep. I was startled with a jolt as the entire universe came whooshing in where the top of my head had been a moment earlier. The rain outside was now raining *inside* of me. A living rain poured down, cleansing the whole of me, yet the rain was also me. I was no longer a body lying in my bed; I was the universe, and nothing existed outside of me. I was one with God and all existence. I had never felt so complete and so alive. An incredible energy cleared its way down through my center, then left where the universe had entered, leaving me lying in a body on a bed. Now I knew, without doubt, my Reality was Spirit, One Self, united with my Creator and every aspect of Creation.

My prayer was answered that day long ago when I set out from a 12-Step meeting, praying to be shown a way in which I could experience freedom from fear. Miracles light my path today, for I do not walk alone, and for that I am eternally grateful.

Nicole Gleason is the mother of beautiful twin daughters, Amber and Brighid. A graphic designer and Web designer, she enjoys writing, teaching, and helping others in whatever ways she can.

Lukie's Love

March 15, 2005. I slipped over the edge that day. It was a simple thing.

I slept on the futon in my brother's extra room. With a wife and five children, Sean's house was already crowded. My sister-in-law, Karen, quickly stepped into the room to add some recycling to the box. The light was out. She mumbled an apology, a brief statement: "I'll just be a second. Chris, is this all right?" It was an acknowledgement of our agreement that when I turned the light off there was no more going back into the extra room. It was my room at night, my space, my little bit of privacy. True, I shared it with the recycle container, but how could she forget and be so thoughtless? She shuffled in and out. I was already crying but mumbled back to her, "Sure, fine." How could she do this to me, step over that thin fragile line of privacy and respect?

I was devastated. Didn't she know her small act of disrespect put me over the edge? I slid down that slippery slope, immersed in despair with nowhere to go. How could she have ignored our agreement? How could she not have noticed my flood of silent tears when she came into my room? It was only a piece of plastic, and it was a brief intrusion—30 seconds—but it could have waited until morning. It was all I had to hold on to at that moment: a simple agreement and 41 years of despair. Well, not quite 41 years. The despair hadn't set in 'til I was 5 or maybe 6 years old. So let's leave it at 35 years of despair. And tonight I hit my absolute limit. It was the final straw. My heart, my mind, and everything else in my life was broken.

I awoke on March 15th to a certain inner calmness. This was to be my last day on earth. It seemed the plan and decision had settled in as I slept. I started with a few aspirin at breakfast, knowing aspirin would thin my blood. A gun would have been faster, but totally out of the question—way too radical and messy for me. And I couldn't do it tonight in their home with all these children. How could I let 4-year-old Lukie open the shower curtain the next morning to find his favorite aunt motionless in a bath of red water? I called the Ramada Inn: 69 bucks—affordable, and my favorite number, too. Definitely a good sign. I hoped their tubs were clean and long enough for me. I didn't like the image of my white knees sticking up in the midst of all that red.

I never imagined my experience in culinary school would end like this, but I didn't count on the despair building up inside until it seeped out of my every pore. The bakery, where I did my externship, was a serious drag, but I showed up for work as usual on this, my last day on earth. Throughout the day, as I baked soufflés and cheesecakes, I held onto the clear image of my body in that tub. It was a lovely shade of red. Every 56 days the American Red Cross welcomed my donation—ironic how I gave blood regularly to save lives, and tonight I'd give it all to take my own. My blood had always been strong and safe and flowed effortlessly. I knew this was the way to go.

All that day I baked, and chewed on aspirin. I picked up a bottle of Grey Goose vodka on my way home. Why not drink the best on my last night?

I told Karen that I was going out for a few hours to get some supper. She eyed me with concern as she changed Meghan's diaper on the floor.

"What's the matter Chris? You look upset."

I looked over at her and the baby. "Oh, it's just been one of those days." *Jesus Christ Almighty!* There I was, pretending to the bitter end. But what was I going to say? "You and your inconsideration threw me over the f----g edge and here I am, razor blade packed and ready to go." How would she respond to that? I turned away from Karen and said goodbye.

I tried to slip out the front door unnoticed. I could not bear to say good-bye to the children. But Lukie caught me.

"Aunt Chris, when will you be back?" he asked in his developmentally delayed way.

He smiled up at me. I caught my breath, forced back the tears, and reached out to him. I hugged him close and kissed him goodbye.

I decided to go to Z'Tejas for a margarita before I hit the hotel. I slouched at the empty table in the farthest corner of the bar. It was Tuesday night—early enough in the evening to give me some quiet. The waitress, Lynn, noticed me and made her way over. My eyes were puffy with my plan and I could no longer restrain my tears.

"Chambord Margarita please," I mumbled to her.

Lynn stepped back, knowing sorrow when she saw it. I opened my notebook so the tears and the sorrow could flow from my pen. I furiously wrote, "Oh God, how will Sean ever explain to Luke and Ben, to Jack and Amanda, that Aunt Chris died last night at the Scottsdale Ramada? What words could he possibly use to describe this final act of despair and sorrow? How will he help them cope with the loss? How will Lukie wrap his 4-year-old mind and heart around the simple fact that Aunt Chris did not come home last night, and she never would?"

In my mind I focused on that lovely shade of red. But these children loved me, and Meghan, the youngest, would never know me. Sean and Karen would be devastated to think that I had lived with them for a year just to die at the Scottsdale Ramada. But at least I would show some courtesy and had a clear sense of boundaries; I wouldn't do it in their home, and the Ramada was only $69 a night.

Lynn stood before me again.

"Oh yes," I said, "I will have another margarita and the shrimp tostadas too, please," thinking, *Maybe a little food will bring some clarity.*

Inside, my heart cried out. "God, I can't stand this any longer. Look at my life! God, do you even see me? Can you hear my voice? Do you know the sorrows of my heart?"

I tugged tissues from my purse and took another sip of my margarita. It was delicious. As I was blowing my nose I suddenly heard Lukie's voice.

"Aunt Chris, when will you be back?"

My heart almost stopped. My eyes peeked over the tissue. There was no one in sight. The bar was still pretty empty. I waited another moment.

"God, is that you? Don't play games with me. Please God, not now. My only options are a razor blade and a bottle of vodka. I don't know what else to do, how else to live. So this is it, God. Give me one f-----g break. Enough is enough!"

Silence. If God wasn't listening it didn't matter anyway. I looked up from my drink. Then I heard Lukie again.

"Aunt Chris, when will you be back?"

I spun around. No one was there. Tears streamed down my cheeks. I closed my eyes and bowed my head. I didn't want anyone to see me crying like this, but I couldn't stop. My body trembled. My heart stirred. Joy bubbled up in me, flooding me. I cried again.

"God, is this you?" I couldn't stop my tears and there was still more joy—this inexplicable joy somehow bursting through the cracks in my heart. How could this be?

"Six months, God," I cried for the last time. "If this is really You, I give You six months to do something about my life." I caught my breath. Once more I ran the tissue over my face, trying to clean up.

I shook my head, put the tissues and silverware on my plate, and smiled. Here I was, looking like a mess and making a fool of myself in the back of a bar, yet feeling alive, feeling some hope, unsure but knowing I had just taken the first step. I caught my breath and looked through my pocketbook for my car keys. Forget the Ramada Inn. I had to go home and kiss Lukie good night.

Christine Power works at St. Joseph's Hospital and Medical Center in Phoenix, Arizona. Going back to a regular job was not in her original plan after culinary school, but Chris started work at St. Joseph's on September 12, 2005, just three days short of her six-month plea bargain with God.

From Monster to Emissary

"Who's that?!" My fiancée screamed in a panic as I drunkenly stumbled over her shoes. She must have turned on the light just in time to see me exit her bedroom with her gun clutched in my hand. How she was able to tackle me before I got out the front door still baffles me. With frantic, superhuman energy, she overpowered my determination to go and make an example of the man who had accosted me in the bar.

At that moment, you would never have convinced me I would one day strive to become a spiritual peacemaker.

In my relentless anger, I had targeted that man in the bar to suffer for all the injustices life had dealt me. My mother had sadistically abused me, isolating me from my siblings and society at large. I was not allowed to interact with any child who was not of my mother's religion. She had brutally beaten the "fear of God" into me while ignoring my need for nurturing and love. For years, a man with high stature in the church had molested me. The father I had looked to for protection let me down—unable to tolerate my mother's abuse, he stayed away from home, leaving me to fend for myself, and then totally abandoned me by dying of leukemia in my 13th year.

All this pain had eventually led me to gang involvement as I sought companionship and a backbone. Joining a gang was a rebellion against control imposed on me by Bible interpretations and religious brainwashing, and an attempt to escape guilt from my overactive conscience. I succeeded, and raged freely.

Wherever I went, I lashed out and wreaked havoc. In the Army I discovered beer's numbing effect, though even beer couldn't eliminate my pain, loneliness, or confusion. My behavior netted me a 30-day lockup in rehab and drove me to declare, "*No mas*! No more!" I decided to seek personal help.

The process of healing and changing took 20 excruciating years. I studied other religious teachings and spiritual precepts, immersing myself in each for a while. I just could not follow any particular "way." I did collect helpful bits from each, but I needed something more freeing and intimate. Overloaded with spiritual theories and beliefs, my ego sent me on a rampage of desperation, descending into helplessness and hopelessness. What I wanted was an experience of Truth.

One day, I ran across a flyer telling of a new study group forming to discuss concepts of God. The terms *God* and *Jesus* triggered great uneasiness in me as I associated them with the painful experiences of my youth, but a dim hope arose. Attending, I heard my views and beliefs expressed by others. I could discuss my blasphemous ideas without fear of retribution. This was great!

And so, my battles became spiritual and internal. My ego asked, who did I think I was, seeking a relationship with God after my chaos-producing romp through life? How could I remotely deserve God's consideration, let alone His Love? Besides, I was addicted to drama. It was crazy to think I could become a positive force for mankind, that I could live my life in a way that might ease the inhumanity I'd always witnessed...but maybe, just maybe, I could use my painful experiences to approach those still hurting and feeling lost. I was elated by that idea—and scared.

In my late 40s, after extensive counseling, I took my first step out of my isolation in a forest and into a social situation, and immediately wanted to help others move beyond their suffering. The drive from inside me to show others the non-religious Spirituality I had found was unrelenting. I thought about all the times and places God must have had a hand in keeping me alive and sane, not to mention out of prison. *Surely*, my ego told me, *I'll be suspect—after all my years of bitterness, hell-raising, and brutality, how could anyone believe I had completely changed?* I still had so far to go in reaching my goal. But my heart was having none of my ego's reasoning. A new desire had been lit within me. My heart said, "Ask that your growth be accelerated."

Maybe I *was* finally going insane! How would I go about accelerating my spiritual growth? The word *prayer* popped into my head. Prayer? I had not prayed since my father had fallen ill, and prayer had failed to save him. I had felt more worthy back then, but I had lived a lot of rough life since the age of 13. How would I measure up in worthiness now? Why would God listen to me now? Yet I went online and typed it in: "prayer."

One site jumped out at me. It stated that we could hear the Voice of God *within*! Everything I read or heard always had to resonate within me to feel like truth, and this did. I entered the site and found comforting guidance that felt safe. The message I found advised extending love to every thought of doubt and judgment. And then I was to bless them! I read the words, "Be open to whatever comes, however it comes." What a challenge. What unconditionality! Trust and be still. Listen quietly with patience. That is all.

My ego's skepticism could not unravel my interest in this new challenge. Spirit was emerging. I would give this "How to Hear the Voice of God Course" a 30-day test. Nothing occurred until around the 75th day on my third time through the program. As I sat wondering what I could do about the interference of my ego, the message came through: "All is fine." It washed down over me. This was not my idea of an answer, but amazingly, it completely removed all stress, turmoil, and anguish. I was left with an emptiness I cannot describe. Was this sweet, subtle bliss? The feeling remained! My 65 years of suffering was gone in a heartbeat!

How, I thought, could this be true? The relief I felt was so great I didn't know how to deal with it. In my mind's eye, I suddenly saw myself that night so long ago, trying to get that gun. But I was seeing my mother's face, not the face of the man who had accosted me in the bar. Then I saw the face of my molester, the faces of bullies who had tormented me. I wanted to exact revenge on them all, but another message came through these visions. It revealed each of these people as reflections of me. I was shocked by the revelation that they were each suffering too.

I melted, wanting to embrace them with forgiveness and compassionate understanding. I forgave myself, too, for participating in and perpetuating that negative form of existence. My thoughts retreated to my recent week-long visit with my mother. I had been able to be myself with her and to speak my truth for the first time. I know she listened and heard me. As I prepared to leave, she hugged me and cried softly, thanking me and saying, "You are my prize-package son." Thank You, God.

I now question nothing of what continues to occur. I apply the lessons I learned from the Voice of God course every day, extending love to everyone and everything. I am a believer! My life has begun to flow with Grace. I praise God that I have this opportunity to start over and to love life. I have found that transcending the dark is not about overcoming it or eliminating it, but becoming greater than it, larger than it, too bright for it. I appreciate being guided here.

Stephen Ruiz was born in 1941 in Los Angeles, California. He served in the Army in Vietnam and was hired by the Postal Service in 1966. Now retired, Stephen lives in Coos Bay, Oregon, and loves hiking in the forests and beachcombing.

The Listener

Oh God, lead us from the
unreal to the Real.
Oh God, lead us from
darkness to light.
Oh God, lead us from death to immortality.
—Excerpt of "Hindu Prayer for Peace"
from the Upanishads

I've always been a listener. I listened to the words of my stepfather and uncles become slurred as they became more and more drunk. I listened to the paranoid schizophrenic ranting of my brother. I listened to my mother rage at me and my sister, "You little holettas, I'll choke you!" Hearing such things let me know whether I was in actual danger. If I hadn't listened, I might not be here today. And if I hadn't listened to my friend Chris a few years ago, he might not be here today either.

I listened when I received his first long-distance call. What I *heard* was totally different from what I listened to. I heard his words: "I haven't been doing very well, but I'm a lot better now." What I listened to was the higher pitch and unsteadiness of his voice. I listened to its volume—too quiet for his words to be convincing. I already knew something was wrong before the call because I "listened" to letters he'd written. There was something just *not right* coming through them.

Chris knew he'd been too isolated and needed to have more contact with people who loved him. He said he'd call me regularly, but it was quite a while before he followed through, and I was alarmed by how much worse he sounded. He seemed to feel terrified when he considered talking about what bothered him, afraid that putting it into words would make it real. I suspected something had already happened and he was afraid of what might be next.

"I always feel better if I talk about what's bothering me," I said to him. "Holding it in is keeping you stuck. Maybe if you talk about it,

70

that will relieve some of the pressure you're feeling so you can start to move beyond it."

Chris was my favorite young man. My being 21 years older was no barrier to freely sharing our deepest, most profound thoughts and feelings. He even helped me heal some old wounds from my dysfunctional upbringing. An open, kind, and compassionate person, he was now in the grip of such paralyzing fear he was too afraid even to speak. He needed healing on a deep level, something that could pierce through the darkness that enveloped him, and set him free. I was deeply concerned and wanted to be there for him. I didn't even try to decide what to do about it. I just asked the question, *How can I help him?* and I continued listening.

He didn't have the will to say what was bothering him during that call, but when I heard from him again, he decided to tell me everything despite the terror he felt. He was traumatized. His voice sounded steady, though I thought he must be devastated as he told me what he'd been through while he was in Washington State: his girlfriend's pregnancy, the abortion, her leaving him.

Now in Oregon, he lived alone in a cabin on a friend's property. As he spoke about what his life was like, his voice became quieter, higher, more unsteady. He hadn't been eating right. He'd been having panic attacks. I wondered if he was having one as he spoke. In a voice overwhelmed by fear, barely audible, he said, "I'm not sure I'm gonna make it."

I was on high alert. These were the words he was afraid would become real, and I had encouraged him to speak them! I had to say just the right words to dissolve his fear, guarantee his safety, and let him know without a doubt what was real. And I had to say them now. What *were* they?

Help arrived in the form of my attention being drawn to something he kept saying in different ways throughout the entire conversation: "When I'm on the other side of this, everything will be okay," or "I know I'll be fine after I get through this." Those words sounded out of sync to me, as if they were in the wrong time frame. I wondered why they were so strongly demanding my attention.

When I heard them again, I was filled with a totally present, vibrantly alive glow, lush with warmth and peace, teeming with Life. It was all around me and in me at the same time. I felt alert, but calm. It was as if I were feeling God's unconditional love for Chris *and* me, experiencing us both as the perfect beings God had made us to be. I felt loved unconditionally by God and felt unconditional love for Chris, and everything was fine *right now*.

All the tension and concern I had felt for Chris melted away as if it had never existed. Perfect, unconditional Love shone through his trembling, barely audible voice, through the pain he had experienced, through the fear that he wasn't going to make it. The feeling of Chris and I united with God was all that existed in that moment, and the words, "You are fine right now," came out of my mouth!

If I had tried to decide what the right words were, I certainly wouldn't have come up with that simple little sentence and expected it to make any difference. Did Chris think I was crazy for saying that, or insensitive, or stupid? I *knew* they were the right words. They came out of one of the most alive moments I had ever experienced. I wondered if Chris just heard them, or if he'd really *listened*. The silence on the line was ripe with possibility.

"Wow, Kathleen. I wish you could be with me 24 hours a day so I could hear you remind me of that every time I forget!"

He hadn't just heard it. He had been open enough to take it in and accept it! He immediately sounded better. I don't know of anything but God's Voice that has the power to penetrate that deeply and initiate healing that quickly. Chris's fear had no chance of standing up to it.

The next few months were bumpy, but Chris was soon back in Michigan. A friend invited him to work in his home repair business, and the physical work helped ground him. When he started training to be a certified yoga teacher he felt he was on the right path. Sometimes I wondered what "You are fine right now" meant to him. What had he felt when he heard those words?

For my birthday he made a card for me, and in it wrote about a story he'd been told of a woman who had been born into a royal family in India. She fell in love with a servant, and in order to be true to her heart, left with him and didn't see her family for years. The two of them had two children, and shortly after the second child was born, she experienced a great longing to see her parents. The little family started on the trip. Tragedy after tragedy befell them. The children and their father were killed. Sadly, the young woman returned to their home to see it engulfed in flames and destroyed. Having lost everything made her insane with grief, and she tore off her clothes and wandered the streets of her village naked. The people feared and abused her, throwing stones at her and calling her names.

One day she wandered near a monk who was speaking to a group of people. There was so much kindness and compassion in his voice and in his words that they pierced her madness and brought her to her senses. She sat down and listened. Some members of the group found a shawl and gave it to her. She wore it for the rest of her life, working ceaselessly to alleviate human suffering. And then he wrote,

"I just want to tell you that you, Kathleen, are like those words of compassion and empathy that helped to pierce the bubble of grief I was encased in. You are the fabric in the shawl compassionately given to cover and warm and soothe. I pray—no, I know—that it is this shawl, this kindness that I shall wear in my own work to bring greater love and compassion into the world. Thank you, Kathleen, from the bottom of my heart, for the *equipment*.

Happy birthday, dear friend.

Love,

Chris

Kathleen Hellenberg worked as a court reporter in Wisconsin, taught the skill to others, and eventually became a legal secretary. She moved to Michigan, married, and stayed home to raise two children. She now creates customized wedding ceremonies.

Initiation

At 20 years old, I lived on my own for the first time in a cozy little apartment in downtown Victoria, British Columbia, Canada. In the wee hours one morning, I awoke to what sounded like a freight train plowing through my bedroom. The walls, the desk, the dresser, and everything on them shook violently. It was an earthquake, and I felt sure my death was imminent. I'd experienced tremors before, but nothing like this! As my heart exploded inside my chest and my stomach crawled up toward my mouth, I sensed an unexpected presence creep over me. It felt as if I were lifted up into the arms of what I can only describe as a Christ-like being—perhaps Jesus Christ himself. A warm, peaceful calm settled my stomach and eased my heart. My body was still in the bed, yet in that moment, I was aware of being held.

I was not raised in a religious household, but have been influenced by living in a Christian society. Ever since I could talk I asked endless questions about the meaning of life, and, not satisfied with the answers, never felt completely comfortable living on this planet. As a small child, I believed life was like a kindergarten with the teacher missing.

Occasionally I attended church with friends, but soon discovered it was not for me.

At the age of 7, the Cuban Missile Crisis confirmed my fears. In school, we were drilled to hide under our desks in case a bomb shattered the windows. Another lesson at school that left a lasting impression was a story about a man who had a near-death experience. When his friend revived him, he screamed, "Let me go! I was free! This is hell here on earth."

Perhaps this contributed to my cynical attitude as a teenager. I'd never asked to be born, and grew indignant about having to endure this thing called "life." Of course, my parents couldn't understand me at all, because they had come through the Great Depression and World War II. What on earth did I have to complain about? True, materially, I was very comfortable, but with the threat of atomic war and talk of emerging environmental disasters, having no spiritual foundation, what was there to be happy about? I think my attitude was very prevalent in my generation. We weren't busy surviving, so we had a lot of time to think and imagine the worst-case scenarios.

All this changed while cradled in the arms of this otherworldly figure as the earthquake rumbled around me. Suddenly I knew there was nothing to fear. Oddly, it felt so "normal." At last I was with someone who would keep me safe.

The next morning, I was still the same person. If someone jiggled my chair, it would trigger that crashing fear brought on by earthquakes. But a seed had been planted, and the roots have continued to grow deeper. Before that earthquake struck, I had hoped there was more to life than just a day-to-day struggle to survive. I longed for a meaningful reason for my existence. Since that night, I know without a doubt there is. Although I didn't receive any distinct or audible communication, the deep peace, comfort, and profound sense of "knowing" spoke directly to my soul in a way that has changed me forever. Since that moment of union, I now know the true peace and connection that is possible in the world, and can no longer settle for anything less. That night was the initiation of my spiritual journey, and it still fills me with awe, wonder, and gratitude to this day.

Colleen Freeman and her husband, Bill, are caretakers for a resort in the small community of Shawnigan Lake, just north of Victoria, BC, Canada. Colleen's passion for the inspirational side of life finds expression through gardening and sculpting in clay.

New Beginning

One terrible September day in 2003, I received a phone call from a stranger who claimed to be the "other woman" in my boyfriend's life. I experienced a sense of knowing before picking up the phone that this would not be an ordinary call and I was about to discover a hidden truth.

After our conversation I fled to my room, brokenhearted and crying. I had reached such brokenness, I was afraid to go on living, yet just as afraid to die. All I could do was lie there, pleading with God to end the pain gripping my heart.

After crying every tear I had inside, I came to a place of complete silence. In that silence I heard a soft voice that carried such authority—a voice I had come to recognize throughout the years as the Voice of Truth that spoke to my heart in times of trouble or need. I didn't hear this Voice often, but when it came, my body automatically responded to it, much as it would to the command of a parent.

The Voice told me to pick up the Bible lying beside my bed. This made no sense because I had never understood the words in that book. It was like a foreign language to me. Nevertheless, I did as the Voice instructed. I opened the Bible to a random page and read these words: "Follow me."

It was as if these words took on a Voice of their own—a voice much like the Voice of Truth. These words pierced my soul and became engraved upon my heart like a fingerprint. The words left me in awed fascination. I wondered how a book written so long ago could speak to me with such intensity. The moment felt magical, breathtaking. To be able to see words written by the One whose Voice I had heard for many years made me feel as though I'd walked out of a nightmare and stepped into reality—an awakening experience.

I was not certain how to follow this Voice. Moments later, the silence within me vanished. My anger and heartache rebelled and wouldn't allow me to sit there doing nothing. I continued to cry out to this Voice, but the more I cried out to it, the more voices I heard. I became overwhelmed, unable to shut out the chaos of all the different voices telling me to do different things. Which voice should I obey?

I followed the instructions of the loudest, angriest one because it was the most prominent. Rushing to my kitchen, I retrieved a knife from my silverware drawer, telling my daughter to get into the car. We had something that needed to be done. My mind was set, my purpose planned. I headed to my boyfriend's school to exact revenge. He needed to pay for his betrayal and to suffer as much as I.

My mind played out every little detail along the way. Images raced through my mind of slicing his tires, busting out his windows, and ripping his body apart with my knife, humiliating him in front of his military buddies.

Halfway there, revolving red and blue lights glared in my rearview mirror. A police officer pulled me over for speeding. When he discovered I had no driver's license, he impounded my car and took me and my daughter to a nearby rest stop. I called a neighbor to come get us.

Through the silent trip home I felt as though I were bleeding to death. When we got home I ran to my room, sobbing with confusion, frustration, anger, and humiliation. I couldn't figure out what I had done wrong or why my plan had failed. I picked up the Bible again, hoping for a sign, hoping to read something that made sense.

Once again my eyes rested upon the words, "Follow me."

"Follow you where?" I cried out loud. "I can't see you!"

I looked down and continued to read:

"Then Jesus said to his disciples, 'If anyone wants to become my follower, he must deny himself, take up his cross, and follow me. For whoever wants to save his life will lose it, but whoever loses his life for my sake will find it.'"

Those words once again left their fingerprint engraved on my heart. It was all I could think about from that day forward. I had to know the truth concerning those words; from whom they were given, for whom they were meant, and why they were taking over my life.

When I went to work the next day, I spoke with a coworker who was also a minister. I asked him a lot of questions, and the more answers I received, the more questions I had. He invited me to go to church with him and I gladly accepted. Part of me was terrified to go. I had not been to church since childhood, yet my mind was made up. I still had many questions and was still looking for answers.

That night as I lay brokenhearted on my bed, my direction in life changed. The way I viewed life changed. Nothing was the same after that night. My body, which had been numb inside for as long as I could remember, came to life with great emotions. The hopelessness and fear had been lifted and the sun shone down upon my soul. For the first time I could recall, my heart filled with joy and unspoken promises. The chains of sin that had once held me back had been broken. I was no longer bound to the life I'd been living. Now I looked forward into that bright sun to the life that lay ahead of me instead of looking back into the darkness of regret I'd just walked through.

Now my life has meaning, direction, and purpose. I am able to focus on this Voice instead of my own misery. I have hope. How I view my problems, the world, and life's situations has changed. I know I don't walk through life alone. I've been given new eyes and am able to see through Someone's eyes who sees beauty in pain, promise in ruins, and the world the way He created it. I can look in the mirror and truly love the person I am in spite of things I may or may not do. I have the peace inside I always wanted, the joy I never knew existed, and the love I thought had died. My life has become a journey in which every day is filled with beauty I never noticed before. It is filled with the many challenges I always craved and opportunities I never thought I'd have as a woman. Every day for me is a New Beginning.

Tonya Lewis was born and raised in Point Pleasant, West Virginia. A mother of two grown children, she is a retired nursing assistant who now works from home.

The Shade

Three years after an auto accident left me paralyzed from the chest down, I asked a family relative, Mary, if her two children could attend a weekend campout for kids with disabilities. Having a disability and holding a degree in recreation acquired prior to my paralysis allowed me to again work in my chosen profession. I love organizing fun and I'm great at planning events; my wheelchair hasn't removed many of my former abilities.

The campout was the first event I had planned as a woman on wheels, and I thought Mary's girls would benefit from working with kids with disabilities.

"Do you think the girls are up to this sort of experience?" I asked Mary.

Mary quickly dismissed them from the room and then turned to me and hissed, "Katie, my children can't be around *those* kinds of kids because it will give them nightmares."

My quadriplegic self sat there stunned. Anger started to build like the flames of a raging fire. I wanted to yell. I wanted to smack this horrible woman for disrespecting the members of my new culture. Livid and ready to blow, I opened my mouth but then quickly closed my lips. A voice from the back of my head told me to do so. I thought for sure Mary had heard the voice too, but she hadn't. She still sat nearby like a lump.

My focus returned to the conversation in my head. The peaceful voice told me to slow down. "Katie, don't say anything to Mary," it told me. My end of this conversation was delivered in thought: *Why not? I have a lot to say here. I'm really mad!*

"You'll see," the voice replied.

I zipped my lips.

Okay. I was angry at a crazy woman and frustrated by the fact that I didn't verbally respond to the horrible things she had just said. My brother, Tom, walked into the room saying he was ready to leave. So was I! He loaded me and my electric wheelchair into my van and he drove me back home. I sat quietly in my chair, which was strapped to the floor of the van.

Tom asked, "What's wrong?"

I snapped back, "Nothing. I need to go home and chill out for a while."

Once at home, I asked my brother to put on my writer pencil arm brace. I have great arm movement for a quad, but my fingers are paralyzed, so special braces hold my spoon and fork, or a pen, and there's even one that allows me to put on my own lipstick. Tom strapped on my writing brace, and I grabbed a pad of paper off my desk and rolled over to sit in front of the living room window.

I closed my eyes and sat silently, trying to get over my anger at people who say mean and cold-hearted things. I heard an internal voice say "Katie, write your thoughts." I took my pen and the following words flowed.

The Shade

Life needs light to see so clear
Deprivation instills fear

You can't keep someone in the shade
They'll wither, choke, and die.
How can they grow?
How will they know
What it's like to try?

Protection by prejudice
Is not the way to teach
Try understanding and compassion
Extend beyond your reach

Cultivate your being
Don't put yourself above
Shed beams of light
Flee from fright
Because everyone needs love

I read the poem and was amazed. I had physically written the words, but I knew I'd had help. Closing my eyes, I took a deep breath and said, "Thank you, God. Thank you for helping me to silence negative reactions in order to bring forth truth and beauty."

When I slow down enough to listen, God is always there. I have daily conversations in my head and listen with my heart. Knowing that I am never alone creates a more peaceful path to roll upon.

Wheelchair-bound Katie Rodriquez Banister's paralysis became a blessing when it led to her finding and marrying Steve. An advocate and mentor in the disability culture with a mission to educate and empower others, Katie is also a poet, actor, artist, and friend to many.

Drive South

I had decidedly mixed feelings about my tenure as an art student in the noise, mess, and what I saw as the spiritual void of mid-1980s Manhattan. I had been influenced and supported by tremendous teachers at The Art Students' League, and the New York galleries gave me access to work by the greatest living artists, including a personal favorite, Andrew Wyeth. But life in New York City was clearly too harsh for me. I didn't want to become the person I thought I had to become to thrive there. After several months, despite the offer of a full tuition art school scholarship, I left without looking back.

Less than a year later, while running an art gallery in Rhode Island and waiting for the summer season to end, I became immersed in spirituality, studying *A Course in Miracles.* This self-study course put forth the extraordinary claim that we each have access to a far greater wisdom than we currently use. This Voice of "Holy Spirit" knew exactly what was best for each of us in every situation, if only we could learn to be still and hear it. I became determined to do so, yet struggled endlessly, never knowing if the voice I sometimes heard was that of a deeper wisdom, or simply my imagination.

One morning I awoke and realized I had absolutely no plans for the day. The gallery was closed until the weekend, and I was open to anything. I checked in with stillness, trying yet again to hear the "Holy Spirit." To my surprise, I heard a quiet, still voice within me quite clearly. It wasn't like hearing a physical human voice. It was more like an inner dialogue that seemed to appear immaculately. The words were not an extension of something I was thinking, and a sense of power and peace accompanied them. I think the Voice was so clear that morning because I was open to it.

It said, "Drive south."

Huh? Well, what did I have to lose?

I got in my beloved Ford and started driving south, expecting I might be off to a local breakfast place. But I checked in every few minutes, and the message stayed the same. "Drive south."

Okay, I get it! I thought. *I'll drive south!*

After three hours of driving south as my still, quiet voice instructed, I found myself entering the state of New York, heading straight for the city I'd been so determined to leave. With some trepidation, but also an emerging sense of underlying purpose, I followed my inner voice as it led me into the heart of Manhattan.

I drove by my old home and walked the paths I'd traveled as part of my former routine, guided now by "Holy Spirit." It said things like "Go into the Pizza Shop" where I had regularly eaten, or "Visit the Art Students' League Studios" and the other studios at which I had spent time.

In each place I initially felt some old memory of the harshness of the city; the rudeness, the lines, the constant pushing, the anonymity, the concrete and steel, the lack of humanity. But these were old memories. This day, each place I visited felt different, lighter, cleaner, forgiven. Everywhere, people went out of their way to be nice and helpful. Everywhere I went, a blessing came.

I had wanted to be freed from my negative feelings about the city and the people there, to forgive them, but had no idea how to go about it before now. I had struggled for months with this while living there. Now, healing was happening before my eyes, and I knew I was not the one doing it. I wouldn't have even been there if not for the "Holy Spirit."

I was filled more and more with gratitude as the day went on. By nightfall I walked back to my car parked at the Metropolitan Museum of Art feeling absolutely complete. My forgiveness of New York had returned. The love I once felt for the city, and my appreciation and faith in the "Holy Spirit" had grown exponentially. Feeling sure my little Voice would tell me to get going on the long drive home after such a long, successful day of healing and meaning, I checking in just to be sure.

"Time to go, right?" I asked.

"Stick around," my little Voice said.

"What?" I retorted. "It's late and I have a four-hour drive!"

"Stick around."

"Okay! Whatever!"

After reluctantly agreeing, I was guided to return to an art gallery I had visited earlier in the day. It was getting ready for an opening that night to show paintings by Jamie Wyeth, the son of Andrew Wyeth. I knew of Jamie's work because of his father, and had enjoyed seeing the show that afternoon. However, it did not hold the influence on me his father's work had. Seeing Andrew Wyeth's work as a young child in Boston was a magical experience, and deeply affected my career path. His work had been so influential I had realized there was no living artist I would rather meet than Andrew Wyeth. But he is a deeply private man and rarely appeared in public. I had put all hope of meeting him aside as an impossibility.

At the gallery of Jamie's Wyeth's exhibition and formal reception, I found myself with some of the top New York art crowd, generally a hard group to get to know. They were approaching me and starting up conversations as this day continued its amazingly positive energy. I was thoroughly enjoying it all, feeling as though just about anything could happen.

Then, suddenly, it did.

Andrew Wyeth appeared in the gallery. Unknown to anyone but the gallery directors, he had arranged to break his hermit-like routine and travel to the city to surprise his son at the show. His appearance was so unexpected that none of the gallery visitors were prepared for it, and he was briefly left alone for me to approach.

I shook his hand, sincerely thanking him for the joy his work had brought into my life and for the influence he'd had on my path as an artist. The deep humility of the man shone through as he bowed in gratitude to my thanks. Here was the man I had so hoped was real, the man who was clearly in the service of love just as I had imagined him to be from his art! It was a perfect meeting for me. Then, just as quickly as he had appeared, he was ushered backstage by the gallery staff.

I was dazed by everything that had happened. The miracles of this day, run totally by spirit, were undeniable. My perpetually rocky relationship with New York had been healed, and I had met Andrew Wyeth! Amazingly, he was just as I had always hoped he would be.

I was guided back to my car with the message, "It is late! Get going!" delivered by Holy Spirit with a tangible sense of love and humor. It was clear that I would never see my "little Voice" in the same way again.

In the 20 years since, my relationship with my "little Voice" has grown and evolved. I have asked Holy Spirit what to do and where to go, and great healing has occurred. But perhaps no other day has held the clarity of Holy Sprits presence more than that amazing day when I became truly acquainted with it, met Andrew Wyeth, forgave New York City, and allowed the day to go just as God wanted it to for me.

I now live with the belief that every day can be miraculous if I can only get myself out of the way. Such days are guided fully by God's

Loving Presence. To me, God's Presence and God's presents are one and the same. I need only listen well enough, and ask to receive them. He does the driving. I just hold the wheel, follow the little Voice, and "Drive South!"

David Schock is a professional artist by trade. He specializes in portraits, landscapes, and figure paintings; 30,000 of his art prints are in circulation worldwide.

On Loan

Marla's friend Chris burst breathlessly through the door.

"Marla's been hit by a car!"

"Chris, that's not funny..." I started to say. His contorted face told me this was no joke! I grabbed my keys, jumped in my car, and sped the two blocks to the highway.

Eight-year-old Marla was the youngest of my three children. They attended school across the highway near our home in a little mountain town tucked among the Colorado forests.

The intersection was swarming with police cars, a fire truck, an ambulance, and a milling crowd. Orange-clad paramedics stood out among the onlookers, preparing to lift Marla into the ambulance.

"Marla," I gasped as I bent down to her. I gazed helplessly at her bloody face and scanned the rest of her limp body. The paramedics had ripped apart the leg of her jeans and elevated her swollen leg.

She mumbled "Mama," then closed her eyes and slid into oblivion. My heart tried to pound free of my chest.

"Take her to my office," a familiar voice said.

It was Dr. Ronin, our family doctor. He had rushed over from his office, just across the highway.

While Dr. Ronin was examining her in his office, a policeman explained Marla had been in the crosswalk when a high school student failed to stop at the red light. He hit Marla at 50 miles an hour, skidding more than 100 feet. She had stayed fused to the front of his car for most of the skid before being thrown to the side. It was a miracle she had not been run over. As her little body grazed the shoulder's gravel for several feet, her skin had been torn away from her face, arm, and leg, embedding dirt and little shards of debris.

The young driver's tear-stained face registered total remorse when he entered the doctor's office and profusely apologized to me. His sincerity made my chest swell with compassion for his pain. I hugged him and said, "It'll be okay." I was trying to convince myself as well.

After attending to Marla, Dr. Ronin explained she had initially complained about her chest, but X-rays found no injury there. He had detected no broken bones, only pulled ligaments making her knee swell, but he couldn't fully explain Marla's unconsciousness and wanted to admit her to Eisenhower Hospital in Colorado Springs.

During the ambulance ride, with the siren screaming, Marla came around and called for me once more before drifting off again. I shut my eyes. *Please, God, help us!* Although I knew the EMTs were speeding down the dangerous winding pass as safely as they could, it was not fast enough for me. *Please, don't let her die, God.*

Once in the ICU, the nursing staff hovered over her, changing clothing, drawing blood, and inserting IV tubes, while I continued to pray. I stayed by Marla's side and the doctor kept me well informed. He was uncertain why there was blood in Marla's urine.

Everything was so clinical, so white. The gleaming chrome of the bed frame, the side tables, and the IV pole seemed so cold next to the heat of my steaming desperation. Hours passed. The test results indicated no major problems. Dr. Ronin said the blood in her urine was probably from a bruised kidney, but he was concerned because she was still unconscious. I prepared to stay the night.

My obsessive need for answers intensified with each tick of the clock, the steady hum of the heaters, and the buzzing florescent lights. The stark room held no compassion. I was frantic, as if my own life were slipping away. As her mother, it was my job to protect her, but I could do nothing but watch...and wait.

I gripped her precious little hand and begged God for her life. Marla appeared to be sleeping peacefully. I drifted off to sleep a few times, but my body jerked awake at the thought that my lack of vigilance would somehow fail to keep her alive. I knew that was ludicrous, but I had to do something to save her.

I had heard God speak to me before, but I desperately needed to hear His Voice now. I talked to Him, then waited and listened. I had never needed His comfort and calm reassurance more than I did in that moment.

Thursday morning dawned with Marla still in a coma. Emotionally exhausted, desperate, and discouraged, I held her small hand, shut my eyes, and once again called on God to please save my daughter. The hours dragged by with no change when suddenly, at 11 o'clock, my mind was washed clean. In that split second, all the desperation vanished and joy entered my heart. My heart had opened completely, and I suddenly realized that this was not about me and my wants. I let go of my desires and hopes, and let God in to make this life-and-death decision. In that moment I gave my daughter away to God's care.

"I'm sorry, God," I said out loud. Then I softly whispered, "It's not my choice whether she lives or dies. That is for you to decide."

I stood there and gazed at her angelic face, remembering my conversation with Patrick just yesterday. A young man, Patrick had lived in a Buddhist ashram and now shared a college classroom with me. I was impressed with his maturity and his comments about the purpose of life. He had given up all possessions to live his life free from worldly entrapments. The dialogue about possessions somehow shifted to his telling me that my children were on loan. I was to take care of them until adulthood when they would be able to live on their own. I agreed with the concept and thanked him for his insight. I didn't know then how soon my faith would be tested.

I sat viewing Marla's tangled blond hair, remembering her pretty green eyes beneath her closed lids. My love poured out to her and I told God, "I don't know if I can bear it if she dies." The tears streaming down my cheeks this time were different. I was feeling love for God and my little girl.

I held her hand, waiting—just waiting for God's decision. By 11:15 I knew that whatever happened would be okay. I waited patiently, wrapped in God's peace.

"Mama?" She opened her eyes.

"I'm here, honey." My heart pumped pure wonder. God was giving her back to me! I had done what I needed to do—trust in God. *Thank you, God!*

Lifting her head a little she said, "I'm thirsty."

"I'll get you something." I pushed the call button. The nurse brought her a popsicle and said that she would tell the doctor Marla was awake. Doctor Ronin discharged her late that afternoon.

I will forever be full of gratitude for this precious life that had been given to me on loan. Her life had been threatened, but God sent her back to me once more. I opened my heart, let go of my desires, and gave myself over to God.

Valerie J. Foster is a 65-year-old retired mental health therapist who focused on working with women and children facing sexual abuse issues. Now a writer, Valerie lives in southern Oregon with her husband.

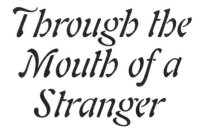

Through the Mouth of a Stranger

I had spent the better part of a year in and out of psychiatric hospitals trying to get a grip on life and understand what was going on inside of me. Now that I grappled with an illness that seemed to have unleashed its power in me to the point at which it controlled every aspect of my life, I struggled to comprehend the nature of life all over again, and what my place in it was. What had first appeared to be a late onset of depression turned into a serious mood disorder in which I experienced hallucinations and had a hard time distinguishing between reality and non-reality.

Throughout the course of the past year I had become very disillusioned with God. I felt that He didn't care about me, nor did He care if anything bad was happening to me. I had even come to the point at which I felt God had abandoned me and that I had been left to fend for myself.

I prayed several times a day, begging forgiveness for something, even though I struggled to know of what to repent, as I wasn't a bad person. But I reasoned that I must have done something in order for God to leave me alone and refuse to answer my prayers.

Through treatment and therapy, I soon discovered I couldn't trust my own feelings. My body was out of whack, and my mind mirrored that condition—if God really wanted to talk to me, I wouldn't even be able to hear or understand anything He said. My growing sense of isolation was compounded by being on medication, going through intense therapy, and facing abandonment by friends and family.

One day a group of us went to a religious service for a friend who was accepting her ordinances. I went for selfish reasons, thinking that while I was in the temple of God I could pray and hope for an answer—something, anything. I had convinced myself that if just one friend from my group came up and talked to me while I prayed, that would be God's answer that I was okay.

After the service I walked into the general reception area and found a place to sit. I bowed my head and started to pray while my friends and others stood and talked with one another. After praying for several minutes I looked up and found that out of the 20 people in our group, there were six still remaining along with a small group of older women on the other side of the room. I felt relieved, though, because I knew God would send one of my friends over to check on me and tell me, once again, that I was okay.

Another 15 minutes passed and I looked up again, but only felt total despair this time. None of the friends from my group were still there. I felt truly lost and alone, and that my answer from God had left the building with them. This time I just lowered my head and cried inside. Nothing felt worse than to feel I was now forced to accept that even God didn't want me.

Several more minutes had gone by when I felt a hand on my shoulder. I didn't know who it was and thought maybe it was a friend who had returned. But I was still crying and didn't open my eyes to see who it was. When I heard the person's voice, I knew it wasn't anyone I knew. It was a woman's voice. She had come over and knelt down beside me. She spoke quietly, saying, "I don't know who you are, but God told me to come over and tell you that He loves you."

With that, I lost control of the rest of my emotions and cried even harder. It was many minutes before I could open my eyes to see who the messenger was. She was one of the older ladies who had been busy talking with her group from the other side of the room. She later told me that she had ignored the promptings a couple of times and didn't want to bother me because she could tell I was engaged in prayer. Finally she could no longer ignore the promptings and came to deliver God's message.

From that day on, I learned that I may or may not ever get a direct answer from God because of my condition, but He will send me an answer through another person. Although I have had several spiritual experiences in life, none felt sweeter than the one this dear lady delivered to me that day.

Had she ignore the promptings or not delivered the message to me, I don't know where I would be today. I would probably still feel lost, abandoned, and struggling for sanity, believing that God isn't there for me.

Kenneth Dyer is 45, a married father of a blended family with eight children. He works as a program director for a day treatment center and enjoys writing short stories and poems.

Four Glorious Days

I spent six months attending Alcoholics Anonymous meetings listening to other people talk about their experiences, and struggling to understand what had happened to my life to leave it swirling down the toilet bowl before admitting my own condition. I finally heard myself say, "I am an alcoholic." I guess my brain took six months to clear up enough from drinking to have this lifesaving insight. I had to find a way to stop drinking and stay stopped. Otherwise, I would die.

This change in attitude gave me a new appreciation for my budding relationship with the 12 Steps and called for me to explore a relationship with God. I had no clue how to proceed. The only thing I knew about God was that if He were responsible for all the suffering I'd seen and experienced, He wasn't anyone I would invite to dinner. But I was counseled by my AA guides to seek a relationship with Him nonetheless.

My childhood Christian orientation was harsh and shame-based; God was a watcher, someone who was always lurking, looking to catch my mistakes—not a friend. As an adult, had I not had plenty of supportive people nearby, I would have abandoned my new quest and returned to drinking—God was no one I could relate to, but a power to be feared and avoided, and prayer consisted of making promises to God to change my behavior for the better as a way of bargaining for favors. Of course, I never kept my part of the bargain long enough to receive any favors. I was doing the best I could just staying sober.

Two years later I was in much the same condition. I was told my life depended on a relationship with God, but I had no concept of any God with whom I wanted a relationship. That all changed the day a doctor diagnosed my wife with breast cancer. Although he was not an expert in the field of cancer, he so strongly suspected the disease that he immediately referred my wife to a specialist. The appointment was set for four days later.

I was livid with God. Hadn't I lived up to my commitment to abstain from alcohol? Wasn't I following the 12 Steps faithfully? How could any loving Power do this to my wife? Or to me? To say I was frightened and angry doesn't quite capture the rage I felt in my heart toward God. I held Him responsible for my wife's cancer and all the pain and suffering I'd endured. If a physical God had appeared, I would have grappled with Him, choked Him, and fought Him to the death. Win or lose, I wanted to satisfy the hatred I felt toward the God I knew.

I have no memory of how I came to stand on a beach at sunset, staring at the clouds and yelling at the top of my lungs, "No deals!" I was done, finished, completely fed up with bargaining, beseeching, or trying to communicate with God. If He was the kind of God who would give my wife cancer, he might as well kill me. I had no use for Him or what I thought I knew about Him.

In seconds my thoughts stopped. I was so upset, so bereft of any hope for myself or my wife, so shocked at the possibility that she had cancer, that my internal dialog stopped. I stood silent, still, without a single thought. Within this stillness inside me, I lost all ability to judge the world. I have no memory of wanting to stop my thoughts;

they just came to a halt. In place of all that inner dialog came a Peace unsupported by the facts.

For the next four days I loved everything and everyone I laid eyes on or thought about. I felt gentle, appreciative, kind, and in a state of love with every moment of my experience. I listened to my children's voices as I would to music. I looked at the color of carrots on my dinner plate as I would a Picasso painting. The play of light and shadow on the dashboard of my truck became a display of beauty so great I could only sit and stare with awe. I had been transported to some state superior to the ordinary, some way of perceiving that left me transfixed with the very experience of life itself.

Those four days occurred three decades ago; the state of joy lasted just those four days. When I accompanied my wife to see the cancer specialist he diagnosed her lump as a cyst requiring a simple office procedure. Immediately, my inner dialog resumed. The calm joy I'd been feeling vanished, evaporating as quickly as it had come. I was once more in the mire of the human condition without any idea what had been happening to me. Of course, I was greatly relieved that my wife had no cancer, but I was also heartbroken to lose the wonderful feeling that had permeated my soul for those four days. I fell into a despair worse than any I had known.

Years later I recognized that despair as the driving force that began my quest for God—not the God of my childhood, the shaming, guilt-giving God I had been taught to fear. I had become a genuine seeker of Truth—something I could speak about with real authority, something I could trust, count on, and give myself to. I honor and appreciate the despair I felt back then. It was my first surrender, my first knowing that I couldn't rest until I found something greater than myself to whom I could relate.

I believe the Joy and Peace I felt those four glorious days was God Himself. The Love inside me was God loving through me. What I thought and shared with others were God's Words speaking to me and through me. The simple appreciation for my existence was God's Gift to me for giving Him a place to offer Love. I wonder if the presence of that transcendent feeling within me hadn't miraculously changed my wife's cancer into a simple lump. I don't know for sure. What I do know is that those four days of Peace, Love, and Joy became my new understanding of God and the object of my search ever since.

I have diligently practiced the 12 Steps of Alcoholics Anonymous. Each step has led me further into the realm of my spirit, toward the place within me that is Holy. I have, by Grace, survived a relapse into alcohol, a genuine cancer diagnosis that cost my wife a breast, and other sundry heartaches that are part of human existence. Yet, within each problem I have found a change taking place in myself and my beliefs that makes even the most awful dilemma a source of learning and forward movement, and every time I've touched upon those feelings of genuine Peace, Love, and Joy, I know I've been hearing God's Voice speak to me.

In my relationships with the world at large I find more space between me and the insanity so well portrayed on the evening news. I know myself. I have no secrets, and I willingly investigate and release any shadow that appears within my consciousness. My commitment to the simple experience of feeling what I call Love, or God, is my life's task. Every time I feel Love, I know I am feeling God and hearing His Voice, and my life's purpose is complete.

Alan Brooks is in his 60s and retired. A "professional grandfather," he has written three books: *A Snake Around the Moon*, *Tracking the Divine*, and *The Mummy Murder*. He lives in the Appalachian foothills with his wife, Sandy, and his rottweiler, Tonka.

Three Words

The jet engines' deafening roar failed to drown out my racing thoughts or deaden my emotional pain. Flying back to my Florida home from Seattle after visiting my son and his family, I now carried the emotional pain and anger he had revealed about being raised in a dysfunctional family. He had been the second of my three children to voice these painful accusations, a shock to my system after so many years had passed.

We had all suffered back then, but it seemed life had become somewhat saner after their father and I had divorced and the fighting had stopped. How could I have been so mistaken? How had I missed seeing their childhood wounds? Could I have done something to help them? Was it too late now? I knew I'd made some mistakes and bad decisions, but it still wasn't clear what I had done, or failed to do, to create such pain for them. Some of their accusations I could relate to, but others left me confused, and they refused to discuss these issues with me so we could find resolution.

An obsessive sense of helplessness tortured me daily. I spent hours mentally replaying the situation in an attempt to find some way to end this painful stalemate and find peace for us all. My heart ached at the thought of losing my children whom I had always loved more than anything in life.

Months of prayer for God's intervention had produced no resolution, and my own efforts to reach out and resolve my children's issues failed. The possibility of our ever healing seemed hopeless. Now, returning to my home in Florida, tears of despair ran down my face. I finally knew this was not something I could control or solve on my own, and again I turned to God for His help. He was my last hope.

I pleaded, "Please, merciful Lord, tell me what I can do to bring about peace and harmony between my children and myself. I know

95

You can heal us, but please tell me what I should do and give me strength to follow Your guidance."

I prayed over and over, choking on each tear. Suddenly I heard a distinct voice coming from inside my mind, commanding and strong, yet gentle and loving. It said, "Just love them."

Only three words, but powerful enough to bring my whole being to attention. For most of my life I had attended and volunteered at church. I had sung in the choir and taken my children to Sunday school when they were young. Many times in my life I felt God guiding me, but I'd never experienced anything like this. I was stunned! The Voice sounded like a real person talking to me, but it came from inside. Now I smiled through joyful tears and felt as though my heart would burst with gratitude. God was really there, and I knew my children and I were in His care.

Determined to do as God said, I immediately confronted the damaging thoughts I'd lived with so long. I spoke to them with a firm, determined voice, saying, "God told me to just love my children, and that's what I'm doing. I'm no longer listening to you, so leave and never return. I am filled with God's love, and I send love to my children. There is no more room for negative thoughts like you."

At first, there was no change. The negative thoughts still ran through my head like a broken record. After two weeks, however, I began to notice the crippling thoughts diminishing, and within one month I was in a more peaceful state. Whenever I felt doubt creeping in, I spoke to God saying, "Lord, I believe. Help my unbelief." Then I felt freer to anticipate good coming from this experience and continued sending love to my children and feeling God's love inside.

As months passed, I noticed changes taking place, not only within myself, but also from my daughter in Dallas. She called, asking me to help her sort things out in her own mind. She requested answers to many questions. I responded with several letters, trying to answer her questions about the past as accurately as I could. I reminded her that different people sometimes remember things differently, so her father and grandmother might have different memories from my own. She never said she was no longer angry at me or that she forgave me, but as we approached the situation together I noticed that her voice softened and greeting cards became warmer and more personal. Gradually, the love between us strengthened and we developed a closer, more loving relationship.

It saddens me that my son and I have not done as well. I rarely hear from him, and several years have passed since my last attempt to speak with him about childhood issues. Sometimes I still sense his anger. Though I've enjoyed some pleasant visits with him and his family, there are still times when I long for him to put his arms around me and say, "Mom, I understand, and I love you too," but I know this must be his choice. I continue loving him.

In the past, I was unaware of God's attempts to communicate with me, but now that I have learned to listen, I hear His loving Voice more frequently. Sometimes it's words, and sometimes just the knowingness I feel when He gently guides my path. I realize, too, that His powerful three words, "Just love them," apply not only to my children, but to everyone around me—the thoughtless driver who cuts me off in traffic, the stranger who is rude, the friend who fails to be understanding—and I can choose to love them. I can also love myself when I fall short of my goals or stumble on my path.

Hearing God's Voice that first time was an awakening. It was a door that opened my heart to a closer relationship with my Creator, reminding me of who I am, my Father's precious child. Now I allow God's love to express through me more freely, and I am grateful.

Marilyn Fowler is single and retired. Having worked many wonderful years as a psychotherapist, she enjoys writing poetry and has written an unpublished memoir.

Succumbing to an Unlikely Death

The argument began innocently enough. While living with my husband, whom I was divorcing, I requested that he leave the children out of our disagreements. I stood just inside his room and told him I wanted it to stop. He sat in his chair, slumped a bit from drinking a couple of beers, and told me to get out. As I backed up, repeating my request, this man I had known to be relatively nonviolent during our eight-year marriage, stood up, grabbed his chair, and raised it over his head to strike me, hitting me in the arm along the way. I was shocked. I knew he wasn't happy we were getting a divorce, but this display of physical aggression was so completely out of character that I felt unsure of what to do. I ran to the phone, intending to call for help. Then I questioned myself and hung up—until I heard him say, "You better be careful or you'll be six feet under."

The words hung heavily in the air. My heart thumped. If he did snap again and actually killed me, I at least wanted this threat on record. I called the police and asked them to come take a report.

Two female officers arrived and took our separate stories. As I heard my husband relate his side I felt sadness well up inside of me. What was happening? I did not want this. I wanted a peaceful divorce. I looked at the officer and told her how he had threatened me while our three children, all under age 8, were present. Tears filled my eyes as I watched the other officer lead this man I loved—had built my adult life around—past me through the house to gather his belongings before being taken to a hotel.

He spewed angry words as he was guided to the police car. "You'd better get out of here because you're not safe in this house."

I watched in a daze, wondering if this was someone else's life I was watching in a movie. Although I knew my husband was angry, and likely shouting words that would not result in action, I couldn't help but feel some fear because he had never reacted to anything in such a violent and threatening manner before.

As night deepened and dark replaced the daylight, my fear grew stronger. I was afraid for myself and my children. What if he returned while I was sleeping? The suggestion from the police had been less than comforting—file a personal protection order in the morning. That still left the night to get through. What became clear to me was the sad fact that if someone wished to hurt or kill me, they could. I could lock the doors and put bells by the windows, but if someone actually wanted to get in, what could I do to physically stop them? What about my three precious children? What would become of them if I were hurt, or worse, killed? I felt caught in the middle of a nightmare with no way out.

I called a close friend and cried while mumbling about my fears.

She said, "Amy, I don't think this is really about you dying. You're taking whatever steps you can to make you and the kids safe. Your husband has left the house and will likely cool off enough to realize the error of his aggravated ways tomorrow. What I think you're working through is the *idea* of dying."

A shiver of warm, flowing energy resonated through my body as I realized the truth in what she said. I cried harder. "And in accepting that I *will* someday die, I have to admit that my children will somehow be okay without me."

In that moment I broke down and realized that this situation had forced me to contemplate my mortality in a way I never had. My mind raced back to a missionary mother's story I had read earlier about her young child who was gravely ill. She was miles from any hospital, had done all she could, and was grief-stricken at the thought her child might die. She lifted her young son up to God saying "I have done all that I can. I give him to You. I surrender."

My sobs poured from the depths of my soul as I considered what I was up against. I could admit that I was eternal or I could shrivel in fear. My children looked at me, wondering what would happen if I were to die. The situation's sadness prompted me to talk to my Creator in a way I had never done before.

With my children watching, I let the words flow to my Creator: "I know I am eternal, part of You, and that even if I die in physical body, I am not really gone or dead. I trust that there are no accidents and that we are all okay, whatever happens tonight. I trust You and I love You."

A new sense of confidence enveloped me as I took precautions to make our house safe while we slept. I gathered the children in my bedroom, wrote emergency numbers down for my 7-year-old, and blocked the doors with chairs. We read books and fell asleep, knowing we would wake up to the light of day.

Later that night I woke, sick to my stomach, shaking, and shivering with a feeling reminiscent of the panic attacks I had experienced in college while in an abusive relationship. I stumbled to the bathroom, questioning whether I should drink a glass of water.

Then I heard the voice.

"Just lie in bed and breathe."

I felt it on all layers—the clearest and calmest voice I'd ever heard. Quiet, yet guiding. Calm, yet directional. My body tingled and a sense of peace began to settle upon me. I felt no hesitancy in following this voice. It came from inside, yet it was also outside of me, extended in space.

Back in bed, I lay down, closed my eyes, and breathed. Feelings of nervousness and fear coursed throughout my body, then gently dissolved as I continued to breathe deeply. It felt as if the air around me swirled and swooshed ever so quietly, intermingled with my own energy. Colors changed, and the images behind my eyelids were simple and flowing like a river. I opened my eyes. The room was dark, but the colors continued in a muted fashion.

The voice repeated, "Breathe."

Closing my eyes, I saw myself as energetic essence, guided to places of darkness and followed quickly by bright, colorful light. I was being shown the places where I held fear, and then the warmth that could dissolve it. As the experience progressed I surrendered, and the fear became neutralized. It washed through and away from me. The tingling in my body subsided, replaced with overwhelming peace. I fell back asleep in complete relaxation.

The next morning I felt a sense of knowing about my nature as a spiritual being that I had not grasped in the past. Through my willingness to trust in my Creator, I was "awakened" to consciously participate in my own spiritual transformation. I had been a bit skeptical of my spirituality in the past, but it was no longer something I could deny. I saw clearly that I am a spiritual being, that God is within and is everything. There is no separation.

As I ruminated on this tranquil blessing, the phone rang. I picked up to hear my husband's voice, quiet and calm.

"I'm sorry about last night, Amy. I'm not going to hurt you or the kids. I want to work this out."

I took a deep breath, hearing the resignation and truth in his voice. "I know," I replied.

The fear had been banished, replaced by God's loving peace and calm. With quiet confidence I proceeded with the divorce, strengthened by my new spirituality.

Amy Christine Bush is a mother and parenting coach who enjoys reading, music, being in nature, and playing with her children and animals.

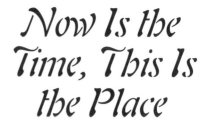

Now Is the Time, This Is the Place

As a middle-aged man who had always enjoyed being in relationships, I married for the first time in my early 20s, and for the second time when I was 28. I believed I was marrying for life both times. When both marriages ended in divorce, I suffered through a troubled period, which led to much soul-searching. Eventually, I became involved with a spiritual study group.

Through a friend I received a list of 25 study groups in San Jose, California, where I lived at that time. I got a map and located all the addresses, to discover two of the meetings were very close to my home.

I called the teacher of the closest location, and Roxsan answered the phone. I felt an energetic zap over the phone lines when she spoke, and later found out she also had felt it. I was happy to hear this group had just started a book, and I accepted her invitation to attend the next meeting, still wondering about the shock I had felt. When I met her, I thought she would be a good teacher for me, but nothing more.

A few months later, Roxsan caught me by surprise when she asked if I could stay after the meeting. Throughout the meeting I had been concerned she would ask me to leave the group because my beliefs were in conflict with those of the group.

After everyone else had left, I was surprised and relieved when she expressed feelings for me. I was speechless and not looking for another relationship. In fact, I had promised myself only to have friendships with females. That promise was short-lived. Roxsan asked me to join her for a Sunday service at her church. Although feeling strained during our first get-together, I felt compelled to ask her out to a musical evening that also took place at church. We continued to date and I found myself greatly enjoying her company.

Four to five years into our relationship Roxsan expressed her strong desire to get married. I said that with my previous track record I would have to hear it directly from God. I did not trust myself to make this decision. Roxsan seemed to accept this reasoning.

A few years later, while Roxsan and I were walking along a rushing river in New Mexico, I began to look at the rocks in the water while Roxsan went exploring in a field a short distance away. As I looked around I heard a deep male voice say "Now is the time, this is the place."

Somewhat startled, I glanced quickly around me, noticing no one near. I wasn't sure if this voice came from within my mind or outside of me, though I simultaneously knew what it meant.

Thinking that I might be making it up, I asked myself, "Now's the time for what?"

"Now is the time and this is the place!" said the voice again.

In that moment I was filled with all sorts of emotions: excitement, fear, disbelief. I gazed over at Roxsan as she walked in a field of colorful wildflowers. This timeless moment was beautiful beyond words. I began to cry, knowing the voice was correct. This was the perfect moment.

Just then, Roxsan turned to me and said, "I think we better head back." We were camping with friends and they had returned to the camp earlier to start dinner.

I called Roxsan over, and to her amazement got down on one knee and asked for her hand in marriage. She playfully paused for what seemed like eternity before saying, "Yes! What took you so long to ask?"

I replied, "I had to hear it from God."

We married each other on Valentine's Day with God as our only witness in a beautiful garden with a magnificent waterfall and are grateful for the continuing blessings we share as friends and lovers.

Paul Lanoie was born and raised in San Jose, California, where he fathered two great kids, Jennifer and Joshua. Passionate about woodworking, he currently resides in Placitas, New Mexico with his wife, Roxsan, and two dogs.

In My Own Backyard

I have always talked to God, but it hasn't always been easy to hear God's Voice speaking to me. As a child I would go outside and climb a tree in our backyard to listen to the wind and watch the sky. I felt that if God were to speak to me, putting my ears and eyes to the sky would be how I might hear Him best.

I was raised Catholic. For nine years I attended Catholic schools, went to Mass six days a week, nine months a year, and never once rebelled. I loved the quiet, holy space in church where I could talk to God. But as I grew I began to question the tenets of my faith, and a strong desire took root in me: I wanted to know how people of other faiths related to God in cultures other than my own. After exploring many religions and philosophies of the world, I returned to just going outside to listen to the wind and watch the sky.

Now, in the fifth decade of my life, I have grown accustomed to hearing God's Voice in many ways—some more striking than others—but within each of these occurrences I have noticed the common link of a strongly felt *desire*.

During the first week of the new millennium I experienced one of the most dramatic episodes of personal communication with God I have ever known. I had reached a point in my spiritual life at which I was feeling a deep inner longing to know God. In my home, on January 6, 2000, I sat down before a large window framing the open sky. I closed my eyes and repeated my one request to God: "Come, Lord, come. Please come into my heart." I longed to feel God's presence within me, to surrender to God's will in all things. I opened the door of my heart, much like opening the door of my home, and said, "Come in, Lord! Yes, please, do come in!"

After several minutes of feeling immersed in this prayer, I opened my eyes and gazed out the window. The midday sun shone brightly encircled by a large ring resembling a halo. I had seen this a few times before, but in that moment the huge halo seemed to communicate something more. I sensed it to be a doorway in the sky leading to where I most desired to go. Just that fast, my heart and soul flew up through that doorway.

In my mind's eye I saw a large bird in flight, winging toward the sun. I soared with the bird, following close behind. I became so thoroughly fascinated by this flight that at first I didn't hear the voice speaking within me. When eventually I heard it, the voice was saying "Go outside. Go outside. Go outside." But I was much too content where I was. Not wanting to break the spell, my heart echoed back, "No, I'm very comfortable right where I am, thanks." I brushed the voice off as a wave of distraction from my mind and tried to ignore it.

But the voice didn't go away. It persistently interrupted me to the point that I became annoyed. Finally, in the hope of resolving the matter, I got up and walked outside. What I saw when I looked up at the sky stopped me in my tracks. There, high in a clear blue sky, was a large feather-shaped cloud striped in brilliant rainbow colors! The sight of it made me gasp. It wasn't a rainbow—it hadn't been raining—it was a multicolored cloud, stretching like a feather halfway across the otherwise clear blue sky. The brilliant colors shimmered and blended together, creating the most gorgeous thing of nature I had ever seen. I stood transfixed, and its beauty made me weep. I wanted to run up and down the street in utter joy pointing it out to everyone I met, but I didn't want to miss one second of its presence. I stood there with tears of joy streaming down my face, saying, "Oh, dear God! Thank you, thank you, thank you..."

Then my gaze averted to the ridge top across the wooded canyon. There I saw such heavenly light among the trees that once again I gasped, so taken by the utter beauty of it all! Then, coming from that ridge top, I began to hear celestial music and the sound of heavenly voices singing. Such angelic song I had never experienced before. I thought my heart would burst! Standing there in my backyard I was transported in ecstasy to another world—to Heaven on Earth.

After several minutes, I watched the vision slowly fade away. I began to wonder how many other people might have seen the rainbow cloud that day.

As the day went on, I asked several people if they had seen the rainbow cloud but no one had. How could they have missed it? Had it occurred for my eyes only? Had I passed through a portal to some other dimension? Was I crazy, or was it God's way of answering my heart's deepest longing?

A few years later I received a beautiful confirmation. For my birthday in 2004, my husband gave me a coffee table book about buddhas, blessings, and prayers, called *The Buddha Book*, by Lillian Too (HarperCollins 2003). I'd glanced at this book a time or two, but it sat there on our coffee table for another year before I picked it up again. When I did, I was stunned by what I read. There, on the second page of the introduction, the author describes certain signs in the sky known to Buddhists in the high mountain regions of the Himalayas—signs that are said to reveal the presence, or passing, of an enlightened being. The author explains that in the Solu Khumbu region of Nepal, in a village called Lawudo, there lived the Lawudo Lama, "a living Buddha who manifested as a meditator-teacher living in retreat in a cave in the high mountains. Few knew him for what he really was, until the time came for his passing on. Only at his death did the Lawudo lama reveal the enlightened mind that had resided in his enlightened body. For 12 days and nights the signs appeared—rainbow clouds, blue skies, and the sounds of angels singing."

The confirmation brought by this passage inspired me to open myself completely to a committed spiritual path. Feeling called to begin again at my roots, I found myself attracted to books about the historical person known as Jesus, and I immersed myself in the purest form of His original teachings I could find. Today, these teachings continue to awaken the Christ within my own heart while opening me to the Presence of Love everywhere I look.

In 2005, I traveled to Israel with a group of kindred souls to visit the sacred sites and peoples of all the major religions represented there. We "prayed" for peace by *being the Presence of peace*. We shared with many people a mutual goal of honoring one another while opening to God's Presence in our lives. I feel at peace in my own heart because God's Voice has led me to an awakening of Divine Presence within me. The seeker has found. And the way—marked by my willingness to open within—was there inside me all along.

Rebecca Zimman is a full-time mother and part-time legislative research consultant. She enjoys living in Northern California with her husband and daughter and several precious furry friends. Her favorite pastime is hiking in nature and writing in her journals.

My Angel

One day, when I was in second grade, I was listening to my teacher very quietly. I closed my eyes for a second or two, and then I saw my very own angel. I was so surprised that I could actually talk to her. Her words, she told me, came from God's heart. She was wearing a dress. At the top of it was red and at the bottom was a patch of orange. It was tattered. The dress had a couple of pockets with white and green dots. Her cheeks were pink. She had brown hair and very much of a smile. She looked a lot like a doll to me. Her name was Lily.

I asked her a few questions. Now that I am in third grade, I don't remember all the questions I asked her or all the answers. I told my mother a lot about it. I told my mother that where she could speak to her angel was in Oregon at a waterfall. My angel told me that.

Sometimes I ask Lily if she can help me solve things. But she wants me to solve them myself.

Sometimes she talks to me first. She usually talks to me when I am very quiet and alone. When I close my eyes, I can talk to her whenever I please. I can even talk to her with my eyes open. I talk to her because she shares God's words with me and it can be comforting.

My angel comes from heaven.

Zoe Stephens is a third-grader in Roseville, California. She enjoys snuggling with her mom, reading books, drawing pictures, playing with her toys, and riding bikes with her mom or dad.

The Day I Got a New Name

I was born James Allan, and later, through my Catholic upbringing, I added another name, Joseph, at my Confirmation. It was not a ritual I fully understood at the time, but others in my family felt it was important. My mom had come from a large Catholic family with nine brothers and sisters, which meant I had around 30 first cousins on that side of the family. With half being boys, they all received a second middle name with their Confirmations too, so it did not seem unusual. I didn't put much stock in the tradition, but it somehow felt important to have something a little extra to set me apart.

In my early 20s I moved from Ohio to Florida, and went to work in the nursery business. The work was satisfying and rewarding in its own way; being in contact with the plants and working outside in nature, I always felt closer to God. Though I stayed in this business for 15 years, I began to teach yoga part-time. How does someone make the leap from nurseryman to yoga? God calls.

My newfound joy and enthusiasm could not be contained. I so loved the connection with myself, God, and others that yoga brought into my life. At first, I taught yoga for free, wondering, *Could I dare to consider following my heart and further discovering God by teaching yoga full-time?* People seemed to be genuinely moved and supported by my teachings and practice. *If only I could get some clear direction...*

One day, sitting in meditation (a practice that had become part of my daily ritual), I heard something clearly inside. It was a word that seemed familiar and yet startled and scared me. I knew it as a name. Until that moment, whenever I felt the presence of God it was just that—a "feeling" of comfort or support. But I had never "heard" God. I dared not believe that He would actually speak to me directly.

In the yoga practice, it is not unusual to receive a new name, one that is given by a teacher when the student is ready. My teacher had actually talked to me about this, as I had been studying with my whole heart for some time by then. On this particular day of meditation my yoga teacher had gone sailing. I tried to call her. I was afraid to tell anyone else what I had experienced. If she gave me a new yoga name, that would be easier to handle than getting a name right from Source. But I could not reach her. For safety's sake, I was her contact while she was out on the water in case something went wrong, but when I could not reach her I seemed to just know she was okay, as if God was infusing me with this knowledge.

I told God that if He was going to give me a new name, then He had better send a burning bush or something clearly identifiable. I told Him I needed a little help with this, and didn't want to risk getting it wrong. Could He understand my smallness and make His intention clear for me? I needed a sign. I felt a bit forward, after hearing God's Voice, demanding something more of Him. Just who did I think I was? But, the request had been made, and I waited, quite sheepishly, for something to appear. I was both embarrassed and excited at the same time. What if God *had* actually spoken to me? Would that make me special, important, or different? All my practices to date had shown me that the biggest obstacle to experiencing God directly was my own ego. I did not want my ego to take the place of joy and love in my heart.

That afternoon, I met with one of my students—a good friend of mine. We had done spiritual work together for some time, and I considered him someone safe to share with. I told him what happened, and as he listened, a big grin appeared on his face. He could hear the truth of it and was excited as well. Energized, we prepared to go to our regular Sunday night activity, a guided meditation.

At the meditation center, I went into the bathroom. Standing at the sink washing my hands, I reached for the paper towel dispenser. There, written in plain text were the words "San Jamar."

I stood frozen in shock. *Jamar* was the name I had heard earlier in my meditation, the word God had spoken within me. He not only heard my request for a sign to make me know this was real, but also honored it. I was dumbstruck and humbled. The name, as it appeared, actually was the style of the paper towel dispenser, but, how perfect that God would honor my request in a lowly public bathroom in a way that was confirming, understandable, and appropriate for me. I could now let go, realizing my strength lies in my vulnerability and humbleness.

There was no time to digest the experience, as the meditation was about to begin. I was finding it difficult to integrate in my mind what my heart and soul already knew: that I was profoundly loved and seen, and so were all others. I half stumbled into the meditation circle, and sat down on the floor as the facilitator began. I don't know what words she spoke. I just closed my eyes and was transported.

In my meditation I was swimming. I came up from under the water on the other side of a lake. There, my teacher sat in a chair. I placed my head upon her lap as she wiped away the water from my face. Suddenly she morphed into another expression of God. She became another venerated teacher: Jesus. The love that washed through me was hard to contain. Jesus stood me up and looked into my eyes, saying, "You shall be known as Jamar, 'one who brings light.'" It was the last thing I remember before opening my eyes to a room of people. Apparently, the meditation was over.

How could I hide the ecstasy coursing through my heart? Traditionally, each person had a chance to share their meditation experience, a sharing that always began with a speaking of their name. Many spoke of how they had seen me in their meditation surrounded by light. This surprised and encouraged me. When my turn came, I recounted my experiences of the day and introduced myself to others for the first time as "Jamar."

Soon after that, I began to teach full-time. I even went so far as to change my name legally, another demonstration of my understanding and commitment. I am fortunate to have found God everywhere in the 10 years since. He speaks to me today in many forms, and I love and cultivate each one.

Jamar Caudy lives in West Palm Beach with his wife, Marlowe, his daughter, Kylie, and their dog, McKinnley. He enjoys kayaking, canoeing, hiking, and playing Ultimate Frisbee. After a busy day of teaching yoga, his greatest pleasure is cuddling up on the couch with Marlowe and watching a good movie.

Just in Time

The end of Ruthie's life began with her zest for travel and adventure. That was nothing new.

Accounts of her various exotic journeys were interesting enough, yet it was her outrageous tall-tale versions that sent the family into paroxysms of laughter whenever she returned. Getting gangrene on her toe after climbing Mt. Kilimanjaro, narrowly escaping a landslide in Tibet, and various other near-death experiences on mountains all over the world kept us all entertained.

I loved my sister like no one else in the world. Our parents had died early on, and we had only each other for immediate family. Ruthie's virtues were manifold: She was courageous, loyal, a devout Christian, and exceedingly generous to everyone she met. Yet Ruthie required infinite patience. Her appetite for drama was inexhaustible. Each new adventure brought greater danger for Ruthie and increased anxiety for me. Did a landslide *really* almost slide her bus off a cliff? Only God knew for sure.

Ruthie and I reached an impasse in our relationship in 1999. When I returned from the Peace Corps in Africa, Ruthie gave me refuge while I looked for work. Our easy banter when I first returned eventually wore off. She seemed disgruntled when I disagreed about something, and I felt guilty that she'd managed to wear down my patience. She demanded ever more attention and unflinching acceptance of all her ideas and actions. It was exhausting, and I felt like a bad sister for resenting her behavior.

"What's the matter with you?" Ruthie asked one evening. "Don't you have a thing to say?"

"It's hard to make conversation after a long day of work," I replied. This tense exchange had become typical, and the stress of walking on eggshells eventually wore me down. I loved her so much, yet I felt tested daily.

"I'm moving into a place of my own near the ocean," I said one morning. "Whatever," she replied listlessly as she moved into one of her moods. Shortly after my announcement she told me, "I don't know when I'll have time to see you again."

She cut off all contact after that. A door had slammed shut, seemingly never to open again. I felt devastated and inadequate. No matter what I did, it was never enough. I would never meet her standards for being a "good" sister.

I resented being shut out of her life for not doing what she wanted, and hurt that she felt I didn't love her. Each time I tried to reach out, she hung up the phone or ignored my messages. A cloud of depression hung over me.

I turned to friends to fill the void, but I still missed Ruthie. I felt extremely alone, exposed, and raw. Never in my life had she been so noticeably absent. It made me vulnerable and deeply uncomfortable in a way so foreign to me.

One morning at the beach, while enjoying the sight of the sunrise over the ocean, I began to talk to God as though He were my friend.

"I feel shut out of her life and hopelessly stuck when I try to reach out to her. When I try to do what's right for me she tells me I don't love her," I explained. "I do love her, more than anything in this world, and wish I could spend time with her again. I want to be kind to her without losing myself in the process. I pray for knowledge of Your will for me and the wisdom to carry it out. I hope You know what to do, because I don't have a clue!"

As these words left my lips, I felt my body relax into the sand. For a brief moment, all was quiet within me. Suddenly, an inspiration emerged: Why not write a letter to Ruthie saying, "What I appreciate about you is..." and then fill in the blanks? This thought was clear, powerful, and electric. My skin erupted with goose bumps as the thought took form.

Yet just as swiftly, a pervading sense of fear began to swallow my excitement. If I were to follow through with this, I might set myself up for yet another painful rejection. My muscles tensed at the thought. I couldn't bear more pain or endure lengthy lectures about how *right* she was and how *wrong* I was. I asked myself, wounded as I felt, could I head back into battle for the sake of love?

As this unexpected suggestion began to settle deep within my heart, the tide within me began to turn. Something bigger and more powerful than the pain and fear was at work here: hope. Hope for a healed relationship with my beloved sister who had the power to throw me into the pit of despair or send me to the heights of happiness.

I felt the depth of my love release my heart from all past hurts. The strong desire to share my sense of appreciation for her replaced the overwhelming fear of rejection. After long reminding myself only of her flaws, I felt free to express why I so loved this difficult person. Images of Ruthie at her best flowed through me as if I were moving from a grainy black-and-white movie into Technicolor.

My prayer had been answered in a way I could not have imagined. I didn't want to miss this chance to reach out only to wonder later what might have happened had I taken the risk. For the first time in weeks I felt peaceful.

I returned home and wrote:

Dear Ruthie,

What I appreciate about you is that you really care about people who are hurting. I appreciate that you drop whatever you are doing to be with someone. You did so much to help Mother. I appreciate your help after my car accident.

Having filled both sides of the paper in five minutes, I realized I'd remembered everything I loved about her again.

I mailed the letter, feeling relieved that I had done the best my heart and conscience could to heal this relationship. The timing was indeed divine. Ruthie called two days later.

"Hi, this is your long-lost sister. Can you come over on Saturday before I leave for Yosemite?"

She had scheduled another trip—this time closer to home and seemingly safe.

After a great meal, we lay on her living room couches and began to reminisce. We recalled happy times when our infectious laughter caused bystanders to smile. When the emotional winds were good, we complemented each other perfectly. It warmed my heart to spend time with Ruthie again. She promised to tell me all about the back-country of Yosemite at the end of August when she returned. We embraced and said, "I love you. See you later."

I didn't hear from Ruthie on her return date. I paced the floor, calling everyone who might know of her whereabouts.

"I don't know where she is—something must have happened to her," I heard over and over from friends and relatives.

Something was terribly wrong.

Finally I heard from the Detective Division at Yosemite. They had found her car, but not her.

"We are very concerned about your sister, and have started to search for her."

I boarded the next plane with my daughter, Carla. A park ranger and detective helped us try to piece together what had happened. Yet a search team of volunteers with dogs found no trace of Ruthie.

On the fourth morning, the search team put words to the thought I couldn't bear: "The conclusion we have reached is that Ruthie is not alive."

I began to cry. Grief I'd tried to bury deep within me came pouring out in great sobs.

We flew in a helicopter to grasp the enormity of the wilderness into which she had disappeared. I silently admitted to myself and God that Yosemite was a splendid place for her to have ended her days.

I returned home feeling both deep sadness and relief that I had searched for Ruthie and had seen her final resting place. I felt the presence of her exuberant spirit nudging me to rise up again and live life with the sense of wonder she so embraced.

Since those agonizing days, my life has taken a new direction. I do not sit on the fence seeking inner guidance, fearing that following it will somehow end badly. During a hectic day, I stop to be fully present with a friend, or pause to gaze at nature's wonders. I help those who have nowhere to turn, and express love to the significant people in my life. Love fills me, and I feel fully alive.

Thank you, Ruthie, wherever you are, and thank you, God, for inspiring me to reach out to her, just in time.

Prior to retirement, Marilyn Sapsford worked as a therapist and freelance journalist. The mother of a beautiful daughter, she now enjoys travel and volunteer work in her community.

Free at Last

God has spoken to me many times throughout the years in different ways. He speaks to me through books, intuition, thoughts, and people, but the first time I stopped long enough to listen to that still, small voice in my mind was in the summer of 1962. I had been stricken with Guillain-Barre Syndrome, a debilitating illness that attacks the nervous system. It paralyzed my body and altered my breathing. Because I was near death due to being unable to breathe, I had to live in an iron lung in Spartanburg Regional Hospital, in Spartanburg, South Carolina. An iron lung is a large metal respirator that encloses all of the body except the head and is used for maintaining artificial respiration for people who have difficulty breathing on their own.

After being in the iron lung for two weeks, I was miserable. I was 21 years old and could not comprehend what was happening to me. It was a terrible feeling not being able to communicate with my family or friends. I was aware of their conversations and their sorrowful, negative feelings. They thought I could not hear because I could not talk above a whisper. It was during this challenging time of not being able to communicate with anyone else that all my energy and attention went within. In the midst of my depression, I began to talk with God. One day, I heard a voice within me say, "Girl, you have a choice. You can choose to be miserable or you can choose to be happy." *How could I be happy in an iron lung?* The answer was, "Change your thoughts to good ones."

With nothing to lose, I began changing my thoughts about everyone and everything in my life. In a short period of time, my attitude and my perceptions changed. I began to enjoy my experience in the iron lung. My awareness of my creator and my union with Him became a driving force within me, and a deep sense of love for others soon replaced any feelings of prejudice and judgment. This experience changed my life.

After three months I was able to breathe on my own. I traded my iron lung for a bed. After a short time I was strong enough to sit up in bed. My limbs gradually began to move, and feeling was being restored throughout my body. I was well enough to be transferred in an ambulance to Charleston Medical Center in Charleston, South Carolina, in October.

Charleston was a new world. Doors opened for me. I met many new doctors, physical therapists, interns, and a new medical staff. Because I was their new interest, they gave me their undivided attention. They kept me busy. My physical therapist exercised my limbs daily. Although they did everything they could to make my life better, they refused to give me any false hope about ever being able to walk again. Eventually, I grew stronger and graduated to a wheelchair.

In December I was released from the medical center just in time for a Christmas celebration with my family at my mother's house in Gaffney, South Carolina, 200 miles from Charleston.

After the holidays I returned as an outpatient to the medical center, and rented an apartment nearby. Although my health continued to improve, being out in the world was much different from the quiet, internal life I had created with God in my iron lung. My old negative ways of seeing things crept back into my life, and I became depressed and discouraged once again. I was young, restless, and longing to live a full life.

One day, in spite of my protests, my husband rolled me down to King Street from the medical center. Of course I did not want to go, because I felt sorry for myself. It seemed as if all eyes focused on me when I appeared in public all dressed up in my metal braces, and I knew this day would be no different. My wheelchair seemed awkward and huge. All I wanted to do was hide. I felt a victim of my disease and deserted by my Creator.

As we neared King Street I heard beautiful singing. A parade had blocked the intersections of King and Calhoun. People were marching and singing freedom songs. They clapped their hands as they marched. Some spectators were cursing, some were crying, and some were singing and clapping their hands. Mesmerized, I sat in my chair on the corner. It dawned on me that these people were the freedom marchers. Oh, how I wanted to be free of my mental anguish!

Leading the parade was a radiant black man. He had a magnificent presence. When he walked by me our eyes connected. We did not speak. A wave of compassion washed over me and a healing took place in my soul. Although the man was black, he did not care that I was a Southern white girl.

The man standing next to me said, "That was Dr. Martin Luther King."

God had not deserted me after all. He had come in the form of Dr. Martin Luther King to set me free from my prison of negative thoughts. In that powerful moment when our eyes met, my life changed drastically. I decided to make a difference in the lives of others by giving of myself in small ways to help mankind. All I could do that day was smile, and smile I did.

Slowly I learned to walk again. I completed my education, nurtured a family, taught school, and volunteered for many community organizations. I celebrated my 68th birthday this month. I am enjoying my grandchildren, traveling, and playing with my Red Hat chapter, the Rocky Mountain Roses of the Red Hat Society. Every day I listen for God's Voice. He always has a message for me in some form. Now I am free at last! Free at last! Thank God almighty! I'm free at last!

Linda Bridges received her bachelor of arts from Limestone College in South Carolina in 1972. Since her retirement from teaching in 1994, she divides her time between South Carolina and Colorado. She enjoys reading and writing humorous stories.

Finding a Personal God

The concept of God as Universal Mind, a kind of intelligent energy, had always attracted my curiosity. In my mid-20s I joined a spiritual study group to learn meditation and to enjoy lively spiritual discussions around a book called *Search for God*. Having grown up in a non-religious home, I did not understand what a personal relationship with God could be. Further, I judged those who said they talked to God or Jesus to be mistaken or deluded, and myself as smart, rational, and realistic.

At one meeting, a man questioned my position that God was an amorphous abstract energy that contained everything in the universe. He asked me a few questions that led to the big question: "If God is Creator and Universal Mind, why couldn't He be both abstract *and* personal?"

I didn't see how, but an avalanche of doubts and questions flooded my mind. I eventually realized my desire was to know God in a personal way, but I felt afraid of compromising my stance as smart, rational, and realistic. How could I release my judgment that people did God an injustice by talking to Him as if He were an invisible person who cared about the details of their day? A small prayer went forth from my heart to find a way to have an intimate relationship with God that would not breach my integrity or intelligence.

That prayer was answered about 15 years later. My spiritual practices had been growing, yet it was an emotional upheaval at my workplace that fulfilled my desire.

My job was as an administrative assistant in a fire department. Several changes led to Ralph, a Bible-based Christian, becoming my new boss. My previous bosses never discussed religion with me, but Ralph would periodically allude to the Bible's authority if I opened a discussion of a spiritual concern. Otherwise, Ralph lived his religion by being respectful and supportive of all the people with whom he worked, instead of being preachy.

His integrity was beyond any level I had seen. He took the blame for anything that didn't work out well and gave credit to others for everything that succeeded. His door was always open for work-related issues as well as personal concerns. For me he had become a perfect symbol of a wise and loving father, brother, friend, and chaplain, as well as a stellar boss. I had never met anyone like him and couldn't imagine life without him.

I knew that periodically Ralph suffered with severe migraine headaches, but he rarely lost any time at work. After only a few months of working together, Ralph suddenly fell gravely ill. He had come down with the flu, complicated by internal bleeding from headache medication. He was in the intensive care unit of a local hospital.

I was distraught at the thought of Ralph lying gravely ill in the hospital. My friends said I sounded as though my lover was dying. Fearing the loss of this amazing man and worried about his family, I called all my friends and asked them to pray for him. I couldn't bear the thought of his suffering or possible death. One friend, concerned about my extreme emotional state, suggested I call a prayer line.

And so it was, so many years after my intention to know God in a personal way, that I was brought to my knees with fear for Ralph. I called the prayer line. The woman who answered asked if she could pray with me. She listened to my request for a healing prayer for my boss.

There I was, sitting in my living room with a telephone receiver held to my ear, yet it was as if a woman was no longer speaking across the miles to a frightened and worried stranger. She told me to still my mind and "go within" where there is perfect peace and a knowing of wholeness and perfection. As she spoke words of faith, wholeness, miracles, healing, love, and God's caring, I was no longer simply hearing hopeful words. I became a tuning fork resonating with Divine Truth. It was as if God's Voice were speaking to God's child in a language I didn't know I knew.

As peace filled me from the inside out, all my fears about Ralph dissolved. I sat straighter and breathed more deeply. I felt lighter. The weight of fear had been taken from me. It was an experience of communion. The prayer she shared with me was God speaking to me and through me. My heart opened in a new way, letting in a new powerful Voice for Love that I could now find and recognize within me. Though I later realized it had been within me all along, it took the intense emotional longing for Ralph's healing to break down my defensive barrier. It was a barrier I didn't know I held in place through the first 40 years of my life.

That prayer changed me. God's Voice became real for me through this experience. I received God's Love and peace. I felt God's Love being revealed to me as a Mighty Creator turning His attention to my specific need in that moment. Only part of that message from God was about Ralph's healing. The main part was about my relationship with a loving, caring God and a peace that passes all human understanding.

I am overjoyed to say that Ralph recovered fully and returned to work with me for 13 wonderful years. His family and our work family were blessed by his recovery. In addition to Ralph's physical healing, however, was another healing that colors every day of my life. I have begun to let go of my need to appear as "smart, rational, and realistic." Instead, I surrender more and more to an intelligence that is greater than my own. The experience of feeling God's presence, guidance, and comfort is the greatest miracle and joy of my life!

Jill Carel works full-time for the fire department and devotes much time and energy to her family and to her interfaith ministry.

Clarity

Shortly after September 11 when the Twin Towers fell and the mood of the country was one of anger and judgment, I experienced a dream of healing. It was as though God took me by the hand and said, "I have something to show you. You must understand you have a plank in your eye, not just a speck. I will provide a special lens for you so that you may see more clearly. I want you to see the world and the people as I see them, and not through your own human eyes."

The journey began along a path where I saw an elderly lady sitting on a park bench. Her face was lined and wrinkled, her hair streaked with gray. Her hands had twisted with arthritis, and she peered at me through eyes dimmed with age. When I gazed at her through God's lens, I saw a woman glowing with radiance. Her soft eyes and loving face revealed angelic serenity, and her skin appeared smooth. I saw not an old woman, but a woman who had lived fully and served God.

We journeyed on, seeing several children at play. Through my eyes I saw a group of loud children showing little respect for anything. Through God's lens, the children appeared as beautiful butterflies scampering about the flowers as though they had just escaped their cocoons.

As we traveled farther, I saw terror in the sky. Planes slammed into buildings. People ran everywhere, jumping from buildings to escape the flames. I was terrified, surrounded by sadness and distress. I couldn't comprehend this scene with my own eyes or bear what I saw. I fumbled, trying to put on the special lens again as a tear ran down my cheek. Even though I looked through God's lens, it was difficult to comprehend man's inhumanity to man. I saw many faces looking to me for help, for answers. Now that I had seen what God sees, I could feel His compassion and I began to weep and pray. The plank had been washed from my eyes.

The journey was coming to an end. God led me into a large room resembling an art gallery. Each piece displayed represented a mystery. I was allowed to choose one of these mysteries of life to view through the lens I now knew held great power. I chose to look at love, and I was soon filled with awe. For the first time I saw the face of God.

I awoke from my dream with a jolt and sat straight up in bed, sweating and shaken. It was a journey whose lessons I shall never forget. My life has been filled with challenges, but this dream helps me to know that God is never far away. I don't always understand what God has in store for me, but now I try to view humanity through God's lens, and have peace knowing He is near.

Tom Halter was born in Evansville, Indiana. He is married and has three children and eight grandchildren. Retired after 41 years in radiology, his hobbies are traveling, writing stories and poetry, and watching football and movies.

The Simplest Thing

A few years ago, my 6-year-old niece developed an inoperable cancerous brain tumor. Our family struggled to grasp the terrible truth of the situation, and, more importantly, how to deal with the possibility of her leaving us. I was hopeful and my faith was strong, but still I found myself questioning. I wanted to speak to someone who could help clear my head, to maybe hear a positive or even spiritual point of view, but I kept putting it off because expressing my thoughts and feelings was uncomfortable for me.

After an especially difficult weekend for my niece, I woke up Monday thinking I should call a particular priest in my parish whom I believed could offer some comforting words. He would listen and I would talk. He would share insight and I would do my best to understand. He would give guidance and I would try to remain hopeful. Still, I didn't call. As I dwelled on this dilemma, the phone rang. It was my brother. His van had broken down and he needed a ride.

I piled the kids into the car and drove to pick him up. Angry and upset about his van, my brother climbed into the front seat and told me to take him home. As we drove, he ranted about his van. The kids occupied themselves in the back seat and I watched the road, lost in my own thoughts—should I call the priest or not? As we reached the top of a hill, I noticed a truck ahead ready to pull out in front of us. I slowed the car and tuned into my brother who was still complaining. As we approached the truck, my eyes struggled to focus on the huge letters painted on its side. At first I didn't grasp the name I was reading. It was so familiar that for an instant I couldn't believe the coincidence, but I felt an intense stirring inside my body and a sharp sense of awareness came over me. A chill crept down my back as I stared at the name.

On the side of the truck, in big, bold letters was the name of the priest I had put off calling. Overwhelmed with emotion, tears filled my eyes. It was a simple thing, just a name on the side of a truck. But there it was right in front of me, an obvious sign from God saying, "Call the priest and he will be there for you." As the truck turned in front of us and the name disappeared, I was in awe.

My brother was still talking as we continued down the road. My heart was light and a warm smile covered my face. God had entered my life, communicated with me, and helped me in such a simple and ordinary way. I was full of joy and wonder at the realization of what had just happened. In that moment I knew I was not alone in this world, nor did I ever have to be as long as my heart was open. I dropped my brother off at his house and headed for home with a definite purpose in mind. I would call the rectory as soon as I arrived home and make an appointment with the priest.

To this day, I have yet to see another truck with the priest's name painted on the side. Perhaps I never will. But this experience was unforgettable. It was simply my moment to be filled with the presence of God. Hopefully it was just one of many to come.

Lisa DeCorleto lives in Connecticut with her husband and two children. She works full-time and spends her off-time with family and friends or doing various church and community service activities. Lisa enjoys reading, traveling, and photography.

Brothers and Sisters

We must live together as brothers or perish together as fools.
—Martin Luther King, Jr.

A few years ago I was in deep emotional pain. I had cheated on my partner of 7 years, and had just come clean about it. I realized I was addicted to sex. In need of serious help, I thought of asking God, but wasn't too sure if I even believed in a Higher Power, what that meant, or how to pray. I also wondered if God would even pay attention to me because I am a gay man.

My partner was a Lebanese Christian. In our house were pictures of the Virgin Mary and Jesus above every door. He told me he felt safe with them in the house and that they would protect us from harm. I didn't grow up believing in that, but in time I grew to like the pictures and even felt they brought some sort of protection to our home.

After a night of feeling guilty and alienated from my boyfriend, I took a picture of the Virgin Mary his mother had given me and brought it close to my heart. I began to sob and sob, because some-how I felt the Virgin Mary loved me. As I wept against the wall, I felt a Love I had never experienced all around me. Like a warm hug, it was so peaceful, so utterly relaxing, that all fear melted away. For the first time I felt truly forgiven. It was as if She said, "I know what you've done, but I still love you because I know you can do better."

Though it was a wonderful experience, soon the old fear re-turned and I brushed the loving experience off as a coincidence. There was no way God would love me because of what I had done.

Months went by, and again I cheated. I felt totally out of control and couldn't understand why I chose to continue hurting someone I so loved. I was repeating the same pattern and badly needed answers.

I went to therapy, though my partner refused to join me. One day after a good therapy session, I got down on my knees and prayed. Though I had been reading a lot of self-help books, I had intellectualized them instead of putting them into practice. Being a huge fan of Oprah Winfrey, I had heard her say, "You need to ask God to use you." Realizing my life was in a mess, this sounded like the only thing left to do. Killing myself was not an option, but the "Jamie Plan" was not working out too well. After looking up Oprah Winfrey's prayer in her magazine, I prayed, "Use me, God. Show me how to take who I am, who I want to be, and what I can do, and use it for a purpose greater than myself."

Immediately after the prayer I felt better, as if the universe really listened to my cry for help. Calm and relaxed, I let the whole thing go, knowing God would answer my prayer. Three months later at my flight-attendant job, one of my colleagues put his arm around me and said, "What's up, my brother?"

Something suddenly clicked. *Oh my God. What if he really was my brother?* This concept of the brotherhood of man was something I'd heard before, but the depth of its meaning had eluded me until now. My heart melted. If he really were my brother, how would I treat him?

All my life I've felt that I am less than others, but on this glorious day I treated everyone on my flight as if they were family members. It brought my heart such joy, and at the end of the day that same colleague said, "You know, Jamie, I really felt loved by you today."

On my layover that night, I reflected upon the three months since I had recited Oprah's prayer and realized God had been trying to talk to me all along. I just hadn't been listening. From the time I had prayed to be used and released from my pain, the message of brotherhood and sisterhood had kept coming up in my life. I have heard that coincidences are God's way of remaining anonymous, and this was certainly true in my case. Although it took three months to realize it, I felt so grateful because God had answered my prayer in a totally unexpected way. The message of brotherhood was the perfect wake-up call for me to start authentically healing and taking responsibility for every area of my life. It softened my heart to know we are all linked. That made it so much easier to love others.

Although deep inside I felt God was speaking to me, I needed to make sure. I asked the Universe for a sign. This time I got a strong feeling to buy the book *God Has a Dream*, by Archbishop Desmond Tutu. Sure enough, this book impacted my life. Chapter 2 affirmed the experience I'd had at work. Tutu writes:

> Dear child of God, before we can become God's partners, we must know what God wants for us. "I have a dream," God says. "Please help Me to realize it. It is a dream of a world whose ugliness and squalor and poverty, its war and hostility, its greed and harsh competitiveness, its alienation and disharmony are changed into their glorious counterparts, when there will be more laughter, joy, and peace, where there will be justice and goodness and compassion and love and caring and sharing. I have a dream that swords will be beaten into plowshares and spears into pruning hooks, that My children will know that they are all members of one family, the human family, God's family, My family."

Thankfully, he also writes about gays and lesbians. This brought such comfort to my aching heart. He writes: "God just wants us to love each other. Many, however, say that some kinds of love are better than others, condemning the love of gays and lesbians. But whether a man loves a woman or another man, or a woman loves a man or another woman, to God it is all Love, and God smiles whenever we recognize our need for one another."

For three years now, God continues to "speak" to me. It's been mostly through people, like receiving a phone call from a loved one at the exact time I need a dose of love. Sometimes it's just a shift in perception, like the Christmas I felt sorry for myself because I had to work...until my eyes gravitated towards 15 homeless people lying in the subway. I had a job, a home, loving family and friends, and no excuse for whining! God guides me daily to become more loving. I am having a positive effect on others as well, which has helped my self-esteem and brings me true joy.

I am still a work in progress, falling off the path from time to time, but there is no going back. I have been touched by God's Love, and healing has become my new addiction. In the midst of my sexual addiction, I thought I had to be "high" and hyper all the time. I have struggled with letting my addiction go, but was guided by the Voice for Love to this passage from the prayer book "Illuminata": "Those who are not sober today risk missing the train of history. Sobriety itself is today's high, for it is ultimately in the most centered consciousness that we find our power to transcend the world."

Now I'm truly ready to fly.

Montreal's Jamie McNiven Smith takes great joy in being with family and friends. An avid reader and nature lover, he speaks English and French, loves to travel, and makes an effort to exude kindness and peace everywhere he goes.

Healing With God

When I was 38 years old I stopped eating, and, like a flower, slowly withered away. I subsequently suffered an acute psychosis—it was as if hell had opened its jaws and swallowed me. Through the following 16 years of psychotherapy, I lived in isolation except for the hours I worked to sustain the costs of my treatment. Although this period was marked by profound suffering and pain, positive things were happening. I was changing, becoming richer within, and beginning to value the simpler things in life.

One evening, out to dinner with friends, I felt profoundly depressed. As usual, I watched everyone eating with a hearty appetite while I sat before my plate of grated carrots pretending to savor every mouthful. In reality I was starving. I remember how utterly desperate I felt when I went to bed. I simply couldn't go on any longer and wished I could die.

In the middle of the night I woke up with a strange sensation, rather like a force or energy rippling like waves throughout my body. It grew ever stronger until my body was vibrating. I wasn't frightened because the effects were warm and comforting and I no longer felt alone in my despair. It seemed someone was with me to share it. This sensation stayed with me all night, and I began to talk, expressing my innermost thoughts as if someone were listening to me. I whispered, "I don't know who you are, but I know that you're here inside me, and I can tell you everything."

Shortly after, I began to breathe in a totally different way. I wasn't frightened but, rather, curious to know what would happen next. I continued talking to the "presence," which had become a part of me, a faithful friend and companion ready to listen.

One day it answered me—through my respiration. I had asked it one of my countless questions, expecting no reply, when suddenly my respiration changed so completely, it was as if someone else were breathing for me. A single inhalation starting from the solar plexus indicated a positive answer, whereas two or more short exhalations, again centered in the solar plexus region, indicated a negative reply. After receiving my reply, my breathing returned to normal.

I could in no way have invented such a complex system of communication through my respiratory system. It was an ingenious method for avoiding further confusion in my mind. I felt exuberant to have found someone with whom to share all my loneliness. I seemed to have found a lifelong friend.

My faithful companion stayed with me and answered my questions. There were moments of terror when I thought I might have been possessed by a devil. I pleaded with God to send it away if it was evil, for I wanted nothing to do with evil. But it remained and continued to answer me.

After a long period of confusion, I decided this strange companion was "good." I spoke to him constantly and he always replied. I talked to him as a child might. When I woke up terrified by a nightmare, he would comfort me and I would feel the warm and gentle ripples within as if he were caressing me. Still, I questioned the identity of this mysterious internal presence, and so began my journey to discover the truth.

I began devouring two or three books a week, but they were not enough to satisfy my insatiable thirst. Those 16 empty years slowly began to be filled. I began frequenting a spiritual movement that taught that God is in every blade of grass, plant, animal, and mineral, and within us. Was it possible the presence with whom I spoke was God? I asked it.

"Are you God, our Heavenly Father?"

The answer was affirmative.

"Are you sure?"

Again the reply was affirmative, but I wasn't convinced. The answers to my questions were always limited to yes or no. This contact, however, was still of enormous comfort to me.

In May 2002, I was in a bookshop and by chance my gaze fell upon a book entitled *Conversations With God* by Neale Donald Walsch. Thunderstruck, I bought all three volumes and began to read as soon as I got home. The author explained how, on a night filled with anger and exasperation, he had poured out his soul in a furious letter to God and God had unexpectedly answered him. This was the beginning of his inspiring and wonderful conversation with God.

I was exuberant, for the God who spoke was extremely loving, simple, accessible to everyone, willing to listen, full of joy, and had a sense of humor. He was nothing like the strict, severe God who judged and punished about whom I had been taught. I found the message unique and revolutionary: All is ONE; there is no separation between one human being and another, between one thing and another, between us and God.

I heaved a sigh of relief. I had finally found Him. Yes, this was the Father I had been seeking my entire life. I gave myself up to His warm embrace, no longer doubting the identity of the mysterious Presence I had felt within me for so many years.

If God had answered Neale, a normal person like me, why couldn't he also answer me? I was afraid; afraid of being disappointed, of not being able to write anything to Him, of having no inspiration, of perceiving only emptiness. But a few months later, I sat down at my desk to start the day reading and meditating in the company of God and the Angels. I took a sheet of paper and a pen, and with my heart in my mouth began to write:

"I love you, dearest Father."

"I love you too. Don't be afraid, go ahead. Search for the answers within you and you will find them. At this very moment, you are blocked by your fear and this prevents you from opening yourself up completely. Little by little you will learn to overcome it and this will be a glorious moment for you. You will open up the way for new possibilities and a new hope. Continue."

This was the beginning of my diary with God, a daily diary in which I open my heart and pour out all my thoughts, fears, worries, emotions, and questions, and I always receive an illuminating and loving answer.

"My dear child, you are right. I have always been with you, I have always heard your cries and am happy that you can finally feel my presence:

I am within every human being, I am closer than your breath. I am your very breath, the breath of life. I am life itself. And now go in peace, let every breath, every thought, every word, every cell in your body be filled with peace at each and every moment of the day. Peace be with you, now and forever."

After so many years, I realize, God, that You have always been with me, You have never abandoned me. I am infinitely grateful for Your Love.

Patricia Williams Scalisi was born and grew up in North Wales in Great Britain. Married to an Italian, she now lives in a small village near the Swiss border where she carries out her activity as a translator.

Mom and the Birdhouse

I am a 49-year-old man from a large Irish-Catholic family. When I was a kid, my mother used to recount a story to which I never paid much attention. When my sister, Mary, 12 years my junior, was about four months old, my mother decided to put her to bed in our backyard for some fresh air on an unseasonably mild spring day. My mother put Mary in an old-fashioned carriage with the hood down. After tucking her in, mom returned to the kitchen and closed the screen door.

As she was cleaning some dishes, she said she heard a voice. The voice said, "Put up the hood." *Why should I put up the hood?* my mother wondered. *The sun isn't in Mary's eyes and there's no wind.* Again, the voice said, "Put up the hood." This time the voice was a little firmer. Almost robotically my mother went out to the stroller and snapped the hood into place. She walked back to the kitchen. She had no sooner closed the screen door behind her than a birdhouse my brothers and I had nailed into the tree a few years earlier fell from its mount and bounced off the hood.

Hot tears ran from my mother's eyes and she shook as she ran to pull Mary from the stroller. My mother sat on the back step of our home rocking back and forth with Mary in her arms, sobbing like a baby herself.

Years later, when I began to have similar experiences, I asked my mother about that incident. "Mom, what was the voice, male or female?" I asked.

Her whole countenance changed. I will never forget the look on her face. It was almost angelic. She looked off into the distance, smiling, and said, "Oh my God! It was neither. It was just a voice."

I asked her why she thought the voice had let her see that birdhouse hit the stroller. Why, in her opinion, did the voice not tell her to take Mary out of the stroller or bring her into the house?

My mother said she had never really thought about it until I asked her. She was so grateful that Mary was safe, she had just accepted it as some kind of a miracle...a miracle indeed!

I've often tried to figure out why God would have my mother witness such an event, instead of just telling her to move the stroller. What I haven't shared is that I had three sisters who died prior to Mary being born. Two were premature and one was born with a congenital heart defect. I was too young to remember them, but it was a very traumatic time for my mother and father. I can only imagine that if my mother had gone through yet another gruesome and unforeseen death of a child, I doubt she would have ever recovered.

Today, Mary has a beautiful baby girl of her own. She is named Joan, after my mother.

John Mulrooney is a stand-up comic with more than 25 years of experience in show business.

Cutting Through the Fog of Uncertainty

I grew up in an abusive and destructive environment with an alcoholic, drug-addicted parent and mentally challenged siblings. We lived in extreme poverty. Our house was almost uninhabitable: The roof leaked, the plumbing didn't work, and my mother did little to help the situation. I tried my best to cope, but found living under these conditions intolerable. Many years of my youth were spent running away from home or being put in foster homes and institutions. My mother took her own life when I was 16 years old, and by age 17 I was living on my own—finally I could chart my own path and create a life for myself that would be nothing like where I'd come from.

I received an education, married at 25, and embarked upon my new life. My husband and I had money, friends, and what appeared to be a happy life. With our boats, jet skis, and vacationing in the best places, we seemed to have it all.

Shortly after my 34th birthday I gave birth to our perfect daughter, who completed our perfect package. There was just one problem: I felt miserable and depressed. I never felt *truly* loved by my husband, and shortly after our daughter was born, I left him to start out again on my own. All I really needed, I thought, was that one true love to share my life with. But with all the love I had to give, no matter how I tried, I was never able to express that love or receive it in the way I yearned to.

Shortly after I left my husband, I met someone. He was kind and spiritual, and treated me as though I was the only woman on earth.

But within a year, our relationship fell apart too. He couldn't commit his heart to me the way I needed him to, and that's when I began to spiral out of control emotionally.

Popping antidepressants, drinking, and living in basic survival mode, I struggled to hold on for my 3-year-old daughter's sake, but it was difficult. At times I felt she'd be better off being raised by her father, who had someone new in his life and seemed much more stable. I was lying in bed one day, contemplating my life, when I was guided to turn on the TV. I saw a spiritual leader talking about God in a way I'd never heard before. Intrigued, I went out and bought his book. After reading just a few pages I thought, if he could ask God questions and get direct answers, why couldn't I?

I put the book down, got a pen and paper, and decided to try it. I began to write, "Dear God...." I wrote a paragraph-length question and outlined all the ways in which I had tried to find happiness. I outlined all the ways in which I had tried to find love. Then I wrote, "Why is this not working? What am I doing wrong?"

I waited patiently for an answer. I listened and cried, but nothing happened. After 10 minutes, I decided if I wasn't going to hear anything, I might as well keep reading. Just as I started to put the notebook away, the answer came. It was so clear, so big, and so profound that it shook my whole being! It said, "My dear, you have been looking for Love outside yourself your whole life. No one or no thing will ever be enough to satisfy you. The Love you seek has been with you all along. The Love you seek is Me. And you will never be satisfied with anything less."

It was not really a "voice," as if it were outside of me, and I didn't receive the words separately in linear fashion. It was more of an instantaneous radical shift of awareness. It was a profound inner knowing that cut through the fog of uncertainty, which I then had to translate into words.

I could immediately see why I had been "seeking but never finding" and why I had been so terribly unhappy for so long. With these words came the knowledge that as this information was inside of me, all the answers I ever needed or would ever need were right there inside of me too. The whole Universe had opened up within me, and I didn't even have to get out of bed to find it! I began to wail and cry as if I were being purged of an ancient misdirection. It was as if the Light of the whole Universe were shining inside of me. I cried until I could no longer cry, and I fell asleep knowing the entire direction of my life was about to change.

From that day forward I have looked within myself for all my answers. Although it has been a major shift in my consciousness and at times enormously difficult, God's Voice has become clearer and clearer as I've moved out of its way. It's not as loud and profound now as it was that first night; it's more a still, quiet voice. I really have to quiet my mind in order to hear it clearly. But as I quiet my mind, the Voice simply emerges. It comes from a very deep place inside of me. It neither comes from my head nor through my ears, but is more of a "knowing" that gets translated into words that sound like my own voice. Sometimes it comes as one instant feeling that needs no translation, and sometimes as actual words, as if in a normal dialogue.

I continue to work on removing the blocks to my awareness of this Voice, through non-judgment and forgiveness, and am being shown a completely different world—a world of Love, of joy, of peace, and of a happiness that has surpassed any expectation I could have ever had. I have now dedicated my whole life to this Voice, and I simply, happily watch where it takes me, with a knowing that wherever it leads, I will go in Peace.

Donna Moldovan is a medical professional living in Atlanta, Georgia, with her beautiful 13-year-old daughter. She enjoys watching movies, eating Indian food, jogging, and taking long walks on the beach.

Journeying to God's Voice

I had just received news that a test done on the cells in my right breast revealed them to be "suspicious," and I must have them removed as soon as possible. I looked at my doctor, seeing the fear in her eyes echoed in her words: "If you don't have this surgery, you'll be dead within two years."

Something inside told me to wait and seek guidance before making any decision. Shortly afterward, I learned that a group of women at the church I attended were studying Native American spirituality and had contacted a woman who had been trained by an indigenous healer to lead shamanic journeys. She had agreed to lead our group in such a journey. Although I had never done anything like it before, I knew the intent of "journeying" was to seek guidance, so it seemed like just the opportunity I needed.

We met in the home of one of our group members. The facilitator asked us to share our intentions and the guidance each of us sought to receive. She then instructed us in the "rules" of journeying and explained that the drum she would beat in the cadence of the human heart was the vehicle by which we would enter our own interior space and return from it. We were to close our eyes and let the drum take us inward.

We first cleansed and blessed ourselves with smudge made from sage, cedar, and lavender. She then explained that when the drumbeat slowed and stopped, we were to leave our interior space and return our attention to the room and the group, opening our eyes once again. She instructed us to envision ourselves entering the "lower world" as the drumbeat carried us inward. In Native American tradition, this is the "earth realm," the realm where "power animals" (guides) are found; where memories, emotions, and confrontations

137

of our own "dark side" can lead to healing. One accesses this inner realm by visualizing an opening in the ground such as a crack or a rabbit hole. The "upper world" in this tradition, the world of sky, is where spiritual teachers are found. If we encountered an animal or person on our journey, we were instructed to ask, "Are you my teacher?" until we received an affirmative answer.

Even though I followed the directions we had been given to access the "lower world," I was unable to get there. Try as I might to visualize going down a crack in the earth or seeing a tunnel to enter, I felt as if I were being propelled upwards after a bounce on a trampoline. The earth's crack I last tried to access was a narrow chasm near where Lake Superior cuts sharply into the coastline, a site familiar to me. I was standing high above Superior, on the rim of the chasm. Not able to descend even when I stepped off the edge, I felt puzzled by what to do next. No instruction had been given about what to do in a situation like this.

In the midst of my bewilderment, a beautiful seagull hovered in front of me, inviting me to climb upon his back. I accepted his invitation and we ascended into a beautiful blue sky, swooping and soaring as we flew. When we landed, it seemed I was standing on something solid, yet my experience was one of standing on air, surrounded by nothing but air. Nevertheless, I began to walk.

The first person I encountered along the way was a very kind older man who was a friend to me. When I asked him if he were my teacher, he replied that he was one of my teachers, but not the one I was seeking. The next being I met was a wolf. It was not an ordinary-looking wolf. This wolf looked murderously ferocious. He bared his fangs, saliva dripping from his jowls. He snarled menacingly, and his eyes pierced my own. I feared he was rabid. Nonetheless, in spite of my trembling, I asked if he were my teacher.

"That depends," he replied. "Are you willing to accept me in all my aspects?"

I heard a shaky yes issue from my mouth. As soon as the yes had been spoken, the fierce creature in front of me transformed into a beautiful young wolf who requested that I follow him.

The sense of being surrounded by air changed as the wolf led me over plains of tundra, across a river into forest, and ultimately to a den where a female wolf nursed young pups. It was a joyous sight that flooded me with loving energy and maternal feelings. At this time, the drum carrying me on the journey signaled it was time to return. I reluctantly left the den to return to my non-journeying life.

Upon my return, I heard a voice telling me I needed to journal about my experience. As I did, it became clear to me that the wolf pups represented the "suspicious" cells in my breast and served as a reminder to nurture myself. Similar to my wolf guide, these cells were at first perceived as fearful and dangerous. Yet if I were to accept them in all their aspects, they could lead me to something healthy and nurturing.

All this happened in 1989. I did not have the surgery. The "suspicious" cells continue to inhabit my breast. By remaining there, they are a constant reminder of when I need to slow down, when I need to give myself "alone" time and rest. They also remind me to care for my body by getting enough physical exercise. It is almost as if they are a prompt to keep me more aware of myself and my needs—spiritual, emotional, and physical—simply by their presence in my body. It is as if they are resident healers.

Who would have ever thought the voice of God could come through "suspicious" cells and the mouth of a ferocious-looking wolf?

Myra S. MacDonald is a former special education teacher and retired psychotherapist. Mother of two and stepmother of two, she currently works with domestic violence offenders. She has had a lifelong interest in exploring world religions.

One Breath at a Time

Slowly opening my eyes, I glanced over at the clock. 7:30. Time to rise and shine on this beautiful April morning. My husband lay blissfully sleeping, one arm resting above his head on the pillow. I leaned up on my elbow, quietly watching the rise and fall of his chest. I gently ran my fingers through his wavy black hair, whispering into his ear, "Wake up, sleepy-head." He stirred, and turning to me with a cheeky smile, snuggled close.

From behind our closed door the clatter of cups and plates could be heard as our daughter Kerri prepared her breakfast. The pungent aroma of fresh coffee wafted through the house, tantalizing my senses.

I quietly slipped out of bed to pour myself a mug. Coffee in hand, I sat outside listening to birds sing their morning salutations. Emerging through the sounds of their peaceful songs, the words "Have faith...and trust that everything is as it is meant to be" wove themselves into the stillness of my mind. I smiled in recognition of the voice, closed my eyes, and drifted deeper into my world of inner silence, waiting for more. But there were no more thoughts, no more words, nothing! That's odd. Usually I am given some form of continued dialogue when small whisperings from within the quietude of my inner sanctum surface in my conscious awareness. I pondered the silence a few moments longer, then with a long sigh opened my eyes and went inside.

It was a beautiful Australian autumn day and the weather was perfect. Although we had planned to meet my parents for lunch the following day, the feeling within my heart impressed me to seize the moment and celebrate *now*, not later. I called Mum and Dad and asked if they could join us for lunch at midday.

Mum was quick to question: "Why today when tomorrow is yours and Neale's 9th wedding anniversary?"

I replied that I wasn't sure why, but as it was so beautiful and my feelings were to celebrate our anniversary today, the date was set. Finishing my last mouthful of coffee, I went to rouse my husband and youngest daughter out of bed. It was Easter school holidays and Olivia was enjoying the quiet time away from the hustle and bustle of classroom life. She was overjoyed at the opportunity to join in our festivity.

Our chosen restaurant was quite busy so we chose to sit outside overlooking the water. The meal was lovely and the company even more so. Olivia took a few pictures reminiscent of the day and we wended our way home.

Whilst washing up the evening dishes, "*Go to Neale now!*" boomed inside my head. Startled at the forcefulness of the voice, I shook the water off my hands and hurried into the lounge room where I found Neale looking quite bluish and struggling to breathe. I immediately rang 000.

The sounds of the sirens and sight of the ambulance's flashing lights resounded inside my brain as we were rushed to the hospital emergency department. Amidst answering all the doctors' questions and watching my husband fight for every breath, my mind went into overload. I sat beside him in disbelief, feeling absolutely numb as the doctors tried to save his life. This can't be happening, I thought. How can this be? Neale looked so well this morning. Even at lunch he was laughing and joking! I kept wishing the day could start over, as I remembered the joy of ruffling his hair before sitting outside listening to the birds sing their happy melodies.

Minutes turned into hours. Just after midnight, Neale's doctors felt his condition had stabilized enough to move him from emergency into ICU. Feeling the enormity of our situation weighing upon me, I gently rested my forehead upon Neale's hand, trying to stifle the sobs threatening to erupt from deep within me. Hot tears silently streamed down my face, dampening the sheet beneath his hand, and again the voice softly whispered through my thoughts, "Trust that we hold you both in Love's embrace...everything is as it is meant to be."

My mind began racing at warp speed, questions zipping back and forth trying to elicit an answer from the voice, but there was neither a sound nor feeling, only a knowing to calm my mind and move my awareness into the safety of my inner sanctum. Succumbing to its gentle caress, my body sighed as a wave of peace washed over me. Calmness took hold.

The sun had just begun to rise above the horizon when a young doctor came to inform me that the hospital didn't have the required facilities to deal with Neale's lung condition. We were both to be transported to Prince Charles Hospital some 100 kilometers away.

The team of doctors assigned to Neale's case at Prince Charles Hospital explained that a rupturing of blisters called emphysemic bullae had formed numerous pneumothorax, or small holes in Neale's left lung, causing it to collapse and the air to become trapped between the collapsed lung and the chest wall. That was why a breathing tube had been inserted through the intercostals into his chest cavity when he had first arrived in emergency.

The transferring from one bed into another had displaced the breathing tube that had enabled air trapped within Neale's chest cavity to be safely released. The internal buildup of unreleased air immediately created an increase in pressure that began compressing Neale's heart function.

Within a matter of moments Neale's heart stopped beating! A code blue was called and once more the doctors worked feverishly to revive him as my daughter Angela and I watched in shock. Miraculously, Neale was again stabilized, and the doctors advised that their only option was to surgically repair the ruptured bullae and hope that the lung tissue itself would heal.

Throughout the next two months, thoracic specialist surgeons performed three more major operations. Each one failed to produce the desired result, leaving Neale totally dependant upon a breathing device.

Since the onset of this journey, the no-name, faceless voice from my inner sanctum had become my companion, a trusted friend in whom to confide when fear, doubt, and aloneness cast its shadow over my being. Each time the voice communicated, a kaleidoscope of light and sound filled the spaces between my thoughts. Its linguistic symphony became words and perceptions my inner ears could hear and my heart could feel.

Finally the doctors advised that each successive operation had greatly weakened Neale's body and they had done all they could do. They explained that his lung tissue and membrane were so fragile and damaged that each time they attempted a repair, it simply tore again within a few days. They urged me to prepare myself, as it would be only a matter of days before Neale's organs failed and he gently slipped into a coma and passed away.

I heard a gasp escape my lips and time seemed to stand still. Then the words "Have faith...trust...all will be well" resounded within my mind. I felt my body inhale deeply as the kaleidoscope of light and sound began its dance between the spaces of my thoughts. For the next few moments the voice began speaking through my vocal cords. I could perceive the gentle yet authoritative manner in which the voice communicated to the doctors. I felt the doctors' vibrations as they intently listened to my every word. My heart skipped a beat when they unanimously agreed to one more attempt at repairing Neale's damaged lung. My body relaxed and the presence was gone.

The expertise of respiratory specialists from the United States and Europe was sought, and after much deliberation, the consensus was that a surgical mesh would be adhered to the outside pleura of Neale's left lung to seal the emphysemic bullae ruptures.

The following morning Neale went into surgery. Time crawled, and I could feel myself becoming quite antsy. Then the voice quietly spoke, "All is well!" When the surgeon came through the door beaming, saying "Neale is in recovery and doing quite well!" tears of joy flowed freely down my cheeks.

Three more weeks passed before we left the hospital to return home. I walked through each room as if seeing them for the very first time. The voice whispered, "Welcome home."

In the ensuing 11 years, Neale's health has continued to ride the white-water rapids of life. When the raft overturns, submerging us beneath the icy cold water, the gentle, loving voice softly whispers between the spaces of my thoughts, comforting me within an embrace that helps bring calmness to my mind and solace to my aching heart with these words: "Have faith...and trust that everything is as it is meant to be." They are as profound within my heart today as they were in 1997.

Sharron Brook's greatest love is being a wife, mother, and grandmother. She is both caregiver and partner to a wonderful and gentle man who is the light of her life, and between them they have seven adult children and 10 grandchildren. Some of her pleasurable pastimes are personal journaling, reflective "first-thought writing," and computer art.

Expressing God's Voice

There I sat at the base of the tall palm tree. I had hiked to the deserted beach earlier that day and had sworn not to open my eyes or move from the base of the tree until it was done—until I had somehow managed to erase all the pain and misery that had eaten away every ounce of life within me.

Only six months prior, I had experienced the most profound joy I had ever known. After years of searching for the deepest truth I could find within me, in a moment of unexpected surrender my mind had been miraculously set free of all judgment and fear. I experienced the truth of who I was for the very first time. It was an experience of infinite love, profound peace, and continual joy. It was an instant of divine recognition—a moment of seeing the world through God's eyes—and that moment had stayed with me for three months as if time had stopped altogether. No longer did I have any fear-based or judgmental thoughts that could separate me from myself, God, or anyone else. I danced in the streets, embraced friends and strangers alike, and could barely contain the overflowing joy and love I felt.

And then, just as swiftly as it appeared, it was gone. Driving down the highway in my car one day, joyfully blissed-out like every other day, I suddenly noticed a fearful thought pass through my mind for the first time in months. Moments later, I noticed another, and then another. It was as if the fear and judgment deep within my soul had somehow been turned back on and given the reins. Not knowing how to react to maintain my newfound sense of Self, I instantly panicked and became lost in the fearful thoughts passing through my mind. Afraid of losing the profound joy and peace that had become my only reality, I attempted to destroy every judgmental, fearful, and limiting thought that emerged for the next three months. I believed this would restore me to that state of ongoing peace, but with every thought I eliminated, I slipped further and further away from peace and into despair.

Six months later, having lost the most profound treasure of my life, I sat at the base of the palm tree without a trace of joy or happiness left inside. In my desperate attempt to hold on to it, I had lost it all and no longer had the will to live. Nothing mattered. Down to skin and bones, I hardly ate, and felt as if my very soul had been lost. By the time the sun had set late that evening, 12 hours after I had prostrated myself at the base of the palm, no liberation had come to rescue me from my suffering. Heartbroken and humbled, I pulled myself up off the beach and walked the 10 miles back home in utter dejection. There I called my friend Candace for help.

A few weeks prior, while in a deep state of meditation and surrender, Candace had unexpectedly opened up to hearing the Holy Spirit within her in a clear and conversational way. She had excitedly called me to say, "You'll never believe what just happened!" She then told me all about this unconditionally loving voice.

With nowhere else to turn and nothing to lose, I called to ask if she would share the Holy Spirit with me. I didn't really know what the Holy Spirit was, but I trusted what my friend had told me was true.

The words she shared with me changed my life. The Holy Spirit spoke to me through Candace about the judgments I had been harboring toward everything I thought and felt. I had thought I needed to get rid of every thought and feeling that seemed to take away my joy and connection with God. But what the Holy Spirit shared was the exact opposite: If I was to experience my connection with God and restore myself to that profound state of peace and love, I needed to learn how to lovingly *embrace* everything within me *without judgment*. The Holy Spirit gave me an exercise to practice unconditionally loving and embracing my emotions. In the midst of listening to the Holy Spirit's words, my deep-seated feelings of disconnection, hopelessness, and despair suddenly lifted, replaced by a profound sense of joy and wonder.

That was my first experience of joining with the Holy Spirit. I was hooked. Nothing I had ever studied or practiced had had such an immediate impact. For the next four years, Candace graciously shared that still, small voice within her whenever I called seeking guidance and support. Then the unexpected happened. We fell in love and married, and everything changed.

It was one thing to ask *my friend* to share God's Voice when I felt sad, confused, or frightened. But my *wife*? I just couldn't do it. I didn't want to do it. I didn't want to be dependent upon my wife for the rest of my life to hear God's Voice, so I started asking that wise and loving voice within her how I could learn to hear that voice for *myself*.

Throughout the next couple of years, the Holy Spirit gave me dozens of different exercises to practice to help me open up to hearing that voice within me. But no matter how hard I tried, I just couldn't do it. I sat for hours and hours in meditation, filled with complete joy and peace, open-minded, willing, and attentive to hearing even the slightest whisper, but all I ever heard was silence. Each time I tried, I started with great hope and excitement, convinced this would finally be the day. But each time my attempt ended in devastation. One day, I said, "Forget it. I give up." And I stopped trying.

But the desire wouldn't leave me. Sure, I could go for a month or two without thinking about it, but inevitably the desire to hear that voice within me giving comfort, guidance, and support anytime I wanted welled back up until I'd return to my wife with my tail between my legs asking her to share that voice one more time. I secretly prayed her help would somehow turn the tide for me to begin hearing that voice for myself.

One day, I was guided to stop trying to hear God's Voice as some separate, distinct, and audible voice in my head. Instead, I was told to practice asking for signs. Before getting out of bed each morning, I'd ask God a question and look for the answer in signs throughout the day. For the first five or six days of trying...nothing. I didn't notice a single sign. But on the seventh day, something wonderful happened. My question that morning was whether or not I was on the right path. Was I heading in the right direction? While I walked to work, I noticed a yellowish-red maple leaf falling from its branch, gently swaying from side to side through the air as it fell. As I watched the leaf, an expansive eruption of excitement burst from my heart, covering my neck and arms with goose bumps that brought an immediate sense of knowing. Just like the leaf, it didn't matter whether I appeared to be moving left or right along my path. In truth I was always headed in the right direction—I was always heading closer to God.

The joy I felt in receiving an answer to my question was tremendous. With practice, I was soon receiving answers in the form of signs on a regular basis. After several months of success, I was guided to take the next step: to practice hearing God's Voice through other people. Once again, I started my day with a question and then listened for the answer through my coworkers, people I'd meet on the street, while watching TV, or through anyone else I'd come in contact with. I struggled to get an answer for the first couple of days, but then, just as with signs, I began "hearing" the answers spoken to me through my coworkers, friends, a cashier at the grocery store, or a song on the radio. Sometimes the answers were the literal words I heard. The context of the words was often different, but as soon as I heard the words, I experienced that same expansive, energetic joy; excitement; and knowingness flood my awareness. I felt the truth of the answer. Other times, it was the underlying perspective or intention behind the words that provided the answer I needed. Before long, I was consistently receiving answers to my questions by simply listening to other people. My mind was slowly becoming attuned to listening differently.

Eventually, I began to feel so contented with being able to hear God's Voice in so many different ways that I no longer experienced the desire to hear some loud voice in my head. Wouldn't you know it? It was precisely when I had given up all desire to hear that still, small voice within me that it finally happened.

It was Sunday morning, March 14, 1999. Like most Sunday mornings, Candace and I were propped up in bed having church with the Holy Spirit. We meditated for a little while after waking up, and then Candace shared a message from God's Voice. That morning I felt especially peaceful and connected listening to Candace share the Holy Spirit's words out loud. Suddenly the Holy Spirit turned to me through Candace and said, "Open your mouth and speak this Voice."

The surprise I felt was followed by nervousness and uncertainty, but because I felt so connected and good just moments before, I took a deep breath and opened my mouth. Out of me came the most beautiful words I had ever spoken. Tears fell from my eyes. A profound feeling of peace and wholeness enveloped me. This was my first experience hearing God's Voice in the way I had always dreamed. I didn't hear a separate voice in my mind and repeat what I had heard; I was completely joined with God's Voice in my awareness as I listened with wonder and joy to the words issuing from my mouth. For years I had been searching to hear a distinctly separate voice within me, and I finally understood why I never could: God's Voice was truly part of me—the voice of my highest self who is joined with God. By looking for it as something other than my own true voice, I kept missing it ever so subtly all those years.

Since that day, I have been able to hear God's Voice within me in a clear and recognizable way. Now I understand why I had to experience firsthand every challenge, misperception, concept, and belief that kept me from hearing this voice. Precisely because of this struggle I now have the understanding and insight I need to truly help others hear this voice for themselves. The ongoing joy, profound peace, and ever-present connection I now experience with God is so fulfilling, so life-altering, and so rewarding that I have dedicated my life to inspiring, teaching, and supporting others to hear this Voice for themselves.

DavidPaul Doyle lives in Ashland, Oregon, with his wife and daughter. His heart's desire is to experience his union with God in every moment, and support and teach others around the world how to do the same.

A New Sensation

As a young child, I was afraid of life; I hid in the closet when people came to the door. As a teen, I fainted before oral reports. I was so afraid of God and the afterlife that I literally had panic attacks thinking about death. Anytime I witnessed a homeless person on the street or a handicapped person rolling in a wheelchair, I experienced dread. I was afraid of being alone, and afraid of financial disaster. Sometimes I was even afraid to breathe for fear of inhaling toxins and pollutants in the air. I begged God to answer my prayers. I asked for health and joy. I questioned whether I had done the right thing in getting married and choosing my career path. I asked for a relationship with my mom and pleaded for a connection with God that would bring me peace. At 38 years old, my life was about to alter completely.

After 14 years of a strong marriage, my husband and I experienced some challenges and made several mistakes that left us homeless. We wound up in my mother-in-law's house, struggling. I felt hopeless, worthless, as if there were no escape.

Then I got sick.

I remember a tearful conversation with my husband while I watched our world falling apart. My greatest fears had become my reality. I was terrified of traveling life's path alone...and I was seemingly losing my husband. I had dreaded becoming homeless...and I was now with-out a home of my own. The thought of death panicked me...and I was getting sicker by the day. I fell into helpless shock, numb to the world. I retreated inside myself and blocked out reality.

My husband asked, "What do you feel?"

My reply was prophetic: "I don't feel anything."

In 2006, after years of health challenges, I was diagnosed with multiple sclerosis. It was something I had feared with great intensity. Many of my female relatives had the disease, and now I was terrified it would take my life, too. I underwent CT scans, MRIs, a lumbar tap, X-rays, and was told I would take steroids for the rest of my life to stop the disease's progression. The doctors said it would only get worse. I would eventually be confined to a wheelchair.

Within months my vision blurred, and my speech slurred. I lost sensation in my hands, legs, and feet. I had trouble walking on my own. I could no longer bathe myself, feed myself, or think clearly. My mind floated in a perpetual fog, and I couldn't focus. People asked if I was drunk, and it felt as if I was.

I begged God for help, to stop the pain, to stop the spreading numbness. But I didn't really believe my prayers would help, be-cause I didn't believe God was listening. An answer never came.

I had to make a decision. Was I going to die and leave my hus-band, my 6-year-old daughter, my potentially purposeful life? Or was I going to survive, thrive, figure out how to heal completely, and then help my relatives and others to heal themselves as well? I chose to survive. I started reading with one eye covered because my double vision was unbearable. I read Marianne Williamson's *A Return to Love*. I read David R. Hawkins's *Power vs. Force: The Hidden Determinants of Human Consciousness*. And in the middle of reading Louise Hay's *You Can Heal Your Life*, I learned a technique for "ex-tending love to my thoughts" through a course on hearing God's Voice.

From these sources, I learned to start extending love to every-thing. I imagined love in a bottle pouring down my head to bathe my brain and flow over my spine. I extended love to my husband, my daughter, my life, and the world. I learned to release all anxiety, let go of confusion, and just extend love.

On my bathroom mirror I posted a quote by Gautama Buddha and read it every day:

> Let me not pray to be sheltered from dangers, but to be fearless in facing them.

> Let me not beg for the stilling of pain, but for the heart to conquer it.

> Let me not look to allies in life's battlefield, but to my own strength.

> Let me not crave in anxious fear to be saved, but hope for patience to win my freedom.

I started meditating and feeling love. I told myself that God was love, so what I was feeling was God. I started listening, really listening, to people, the world, and God. As I meditated outside on the back patio, I listened to nature: the cooing mourning doves and the melodious wind chimes. I watched belted kingfishers fish in the pond, hummingbirds buzz around me, and the squirrels crunch on the peanut shells I'd thrown them. This was God for me. I never heard a "voice" respond. Instead, I acknowledged God all around me and felt His loving Presence within me.

Once I committed to listening and feeling, I found it possible to actually live in the present. I used to worry about the future: How would I make it financially? Would I heal completely? Would my husband and I save our marriage? I felt so guilty about my past: Why had I done such and such, and why hadn't I spoken up? I had rarely lived in the present. Now, I felt peace in the present. When I listen to God and feel God, I am completely in the present. I silently ask God a question, then empty my mind, breathe deeply, and listen. What I feel is my answer.

It's truly amazing how you can change your life so completely if you want to. I may not be fully healed yet, but I improve daily. I experience more peace than ever before. I listen to God every morning and send out love to the world. The love I extend surges like a wave. I send it over and around the globe, and it comes back to me, pulsing like a heartbeat or the ocean tide.

I now have enough sensation in my hands to write. I have enough sensation in my feet to walk. I see well enough to participate normally in life. I don't fear things over which I have no control. And I surely no longer fear God. I know I am truly blessed with a loving husband, a beautiful daughter, and a connection with my higher power.

A woman I met recently in a doctor's office told me, "You are the most peaceful person I've ever met."

How about that?

Rosalie McClung studied comparative literature at U.C. Davis before teaching language arts, humanities, and short story publishing for 10 years. Today, Rosalie writes and illustrates children's books, self-help books, and short stories. In her spare time, she also draws, paints, knits hats, and cooks her family's Sicilian recipes.

Twist of Faith

As a child I was adopted into what the world would characterize as a caring, loving, and deeply religious household. Although I wrestled for many years with the dichotomy of a parental figure's mood swings and the teachings of the church I was raised to believe in, I don't think anyone noticed the nightmare I was trapped in. I can't remember a single day from my childhood that we failed to bless our meals before eating, hold family prayer, or read from the Holy Scriptures. Yet with all outward symbols of a faith-based life I still feared that this family member's dark side would wreck havoc on our family. For most of my childhood I felt lost and alone, completely abandoned, and ensnared by a life I couldn't alter.

Outwardly we seemed the perfect family: upper middle–class income, active in our community and church. Yet our private lives were a strange combination of prayer, service, and abuse. Random beatings interwoven with cavalcades of screaming, yelling, and broken dishes provided the background for daily life.

Nightfall was the most feared. It was then we could be locked in a dark room to endure the worst nightmare a child could imagine. Your family is supposed to love and protect you, not torture you physically and sexually. What child could imagine a family member using them for sexual gratification? How can a child rationalize physical abuse that seems to be inflicted for no other reason than to satisfy some dark, twisted urging? Not one of my brothers or sisters escaped the daily torrent of abuse, yet through the grace of God we all survived this living hell.

Although all of the physical needs of life—food, clothing, shelter—plus an education were provided, I felt bereft of any real love. I longed to be held and comforted. Although I had six brothers and sisters, I lived with a deep, perpetual sadness that could only be described as loneliness.

Because of my childhood and the unshakable feeling that I had been rejected, ignored, and cheated out of God's Love, I began to seek that one experience in life that would help explain or justify all the pain. Having rejected, out of prejudice, most of what I had been taught in church, I studied in earnest the teachings of world religions. Finding a comfortable niche within my mind, I fully embraced the Eastern philosophy of Buddhism. For years I studied the art of meditation, dedicating my life to the path of peace. My first teacher was a Tibetan Lama, and then from 1996 until 2002 I studied Surat Shabd Yoga under a Sat Guru. Although my meditations yielded a profound sense of peace, I still had not experienced direct communication with God.

During the years of meditation it became quite clear that I needed to forgive myself and my family for past mistakes. The forgiveness process was just that—a process. Sometimes I revisited a single event in my life numerous times before I finally felt peace of mind. Having worked at opening my heart to the experience of love, I was finally ready to take the next step.

It was through a friend that I was reintroduced to the habit of scripture study in March of 2000. Almost immediately I recognized the message of God's Word as the piece of the puzzle for which I had been searching. With an eager heart I began a daily study of the Holy Scriptures, although I did substitute common Christian terms for their Eastern counterparts. For almost two years I swapped the image of Buddha for that of Christ. My painful childhood prejudices had come home to roost in a very subtle way.

Slowly I came to understand the image of Jesus in a totally new light, but my big breakthrough came after asking God to help me understand the real meaning of Christ. Within days I felt a presence in my heart I had never known before. The old prejudices against my Christian upbringing ceased to exist, and I could now finally accept the teachings of Christ in my life.

I was moved to begin a discourse with Jesus Christ one day while I took my morning shower. At first my behavior seemed odd: Was I having a profound spiritual experience, or losing my mind? Strangely enough I felt perfectly comfortable during my morning ritual. As I spoke aloud, I felt no sense of embarrassment at my nakedness. In fact, opening my mind to a loving brother was quite liberating.

Through the months our conversations seemed to produce a pattern: I would talk or think aloud and follow that with a brief moment of reflection whereby I would feel the answer had been received. Knowing Holy Spirit had provided an answer, I rarely felt it necessary to revisit a question. This happened most often during my time of reading and reflection; the answer just seemed to be there, ready for me to acknowledge. I absolutely loved this new experience of receiving God's Love.

As I began to accept God's love more and more, I started to see my life as more than a twisted nightmare from which I needed to escape. I began to recognize the value of my childhood as I started to play with the idea of forgiveness for myself and my parents. The more I was willing to let go of the past, the less painful it seemed to be. Gradually, I began to see the life I was always meant to lead.

As I accepted this gift of forgiveness I noticed an inexplicable calm in my life. One evening as I sat on my front porch reading from the Bible, I was struck with an overwhelming desire to know a specific answer to a nagging question. It was Thursday, the night our local church held its prayer circle. I drove the seven miles to church.

Walking in minutes before the service was to start, I quietly sat and started to meditate upon my burning desire. During the prayer service I felt a profound sense of peace. Reflecting upon my willingness to experience God's Word and receive an answer, I remained unprepared for what was about to happen. I felt as if my whole body became surrounded by Angels. It was as if every fiber of my being had instantly come alive, and my heart sang a song of gratitude I had never known existed. I knew a comforting presence was watching over me as I heard an undeniable voice speak to me within. It was a loud, booming voice, foreign, yet at the same time peaceful and comforting.

Filled with the knowledge that I had experienced something divine, I left that night knowing my question had been answered. The ride home was truly magical. Time seemed to stand still as I basked in the warmth emanating from my heart. By the time I returned home I had no conscious memory of the original question or the answer I had received, yet I was perfectly comforted knowing that a part of me had been touched by the hand of God

After that extraordinarily healing night, every time I prayed or sat for meditation I would do so with the intent to hear the Voice of God. As I continued to accept the love of God for myself and extend that same love to family and friends, my discourses with Holy Spirit became more frequent. As my prayer and meditation routine progressed, I swear I could hear an audible voice, but it was so soft I could barely make out the messages. Still I was thrilled to know that the presence of Holy Spirit in my life was real.

As I drove to church one Tuesday evening to attend a class, I narrowly escaped an auto accident. A young driver recklessly maneuvered a very expensive black Mercedes convertible onto the road in front of me. I slammed on my brakes, thinking, *What kind of father would give an irresponsible child such an expensive gift?* Within seconds I heard a very real voice say, "What have you done with the gifts your father has presented to you?" I pulled my car over as tears of joy streamed down my face.

The impact of the moment hit me full force. For the first time in my life I truly understood the value of hearing God's Voice. No matter what I was experiencing, I could trust that still, small voice within to offer meaningful guidance and wisdom, as well as insights. I felt amazed, realizing I could attune my mind to receive communication from God whenever I needed or wanted Him.

I idled my car on the side of the road and counted my blessings. My life was not about the suffering I had endured, but was a precious gift that was allowing me to learn and grow. I felt a deep sense of gratitude for having been given the gift of forgiveness in my life, and I knew in my heart I was privileged to walk this journey with those who would facilitate my return to God.

Russell Hill is a graphic artist and Internet applications developer. The father of two wonderful children, he enjoys a healthy passion for hiking and whitewater rafting.

Falling in Love

Tony had such an overpowering presence that I actually felt him before I saw him. When he walked into the restaurant I was sitting with my back to the door. I felt an electrifying energy behind me. Having never felt such a sensation, I immediately turned to see who had walked in. I watched him walk by and take a seat facing me. Though he was not the most handsome man I'd ever seen, I couldn't take my eyes off of him. He obviously felt the same because he couldn't stop looking at me either. We were mesmerized by each other.

The electricity between us must have been felt throughout the restaurant, because the next day the waitresses and a friend of mine enthusiastically arranged to bring us together. They gave him my phone number and he called that morning. We talked for hours and were pleasantly surprised about our instant connection and the chemistry between us. He was so charming and complimentary that I knew I could fall for him. Even his voice had a mesmerizing effect on me.

That was the beginning of our stormy long-distance relationship. His work required travel for months at a time, so we took turns visiting each other. I could handle the distance between us, but when he told me he was seeing other women wherever he traveled, I was devastated. I repeatedly tried to end our relationship but could not let go of him. I kept going back, hoping he would choose me over all the others. I was willing to wait.

After a long two-month separation Tony was finally coming to visit. I was so excited! When he walked in the front door I could hardly contain my euphoria. His physical presence was impossible to resist. After we visited for half an hour he casually mentioned he was going on a ski trip with new friends and he would not be able to spend much time with me. I felt my stomach drop. I had waited so long to see him and couldn't understand how he could so nonchalantly stroll in and out of my life. It seemed every time we had a chance to spend some time together, he had some excuse for ending our visit earlier than planned. His apathy felt like a slap in the face. He had just met these people and he was choosing them over me.

Painfully, I realized that the feelings I had for Tony would always be one-sided. I would never be as important to him as I wanted to be. After more than two years of putting up with his detached aloofness I made the heart-wrenching decision to end the relationship for good. I could no longer accept his emotional crumbs.

After many hours of uncontrollable crying and wondering if my heart could survive this pain, I calmed down enough to realize it was time to take a deep, hard look at myself. I couldn't understand why I'd continued to let him treat me this way and why I kept going back for more. I wanted a committed relationship, so why was I attracting men who were not emotionally available? I had been married three times to such men and had done a lot of spiritual work on myself, but I kept making bad choices. Something was missing.

I realized I had deep self-worth issues I had never addressed. I found a book titled *How to Raise Your Self-Esteem* by Nathaniel Brandon and read it eagerly. One of the first visual exercises in the book particularly spoke to me. I made myself comfortable on my sofa and began the process by envisioning a mountain with a pathway all the way to the top. I imagined a perfect fall day with a brilliant azure sky and crisp clear air. I could smell wood burning in the distance. A rainbow of colorful wildflowers and fragrant evergreens adorned the mountainsides. A brook with fresh, clear water meandered through the forest. I walked up the path, indulging myself in the serenity and beauty, and began shedding negative feelings that were a constant burden in my life. As I did this, I noticed that my mind and body felt lighter, and a joyous peace filled my spirit. I could see soft white light emanating from me. As I neared the mountain's top, the climb was so effortless I practically skipped the rest of the way up.

When I reached the peak I was exhilarated. Breathtaking vistas spread for miles and miles. I felt as if I were on top of the world. This jubilant feeling was short-lived, however, as I noticed a dark cloud slowly moving towards me. I knew this cloud was the accumulation of years of my most negative feelings. I turned toward it and said, "Oh, I know you. I've been running away from you most of my life."

I was suddenly interrupted by a strong, loving voice so clear and distinct I could not ignore it. It sounded like someone else speaking to me inside my head. A knowingness that this was the Voice of God within me permeated my heart and soul.

"You need to love it," the Voice said.

Instead of running away, this time I gently wrapped my arms around the cloud and held it and loved it as I would a child in pain until it completely dissolved. Instantly I felt a calmness and joy of spirit I hadn't felt in years. The peace and joy continued to increase until I was in a constant state of rapture. For days I experienced a joy and love of life that I believe was heaven on earth. The feelings were similar to the ones I had felt in the past when falling in love. Then I realized I *had* fallen in love with someone—ME!

Acknowledging and loving that negative, fearful part of me healed my heart. Hearing and listening to God's Voice that day was the most powerful and beautiful experience of my life. The joy I experienced permeated every facet of my life. I have a much more loving and positive attitude toward everyone, and have stopped complaining. Even my looks have changed. Friends and family tell me my skin glows with soft light and my eyes are clearer and softer.

I now thank Tony for helping me look at myself by taking me down to my lowest low so I could rise up to my most wonderful high. I know that I am ready to receive the love I truly deserve—unconditional love. A magical and beautiful new way of looking at the world has opened up to me! Thank you, God.

Janet Calledare works in the health food industry, meeting and helping people from all walks of life. She has a deep love for her children, family, and friends, and enjoys renovating homes and creating things, from jewelry to flower arrangements.

Love in its Purest Form

In my mid-20s, my strong belief in God faltered after losing three very young people who were close to me. I cried out to God, "Why did you take these people?" Heartsick and bitter, I fell ill for a few days and disconnected myself from everyone around me.

Not long after, while sitting stoically in church with that bitter chill in my heart, my pastor called for anyone who desired to come forward and take communion. Feeling unworthy of such an act, given my state of mind, I remained in my seat while others gathered in divine celebration at the altar.

Suddenly, I felt a presence around me. I tried to shake it off, but it would not leave. No words were spoken. No revelations came to me, and there was no loud clap of thunder or booming voice, just a simple feeling of peace and an inner knowing that all was well. It was as if someone were telling me it was okay to just sit there. I felt my misery was somehow understood and I would not feel that disconnected sadness forever. Tears of joy formed in my eyes and a gentle smile crept across my face. I sat in a state of amazing grace. Though I didn't realize it at the time, I now know God was speaking to me as I sat there in wonderment.

Years later, reading about someone else's experience connecting to God, the exhilaration and joy I felt on that day in church so long ago resurfaced in my consciousness and stayed with me for days. When others noticed my tranquil demeanor and mentioned the change they saw in me, I decided to allow myself the quiet time I needed for contemplation.

My decision to examine my life raised many questions, and I wondered why an on-again, off-again cycle defined the relationship I had experienced with God through the years. Why, I wondered, did I look outside myself when searching for a connection with my Creator? While pondering that thought, the words "go within" began swimming in my head.

I gravitated toward a guided meditation program I'd recently purchased and began incorporating meditation into my daily routine. Soon I fell in love with this quiet time of the day. Much of the peace I'd been seeking was found in this practice. However, I was unprepared for what was about to happen as I comfortably positioned the headphones over my ears one day.

During this meditation, I discovered I was thinking "you" statements to myself, and asking "you" questions of myself. It was bizarre. *What is this "you" stuff?* I wondered. While sinking deeper and deeper into relaxation, I discovered myself spitting and sputtering about the fact that my husband was not grasping spiritual ideas the way I thought he should. When I realized how judgmental I was being, I focused instead on thoughts of love, and quieted my mind. As I rested I heard, "Why do you think that he should learn this faster than you did?"

Before I realized what I was doing I looked up and said, "Yeah, why do I think that?"

Who was I talking to? Did I expect an answer? I can't describe the feeling of utter foolishness combined with the "divine knowing" that I *wasn't* talking to myself. Closing my eyes I timidly asked, "Oh, is that You?"

The response nearly knocked me off my chair. "Yes, my child, I am right here. I have always been here; I will always be here."

Yes, my child? I don't talk that way to myself. *Yes, my child?* Why would I say that to myself? It was clear something was happening, but as much as I wanted to believe, I still had doubt accompanied by a feeling of disbelief, uncertainty, and a little fear. Was I losing my mind?

Later that day I related the incident to a dear friend of mine.

"Are you the kind of person who goes around making up stories?" he asked.

"No," I said, "of course not."

"Are you a liar? Do you say things just to hear yourself talk?"

"Certainly not! You know me better than that!"

"Exactly," he said.

My eyes welled with tears. "Oh...I see what you mean," I said humbly. I was awestruck.

Driving home that afternoon, I felt so loved, so special, so cherished. I knew then, without a doubt, I had heard God's Voice. Since that day of profound realization, I can think back to the many times I had heard God's Voice yet didn't know it was Him.

My life has been forever changed. I am learning to notice, to observe the many moments of my day. Life is no longer a blur of activity to simply be repeated the next day. My mind is not chattering incessantly, nor wandering nomadically. There is purpose, there is positive thought, and there is love. I know now that God's Voice has guided me all my life, and continues to do so daily. This Voice for Love has inspired me to take loving action today and not wait for the tomorrows that never seem to come. Conversely, this Voice has shown me the importance of "standing still," not in the literal sense, but in a way that helps me connect with my spirit. Sometimes I need only to sit, close my eyes, and quiet my mind. Other times I might choose to take a walk or go outside to enjoy the beauty of nature all around me. Oftentimes I hear God's Voice in the blissful moments just before falling asleep, and I know that tomorrow will be the best day of my life, ever. This Voice is love in its purest, truest form. I know I am being blessed and I am grateful.

Sharon Caldararo is a happily married wife and mother of three extraordinary children and five (and counting) glorious grandchildren. Visiting nursing homes and connecting with elders is one of her greatest joys.

Don't Judge a Book by its Cover

Joe and Sally asked if I would spend some time with Nancy, their 15-year-old mentally challenged daughter. Nancy had been placed in a special needs class in a public high school and was reading at a second- or third-grade level. The kids at school bullied her and called her "dummy" and "retard." The stress had caused Nancy to have headaches and stomachaches, and to bite her nails until they bled. Though she hadn't experienced any trouble of that kind in grade school, blossoming into womanhood in high school and being rejected proved very difficult and painful for her. Her parents believed if they sent her to a special needs school she would regress even more. But clearly, her present situation was not ideal.

"We think," Sally said to me, "that you might be able to help her understand why she is the way she is and find some peace with it. Would you please try to help?"

I agreed, and the family drove four hours to my home the following weekend. I allowed Nancy some time to get comfortable with me before we started. When she seemed relaxed enough, I sat across from her and began to speak.

"Nancy, why do you think the kids in school are bullying you?"

"Uh, I don't know," Nancy replied. She stared down at the tabletop and twisted her fingers.

"Why do you think you chew your fingernails?" I continued.

Again she replied, "Uh, I don't know," and avoided eye contact.

When her answer to the third and fourth questions garnered the same apathetic response, I was at a loss as to how to handle her. In desperation, I asked myself the magical question I always ask when I don't know what to do: *What would LOVE do?*

I suddenly felt myself shudder and shift and began to feel really nasty and ugly.

"No wonder everybody calls you a dummy and a retard," I mocked. "You keep saying, 'Uh, I don't know,' to every question I ask you. If I kept hearing that all the time, I'd call you a dummy and a retard too."

Part of me was shocked to hear what had issued from my mouth. Was this the answer I received to my question of what would LOVE do? I let it continue. I babbled on and on for at least a minute, mocking her, repeating what the kids in school had said to her.

Oh my God! What was happening? I felt a strange mixture of horrified panic on the outside, and stole a furtive glance at Nancy's parents to see how they were affected by this, yet inside I felt a deep peaceful stillness. I had never spoken to anybody in such a callous and demeaning way, especially to someone with special needs. If anything, I was usually more compassionate and understanding than normal when interacting with a child such as Nancy. I could sense that her parents were shocked. They must have been wondering whatever had possessed them to think I could help their child if this was the way I was treating her. I had no idea what was going to come out of my mouth next, and worst of all, I remembered a cassette player was recording the whole thing!

Though my words and behavior shocked me, and though I was aware of the parents' concerns and could feel Nancy withdraw, I knew I had to trust that what was happening was supposed to happen and I let this process continue.

"Please, God, help me to help your child," I prayed.

I let go of any attempt to control what was happening. "Do you believe God is inside you?" I asked firmly.

"Uh-huh" she whispered.

"Good!" I snapped. "From this moment on I don't want to hear another word from you!" I suddenly felt my body shudder and shift and become my usual calm self again. I continued softly, "I want you to let God use your tongue, your throat, your teeth, your breath, your mind. I want you to let God do all the talking."

"Okay," she replied shyly.

To put her at ease, I asked her to take a deep breath in through her nose and puff it out loudly through her mouth, like a dolphin. Slowly, she repeated that cleansing breath three times, and when she was relaxed I began asking her questions.

For 15 minutes, she spoke confidently, with no hesitation, clearly enunciating every word. Sometimes she used three- and four-syllable words to answer my questions. She told us why she chose her mother, why she chose her father, and why they were perfect for her life's expression. They would, she explained, provide her with the support and nurturing she needed to do God's work.

When I asked the next question we were not ready for her reply. "Why did your soul choose a body that would look and act retarded?"

She paused, smiled, and tilted her head ever so slightly to the right. "That's so simple," she whispered, "I came to teach LOVE. It would be easy for you to love me if I looked like you and walked like you and talked like you. But will you still love me when I drool, when I chew my nails until they bleed? Will you still love me when you have to change my diaper? I came to teach LOVE."

A sacred hush filled the room. I couldn't speak. Her true beauty and grace and the courage of her soul took my breath away. Tears filled my eyes.

The tape recorder clicked off.

Many hugs and more tears were exchanged before Sally and Joe took Nancy and left for home. They were filled with joy, peace, and gratitude for the whole experience.

Nancy had remembered her mission and had allowed God's Voice to speak through her. Joe and Sally saw the perfection of their child and realized how they were to serve her.

The whole experience was both humbling and frightening for me. I learned to surrender and trust that all was in divine order, especially when LOVE came through as "tough love."

Two months afterward I received a card from Sally informing me Nancy was going for her first professional manicure because "God doesn't want me to chew my fingernails anymore." She added that Nancy hardly said "Uh, I don't know" anymore, and had been invited to join a girl's club.

Whenever I hear anyone say that God only talks to special people, I have to agree. I'm so grateful God used Nancy to show me how special we all are!

After completing 16 years in the military as a physical education and combat training instructor, Caroline McIntosh enjoys traveling, writing, teaching, and following her adventurous heart wherever it leads her.

God's Whispers

I had everything a woman could want. My loving, caring husband was a successful businessman who provided for every want and need. We had five beautiful children, but living in an apartment in São Paulo, Brazil, a city constantly growing in population, was becoming a threat to my family. The city had grown dangerous, and my children needed protection from the sort of life it now offered. I had to impose strict limits on their activities and issue constant warnings.

One of my husband's dreams was to have a farm, so we talked about moving to the country where I could give my children a healthier life. He would continue to take care of the companies he owned in São Paulo during the week, and on weekends he could be with the family.

We decided to move to a city 250 kilometers from São Paulo. I had some relatives living there, and, being a seeker of the Truths of God, I was interested in several movements in that city. We were on the road to a more enjoyable life, and harmony continued to bless us as a sign that we were on the right track. By this time, my eldest was 8 years old and my youngest was 1.

We bought a nice house in town where we could stay until we'd found some land on which to build a farm. At times, I sat on the sidewalk and watched my kids play on the street, running, laughing, and having a life I knew was not possible anymore in the big city. My husband was satisfied with our choices, and his coming and going every weekend didn't bother him. Some months later we bought a beautiful piece of property and started building the house of our dreams.

Then an unexpected yearning filled my heart to legally separate from my husband. What a strange feeling! The feeling grew stronger and stronger. What was this? Why was I feeling this way? After working to make all our plans become real I was simply sending

166

them down the drain. I kept asking God why I was feeling this weird compulsion. Had I offended Jesus by marrying a Jewish man? Was I being punished because of my interest in reincarnation? Had I been captured by a negative energy because I was trying to deepen my inner experience of God?

I had no clues and no wise creature to ask for help. Maybe I was being asked to forget my newer beliefs and keep to my traditional religion's beliefs. Or perhaps God was asking me to sacrifice all this happiness in His name. I truly had no idea. The feelings just came upon me and could not be pushed away. I was suddenly thrown into a dark hole. Lost in my feelings, I cried and prayed for answers, but the feeling that I must separate from my husband only grew stronger. I asked God to send me signs. Still, everything around me remained the same. My love for my husband and my children had not changed. Our lives were perfect and our farm project continued smoothly as planned. I was in terrible conflict.

After days of deep praying, a sudden and enormous peace filled my heart. Although I felt more centered, I asked God why I should legally separate from my husband. Though I didn't consciously hear an answer, a certainty grew within me—I should follow what I was feeling.

"Okay," I told God, "if this is a test of loyalty, I will do as You ask."

When I told my husband, chaos took place. The following weeks were a nightmare for him. While darkness was everywhere, peace grew in my heart. I felt more and more sure I was doing the right thing. My family and friends always worried about my search for Truth. Now they were sure it was leading me to insanity. Who in the world would want to split such a loving family? My mind said I was crazy but my heart felt all was well.

My husband knew of my studies about life and had difficulty understanding my experiences. My only explanation for the separation was that I needed more freedom from the cultural ties of our marriage to continue my studies. Of course, that was the worst thing he could hear because it meant I would be free to be in another relationship.

God, what a challenge I was being drawn into. Would we have to split the family? I'd never be able to see him separate from the children. If one of us had to choose with whom they would stay, I'd leave them with him. And where was I to live? Following my heart in the face of the love I held for my family meant I must be ready to sacrifice everything.

I deepened my prayers for my husband to find peace with this situation, and, little by little, thoughts of how to maintain harmony in the family arose in my mind. I told him we could continue living together on weekends and our plans on moving to the farm would continue. Nothing would really change, but we still had to legally separate. Miraculously, he finally accepted my exotic plea and we went for our legal separation in peace.

Two years after our legal separation, my husband's company went bankrupt. His world was in turmoil, and my heart was aching to see his condition. He lost his credit and could not work until everything was cleared up by the law. He became an invisible man to society. How were we to survive with a family of seven?

I prayed to God to give me a peaceful heart and mind. I could not lose myself in my worries. I had to help my ex now. God answered me by filling my heart with peace. I couldn't think of the future. My mind stayed in the moment, and, supported by God's strength, I helped my ex-husband to make the right decisions. My love for him spoke louder and I decided to start living as his wife again.

It was then that we were told by the lawyers of the importance of being legally separated for two years. In our country, when a legally separated man of more than two years goes into bankruptcy, his ex-wife is totally left out of it. What I owned due to our separation would remain untouched. Though the court held all of his assets, our separation gave us the means to live and not fall into despair. God had lovingly protected my family, gently guiding me through the yearnings of my heart.

My journey in search of God's Truth led me to be open to my feelings enough to hear and believe the Whispers of God, and know in the depths of my soul that God's Voice guides me and protects me. I now live in the moment, knowing I will be strengthened and guided as I face my challenges. I have faith that whatever happens is meant to be, that where I am is where I should be. I also know I have what I need to grow spiritually, and that there's always a positive side to everything that seems at first glance to be wrong.

Susana Silbermann is a 59-year-old Brazilian woman. She has five children and six grandchildren. She enjoys reading and learning about psychology, neuroscience, education, art, philosophy, and anything related to human behavior.

Simple Synchronicity

Every painting is a journey. This one started in my art studio. I began by painting a primer of white gesso on a large stretched canvas, a process I did for every painting. It was a ritual I performed to get to know the canvas, and one into which I would pour myself for the next few months. The primed canvas under my fingers would soon take form, and at this moment I was in control. Once the paint started to flow, the art took over and led me. The painting for Parkview Hospital was no different, but little did I know that the journey on that blank canvas would be one of my favorites.

When asked to present an idea for art in the lobby of our largest area hospital, I knew at once what to paint. A family scene came to mind of an old Fort Wayne downtown street and an aerial map of the hospital area all woven together. I liked my idea, but it was missing something. As usual when this happened, I presented my subconscious mind with the task of finding the missing ingredient. I opened myself up to what was around me, having faith that some missing ingredient would mysteriously bubble forth with an "aha!" moment.

I went about my normal routine, and, as always, an undercurrent started to form that looked for the solution. Maybe someone said something or I saw a phrase in a magazine. Anything might have brought that current of an idea to the surface. When that happened, my mind grabbed at those images bobbing around me, as if I had a limited time to pull them in. The phrases, the visuals, the feelings all came rushing my way, formulating a great idea.

When I asked my art class, one of my advanced/portfolio students presented the idea of an angel. I heard the idea of an angel, and hardly anything more of her presentation. My "aha!" moment had arrived. Bubbling up in my mind, I saw images of Michelangelo's ceilings, Chagall's vivid skies with angels afloat, and Nana's shelf of collectable angels. My mind was riding the rapids of thoughts, and the rippling effect of my student's idea flowed with the current. Unbeknownst to me, the beginning of the angel's magic had started.

I researched angels, surprised to find out how deeply rooted angels were in our society. Ancient works by Greeks, Romans, Indians, Japanese, Assyrians, and Egyptians had all recorded angelic figures. Angels were protective symbols, messengers, guides, and comfort-givers who graced our temples, tombs, churches, and palaces. Angels crossed religious borders: Christianity, Islam, and Judaism all embraced them. I found angels of several races and both sexes who seemed to cross every social class. Angel encounters were written in our oldest texts—the Bible's Old and New Testament, the Koran, and Hebrew Scrolls. Art Museums dedicated wings displaying Greek angel vases, Buddhas with angels, and numerous Christian oil paintings sprinkled with angels. The more I learned about angels in our society the more I knew that was my painting's missing ingredient.

I felt references to angels endlessly. I heard angels in songs on our airwaves and found them mentioned in our literature. I remembered Raphael's angels, but I didn't know about the numerous angels in Emily Dickinson's and Edgar Allan Poe's poems, or James Taylor's lyrics. Angels were represented in every sign of the Zodiac.

The first day I transported my portable painting studio to the hospital lobby was a cold January day. The blank canvas fit like a glove in the back of my van. I hauled in my paints and set up shop. People looked at me with questioning faces as I unloaded my studio.

I knew the importance of painting those angels in public. I especially wanted to share that process with the employees, but on that cold, uninviting day I doubted my efforts would be effective. I was sitting on the spot where my parents were born, where I was born, and where I gave birth to my two sons.

I slowly grew emotionally attached to my new space and settled in to a routine of hauling my work out two mornings a week and painting all through the winter. The painting started to come alive and I began to see the effect of angels on others.

If I had been in an elevator with a stranger, chances are we would not have talked, let alone exchanged meaningful information. But painting in public acted as a magnet. As people grew interested in what I was doing they started conversations that often became profound. Emotions were raw in the hospital lobby. I had never considered this component to my painting. People nervously waiting for medical results visited me. I helped pass the time for patients' loved ones and redirected their focus. I listened helplessly to stories about aches and pains and suffering from total strangers. Hospital volunteers were entertained with thoughts of Old Fort Wayne, Indiana, as we all tried to remember names of stores on the 1950s streets intertwined throughout my painting. I had employees stop to see what was happening as they switched shifts.

Each time someone stopped I pointed out the angels, which were disguised as birch trees in my woods. The effect was magical when they saw them for the first time. Hospital employees were my favorite visitors. I wanted them to understand as they spotted the angels that their profession of caring for the sick makes them our community angels on earth.

It was surprising to discover that so many employees collected angels. A doctor showed me an angel pin on her jacket. A nurse showed me angel stickers she used to reward patients. A rabbi quoted scripture about angels and a priest talked freely about our guardian angel's presence. The more I painted, the more magic surrounding angels I experienced.

The most powerful moment during the painting was a simple synchronicity. Two ladies in their 60s approached to observe my painting. It was obvious they were troubled, aimlessly wandering the hospital to kill time. One had red, swollen eyes, and they both looked very sad. You could tell they were sisters by their voices. They said they were here to visit their other sister. I tried to lighten the mood and talked about my own sisters. Sisters were special, I told them, and I had two sisters also. I explained the painting and pointed out the birch trees and asked if they saw the angels on the path in the woods. I was unprepared for their response. As soon as they spotted the angels, they burst into tears and fell into each other's arms. Wrapped around each other, one of the sisters looked over at me with tears streaming down her face and said, "We just took our sister off life support. I had just commented that I wished she would send us a sign letting us know we had done the right thing. She collects angels!"

Goose bumps traveled up my arms as I watched the sisters leave my table looking completely different. They walked taller, arm in arm, with more direction than before.

As I finished and signed my name on the painting I was not ready to let go of the angel experience. I wanted to sit in the lobby where the emotions were raw and where people were drawn into my painting, feeling the magic. I had no idea that that journey of simple lines and various tones of color would be so powerful. I know there were people who walked by my painting and never saw what was hidden in the woods. I also know there were employees who walked by that painting seeing only the angels I painted for them. For me that painting was about moments such as those played out by the sisters. I took part in being the final message of a life, a powerful parting gift, a sign from angels made by my colorful strokes that offered comfort. That beautiful ancient symbol that enriched my life through this painting had also started the healing for two sisters.

Vicki Junk-Wright lives with her husband, Ted Wright, and their two sons in Indiana. She teaches art and does commissioned artwork. Publications that feature her work include *The North Light Book of Acrylic Painting Techniques* and *Mastodons on Parade*, published by Indiana and Purdue University. In 2006, she was awarded the Robert Rouschenberg Foundation Grant for her work with special needs children.

Painting by Vicki Junk-Wright. Copyright 2007. Used with permission. Not to be reprinted without express permission from the artist.

Overcoming My "Autism"

An earsplitting emotional meltdown exploded from my 7-year-old son, Jake, in his car seat behind me. Despite my efforts to prevent these meltdowns, sometimes they still occurred.

Jake displayed all the symptoms of severe autism. He experienced huge challenges in making sense of the world, especially of people. Both his expressive and receptive communication skills were severely impaired. Ordinary lights, sounds, and touch were unbearable to him at times, and he was extremely hyperactive. Everything seemed natural and easy for his 10-year-old brother, Derek. I felt enormously blessed as mother to both of them and learned to embrace the learning opportunities they each brought to my life.

I worked with Jake extensively to help him overcome his challenges. I knew in my heart that through God all things were possible, and I believed in the teachings of Jesus and in miracles. I kept believing, hoping, and searching for answers and guidance from God. I often turned to God in prayer for support because life with Jake made even the most ordinary daily events huge ordeals. Keeping an organized schedule was virtually impossible. There was no way to force Jake or to make him conform. He did the best he could. So did I.

This particular day, as I drove with Jake hysterical in the back seat, I struggled to understand why things had to be this way. I couldn't figure out what there was to learn here or think of anything I could do to help Jake when he got like this. I desperately let God hear about it! It was this day I first heard God's Voice.

It was summer vacation for Derek, and he wanted to go to a friend's house to play. Jake had an afternoon therapy session, so I told Derek I'd drop him off on the way. Jake's therapy took place in a large gym-like room with swings, trampolines, and climbing equipment. He *loved* to go.

We cheerfully piled into the car and I explained to Jake we'd be dropping off Derek at a friend's house first and then go to therapy. He made eye contact with me briefly, then looked expectantly out the window.

On the way out of our neighborhood, I turned left to go to Derek's friend's house. Jake knew we turned right for therapy. I made the left turn and he panicked.

"Back this way!" he exclaimed in alarm. "Back this w-a-a-y!"

I tried to explain the situation. "*We will* go that way Jake, but first...."

My words went unheard. Jake was working himself up to a full-fledged tantrum—biting himself, kicking, screaming his frustration and rage, and disintegrating into a hysterical mess.

With Jake ratcheting up his squalling to a brain-vaporizing pitch, I dropped off Derek at the friend's house and started driving toward the gym. It was too late. Jake had dissolved into hysterical sobbing, his small, pale face beet red with blotches blooming over his forehead. Mucus and tears streamed down his chin. I was lucky he was restrained in the car seat; when he got worked up this way, he would often attack anyone nearby, and I was the usual target. Jake continued to kick the back of the front seat while I tried to remain calm and explain things to him.

"Jake, we can go to the gym now. It's okay, but you have to calm down to go. I just had to drop off Derek first."

He still could not hear me.

"Look out the window, Jake. Look where we're going."

He was so upset, he seemed oblivious to what was going on around him. He focused totally on his misery and disappointment that things hadn't gone as expected. I knew from experience this would be a 30- to 45-minute meltdown and another hour of cooling down afterwards. Therapy was only an hour long. We wouldn't be able to go that day.

After waiting in the therapy parking lot 20 minutes with Jake still consumed in his misery, we left for home. I called the therapist to explain why we hadn't shown.

"Yes, I'm aware I still have to pay," I told her.

I had the door that led from the garage to the house propped open with my purse. Jake remained in the car, sobbing with his shirt pulled over his head, refusing to get out.

Now it was my turn for a meltdown. Tears began streaming down my face and I pleaded to God out loud.

"See? This is why I want him to be able to understand me! He loves to go to the gym, and he couldn't go today because he didn't understand enough to hear and trust me!" I was sobbing and frustrated, having finally reached the limit of my patience and control. Without warning, a deep and loud voice suddenly pierced my consciousness like none I had ever experienced before. "How are you any different than your child? Why don't you trust where *I* am taking *you*?"

I froze in my tracks. The voice seemed to come from all around me. It penetrated my self-pity and stilled my awareness to that moment alone. Usually I felt God as a quiet presence within me, and have wondered whether I've heard Him right. This time, there was no doubt.

As I straightened up and sat still so I could soak in what was being said, a huge wave of relief rolled over me as the truth of those words flooded my mind. It felt as if a weight had immediately lifted. I realized I *was* very similar to Jake when things didn't go as I expected! In my life there were frequent unexpected turns, and often my focus turned to my own discomfort. Surely God, who had a *much* larger perspective in mind than I did, knew the necessity of these turns. Maybe when things didn't go the way I expected them to, I could *settle down and listen*, just as I wanted my son to do. If I listened, I could learn things! I wondered how often I had missed hearing Him before. He must have felt as helpless as I did trying to reach Jake. Hearing Him was all in my control. I just hadn't understood that before.

Wiping the tears from my face, I silently said inside myself, "You're right, God. You love me, so I will trust that You know the way. I'm going to start listening better." Filled with joy, I called out to Jake to take his time. I'd be waiting for him whenever he was ready to come in.

I am so grateful God showed that to me. It has helped me let go of what I can't control, and focus on what *is* in my control. Now whenever I experience those unexpected turns I can't control and start to fall apart, I try to shift my focus to Who is actually in the driver's seat of my life. Only God can get me where I truly want to go. I must remember that sometimes my role is to quiet down and try to listen. I never know who else may be benefiting from the unexpected turn, or what new understanding I may gain, but I can trust that God knows these answers. I need only work on my focus and listening skills to hear His reassurance and guidance. I'm still far from perfect at it, but it does get easier to hear God the more I try. It's what I always tell my son, "If you want to get better at something, it takes practice."

I can hear God quietly say, "Exactly!"

Tara McClintick is a Son-Rise mom, previously an Early Child Special Education teacher. She loves working with children and is passionate about natural healing techniques.

Tap, Tap, Tap

In the summer of 1998, I was a single mom with two children: a daughter who was 4 1/2 and a son who was 1 1/2. They had different fathers, whom I had never married. At that time, I was not receiving child support. Even though I had a degree in pre-med and had worked in the medical field prior to having children, I was struggling to make money as a self-employed massage therapist, doing my best to not place my kids in daycare. Were I to pay for daycare, I'd barely make a living at my low-paying job. On the advice of a lawyer, I filed a lawsuit to receive child support from my daughter's father. I was told the original agreement I had made with him giving him joint custody was illegal without child support.

One sunny summer afternoon I heard a knock at the front door. With my baby son in my arms, I answered it. Two Child Protective Services workers stood on the front porch.

"Are you Theresa Miller?" one of them asked.

"Yes," I answered.

One flashed me an ID and said, "We are with Child Protective Services and we'd like to ask you a few questions."

It felt as if the ground had dropped out below my feet. I said to myself, "I can't believe he really did this." I automatically assumed that my daughter's father was using Child Protective Services as a legal maneuver to throw out my case.

The two of them played "good cop, bad cop" and questioned me in an intimidating way, saying, "Are you a part of a cult? Are you a cocaine addict? Why are you still nursing your son? Are you mentally ill?" and most unbelievable of all, "Is your son's father sexually abusing your daughter and are you allowing it to happen?"

When they left I was shaken to my core. A few weeks earlier at a school event, my daughter's stepmother had said to me, "You are about to get everything you deserve." This must have been what she meant.

After this experience, my daughter's father filed an emergency motion to suspend my parental rights for three weeks pending a psychiatric evaluation. Even my family had turned away from me. Because my ex was married and wealthy, whereas I was an unemployed single mother, they felt he had more credibility and believed his story. I felt as if I were being crucified.

Although Child Protective Services threw out the case based on lack of evidence, I felt terrified and despairingly agreed to sign a "contract" with the father giving him sole physical custody, which meant I would receive no child support. In addition, he dictated our "visitation schedule," which forced me to do all the driving to pick up and drop off my daughter. I lived an hour away from him, making it even more difficult to get a job that would support me and still have the flexibility to allow me to spend enough quality time with her.

In the midst of this, something happened that would turn out to change the course of my life in ways I could not have imagined. A week after my episode in the courtroom, feeling desperate, isolated, and nearly suicidal, I read about Wayne Dyer's new book about St. Francis of Assisi. He talked about St Francis's famous prayer:

Lord, make me an instrument of Thy peace;
Where there is hatred, let me sow love;
Where there is injury, pardon;
Where there is doubt, faith;
Where there is despair, hope;
Where there is darkness, light;
And where there is sadness, joy.
O Divine Master,
Grant that I may not so much seek to be consoled as to console;
To be understood, as to understand;
To be loved, as to love;
For it is in giving that we receive,

It is in pardoning that we are pardoned,
And it is in dying that we are born to Eternal Life.
Amen.

Something inside me clung to that prayer to save my life. I prayed it over and over during those three weeks, truly asking to become a servant of God's will in the world, asking to be of some use, because clearly I had no power of my own.

About a year and a half after this experience, I spontaneously began feeling a gentle tapping on my left shoulder almost every day. Whereas I would ordinarily be startled by something so unexpected, it felt comforting. For several months the tapping continued, gently, but insistently. Then one evening while I was washing dishes at the sink in a rare moment of quiet solitude, I felt the now familiar tap, tap, tap on my shoulder. I turned my back to the sink, folded my arms across my chest, closed my eyes, and said in my mind, "Okay! But how do I know that you are from the light?"

Immediately I heard a Voice inside my head that sounded separate from my own thoughts. It said, "Well, go into your heart and see." I allowed my conscious awareness to drop to the level of my heart center and immediately felt a huge wave of love and peace. It was as though a million angels were hugging me and loving me beyond anything I had ever known. In that moment, I knew this Voice was not only benevolent, but a part of my destiny. I said in my mind, "Okay. I will communicate with You unconditionally from this moment on. I will be Your servant."

As I began to join with this Voice more and more, I experienced a loving, gentle guidance that would first direct me to connect with my heart center, and then to connect with my higher self by repeating the phrase "I am that I am," like a mantra. When I did this I would feel a deep calm centering, and at the same time, an expansive feeling would come over me as my mind aligned with my Higher Self. Then the Holy Spirit's loving Voice would arise in my awareness, giving me whatever instruction I was to follow.

This Voice, which I have come to know as the Holy Spirit, has explained to me that meditation and allowing my everyday, individual consciousness to surrender to my Higher Self is the key to connecting with it clearly. With continued practice, I have become able to access this state within seconds.

The situation with my daughter's father eventually became cooperative, and my daughter and I now spend a lot of time together—time that is beyond the confines of our "contract." This arose completely out of my willingness to listen to this Voice of Love, which helped me learn to love myself and move every relationship in my life toward healing. I now believe that God's Voice *is* the Voice of Love, and Love is what I Am.

A blessed mother of two children, Theresa Miller has worked in the conventional medical and holistic healthcare fields since 1988.

A Homeless Man

A homeless man named John living in a rescue mission shelter, and a single mother in her 30s were in my week-long job-training class answering service calls for a telephone company. The evening before the final class, as I stood at my kitchen sink washing dishes, something unexpected happened.

It was as if time stood still for a moment as my hands lay idle in the warm dishwater and I became acutely aware of my senses. I heard a voice within me say, "Tell John to call his father." I did not perceive the voice to be outside of me, as if someone were physically speaking to me, but it did not sound like my own stream of thoughts either. I didn't know what to do or what to think, but I could not deny what I had heard. Later that evening, in the same clear but unexpected way, I was told the single mother in my class was experiencing difficulty and confusion that would ultimately enlighten her. I did not understand the reason for her difficulty, but the communication was clear.

By the next morning I had decided against saying anything to either of them, not wanting to seem too spiritual while at work. When I saw the mother waiting for me at my door before class, I invited her in to talk. Even though I'd decided to tell her nothing, I changed my mind and explained I knew she was experiencing great stress and difficulty in my class.

"You are the best student I have," I told her, "but last night I became aware that there is a reason you are having difficulties. Do you understand why?"

She began to cry. "Oh my gosh, I know why," she said. "My son has a learning disability, and now I know how he feels." She experienced new compassion for his challenges in learning.

Because of this positive outcome, I decided to approach John. During class while the students were bringing up real customer files in the computer, I called John up to my desk and quietly told him what I heard while washing the dishes.

He looked down. "I haven't seen my Dad for 10 years," he told me. "I'm not sure where he is anymore, or how to contact him."

When he rejoined the class as the rest of the students pulled up Pennsylvania files, his screen showed a Virginia listing.

"Who's that?" I asked him.

"It's my father's account," he answered. "That's his number!" He pulled a tiny piece of paper out of his front pocket that had been posted on the bulletin board at the mission. It read, "John, call xxx-xxx-xxxx." He had no idea who had put it there, but that was the number on his screen.

"Wow, now you have no excuse. You have to call him!" I said.

The following Monday I arrived at work to learn one of the employees I had trained and become close to was dealing with tragedy. Her father-in-law had killed his wife and then taken his own life. Upset and late for an appointment, I nearly walked past John without stopping. He asked me if I had a moment, and I said, "No, I can't now." He said quietly, "Just one minute?"

Time stopped and I looked at him. "What?" I asked.

"I didn't do it in time," he said.

"Do what?"

"I didn't call my dad in time. He killed himself yesterday morning."

As I sat down heavily, the same calm Messenger who had communicated with me before began speaking through my mouth. I told John that he did not have to feel guilty. His father had reached out to him, and somehow, through God, his father's message had come through me and the note on the wall. I told him to feel the love his father extended, not the regret for not calling him. Because he was in a similar situation as my friend who was also dealing with a suicide, I put them in a room together where they could talk to each other.

It was then that I realized how connected we are to one another, each playing a part in each others' lives. With the help of this communication and guidance within me, I felt in my heart how important it is to reach out to others. It has shown me that I too can be a messenger for God, and it has brought a sense of peace and love into my life and encouraged me to be still more often...and listen.

Grace Ross has a BA in psychology and is a certified Workforce Development Professional who serves as a career advisor and teaches stress management classes.

Awakening

My hands trembled as I clutched the steering wheel and repeatedly prayed, "Please, God, help me see him through Your eyes." It had been three days since I'd come home to find my husband unconscious from a drug overdose. Now I was on my way to meet with him and his doctor at the psychiatric hospital.

The doctor warned me. "Be prepared to hear some very difficult stuff."

I wondered what could be more difficult than what I already knew.

Six years earlier, I had awakened one night with a deep sense that something was wrong. It was 3:00 a.m. and my husband was not home. This wasn't unusual; he was a nurse. But I couldn't shake the persistent feeling that he wasn't just stuck at work. I needed to get up. When my children were teenagers and I worried because they were late, other reassuring thoughts always calmed my fears. But this was different. My heart raced. My stomach turned. I started to pray, "Please, God, show me where he is!"

At that moment, I thought I heard my husband crying. A clear and distinct thought came to me: "He's by the pool." Although it wasn't possible to hear someone crying from that distance, I didn't question the thought. I walked across the entire complex to the pool in my nightgown.

I found him there, bathed in that eerie pool light, drunk and crying.

"I'm a terrible person," he said. "You shouldn't be married to me." He went on to confess he regularly got drunk after work, and had been with a prostitute that night.

Such information could be expected to provoke anger, but what I felt was fear and denial. My thoughts spun in the night. This can't be! He has been my higher power, my source of security and self-esteem. *Drinking problems are common among healthcare professionals*, I thought...*we'll just get him some help, and everything will be fine.*

Five years later, in the waiting room of the rehab hospital, I cried and my husband reassured me. I desperately needed to believe him, a need I had clung to for the past five years as he started and stopped more rehab programs and jobs than I could count.

All through this period, I continued to have strong nagging thoughts that all was *not* well. Still I ignored the sick feeling in my stomach when he made excuses for not coming home. I ignored my own wisdom that his excuses for quitting jobs and leaving support groups were neither reasonable nor credible. I ignored the Voice of God that spoke through others who told me the truth: My husband had a serious addiction problem. I chose to believe his lies because they supported my fantasy of how I wanted my life to be. I wanted marriage and a normal family. I had been a single mother at a very young age, and thought being married would erase my shame. My husband became my perceived redeemer, and I wasn't about to let go of that.

After moving twice in search of the magic environment that would solve everything, I decided church would provide the spiritual nurturing I so badly needed. But sitting alone among the other couples at church, I found myself embarrassed by my husband's absence. Then God offered another way. Driving home from work one evening, feeling depressed and lost, I had the thought to start a spiritual support group for women.

That afternoon I picked a date for the first meeting and asked people to join me. We met twice a month to pray and meditate on various aspects of our spiritual power and to support one another. Leading the group kept me spiritually focused between meetings as I joyfully prepared for them.

That focus proved to be crucial when my husband came home one day and confessed to using narcotics he had been stealing from the hospital. I felt a moment of panic, but because I had been strengthening my spiritual support system and intentionally connecting with God, it was easier for me to recognize and listen to the intuitions God used to guide me. When the idea came to me that the appropriate way to respond to my husband's drug use was to return to church and immediately contact a support group for people affected by the addictions of others, I listened and acted.

A class was offered at church based on Maria Nemeth's book, *The Energy of Money*. The underlying philosophy of the book was that the way we handle money is the way we handle life. One week into the class, I was working on a "money biography." After responding to most of the questions with, "I don't know," or "I can't remember," I had an epiphany. "Oh my god," I said out loud. "I have been handling money completely unconsciously, and that is exactly how I've been living my life—unconsciously. In a moment of complete surrender, I said a prayer that changed my life: "Dear God, please wake me up!"

That prayer ought to have come with a warning label! The very next day I came home to find a trail of excrement that led through the house to where my husband lay passed out in a puddle of it. The image was an apt but devastating metaphor.

So it was that I found myself driving to the hospital to meet with my husband and his doctor, chanting the prayer, "God, help me see him through Your eyes. Let me see the perfection in this moment."

As I sat in that stark hospital room, listening to my husband confess horrifying behavior related to sex addiction, I remained calm. As the behaviors he described became progressively more shocking, the Voice of God became progressively louder. That strong Voice in my head overpowered all other sounds in the room. "All is well," it said. "Your peace and safety lie in your relationship with Me."

Finally my bewildered husband stared at me. "I don't understand how you can be so calm. I am a monster."

I believe the Holy Spirit spoke directly through me then. The words issuing from my mouth were God's. "You have done some terrible things," I said, "but I know the truth of who you are. You are a child of God, and, for no other reason than that, I forgive you."

As my husband continued to live lost in addiction and denial, I was led through continuous miraculous communication with God to divorce him. One of God's most powerful instruments of communication turned out to be my 6-year-old granddaughter. She came to visit shortly after my husband went into the hospital. Although she knew nothing of the situation or where her grandpa was, she walked through the door, asked for paper and crayons, and started to draw.

She seemed trance-like as she described her drawing. First she drew what looked like a tornado at the center of the page. "This is a big wind," she said. Next she drew two arms reaching out of the tornado. "This is grandpa."

I had to remember to breathe as I watched her continue.

"This is an angel," she said of the little yellow figure reaching up to grandpa's arms.

Then she drew a crying figure on the opposite side of the tornado. "This is you," she declared.

"Why am I so sad?" I asked.

"Because your knees are bloody," she said as she drew red scribbles on my knees.

She set the crayons down and was herself again.

I thought God might be speaking to me through her drawing, but the bloody knees might also just be a 6-year-old's idea of why grandma would be sad. The full meaning of the picture became clear the next day. After spending at least an hour literally on my knees crying out to God for guidance, a pain shot through my knees and a blinding light of clarity filled my head.

That's it," I cried. "My hope lies in staying on my knees and bringing my pain to God." I looked carefully at my granddaughter's drawing. It became clear it was not my responsibility to save my husband. He had an angel ready to help him. My job was to help myself with prayer.

The Lord was truly my shepherd throughout those extreme times. It was because of them that I gained an ever greater trust in the guidance of God's Voice and a clearer understanding of the many ways God's Voice can manifest. God never gave up. He even called out to me in a child's drawing.

I have moved forward in my life with courage and faith and am fulfilling my life's purpose in a new career coaching others through their own experiences of transformation. I have also found the courage to love again. I am in a new relationship that far exceeds what I could have ever imagined, and God continues to guide my path.

Having worked in the field of elementary education for 18 years, Kare Castle currently serves as a literacy specialist and life coach. In addition to enjoying time with family and in nature, Kare's passion is writing books for children.

Ugly Teddy

The frigid Michigan wind chilled me to the bone as I hugged my inadequate dress coat tighter and hurried through the darkness to my company's annual Christmas party at a posh hotel. I hadn't looked forward to attending this occasion. It was just another obligation—a component of the treadmill life I led. Parties held for the sole purpose of prescribed merriment are particularly fearful occasions for me, and this one simply mirrored my loneliness as I entered the dimly lit ballroom full of chattering couples and shimmering lights.

The entryway table displayed an array of door prizes. I'd never won a door prize before. I'd never won anything in my life and didn't expect to, but my eyes gravitated to a handmade teddy bear propped in one corner. Instead of the cute cuddly child's toy one would expect, this bear was particularly ugly, and my attraction to it was unexplainable. I didn't want a teddy bear, and there was no room for such an unnecessary item in my cramped apartment, yet I reached out to pick it up. The moment I touched the bear, a stillness welled within me that seemed to dance apart from all the music and the chatter of the party. As the partygoers faded into the background, I was overcome with a feeling of absolute certainty that this teddy bear belonged to me. It can only be explained as an unshakeable knowingness that supported not a shred of doubt, not a molecule of uncertainty, as if the ugly little bear was already mine.

Never before had I experienced such certainty, such a powerful sense of knowing the outcome of an event that had yet to unfold. Throughout the evening, I felt preoccupied by the awe of this experience. I wondered when the drawing for door prizes would occur, anxious to know when I could actually receive my teddy bear and leave.

At last the moment arrived as the music stopped and the lights brightened. The emcee began drawing names for the door prizes. As each recipient stepped up to claim his prize, everyone clapped and cheered. Still, the ugly little teddy bear remained on the table. Then I thought I heard the emcee call my name and rose from my chair. Only after I had risen did he actually call my name. The first voice I'd heard calling my name was not that of the announcer. It was inside my head. Yet I heard it just as clearly as I did when it came through the microphone. I had not realized the first voice did not belong to the announcer until he actually spoke!

Why had this happened? To have such a powerful knowingness about such an insignificant event as winning a silly door prize made no sense. My sense of awe about winning the bear and hearing my name called inside my head before the announcer called my name held an aura of divinity about it. But why such a waste of divine direction on mere trivia?

I awoke Sunday morning facing the ugly teddy bear whose misshapen head rested on my pillow. The magic of last night's encounter had faded away like the dreams that feel so real just before you wake. I touched teddy's hand-stitched face with the back of my hand, but felt nothing out of the ordinary. Whatever had filled my consciousness last night was gone. Maybe it had been an overactive imagination and had never really happened at all.

Thin morning light filtered through my bedroom window, making me sigh in the starkness of my own reality. I must now resume my customary struggle with a life that seemed drab, empty, and purposeless. My marriage had ended six years previously, partly because I felt I needed to pursue a new path to give my life some meaning. But now, alone, lonely, and broke, that path seemed to be leading nowhere. I neither felt fulfillment nor had achieved the ability to support myself. God had given me many helpful experiences, but none of them seemed to apply to my everyday quandaries and feelings of discontent. I desperately wanted to leave corporate life and live near my son in Arizona, but I lacked both the money and the faith to make such a big change.

I rose and wrapped myself in a robe on the way into the kitchen. There I flicked on the coffeemaker and sat at the table as brewed coffee began to drip. It seemed useless to even dream about moving to the warmth of Arizona. I was trapped here, grappling with the uphill corporate battle and struggling to make ends meet. I'd be stuck here in Michigan until I hit the grave. The smell of coffee filled the kitchen, but failed to lift my spirits. I had prayed to God for guidance before, but now I prayed in earnest. "Please, God, how can I create the life I so long to have? Should I take a chance and move to Arizona, without even having a clear direction on how to support myself there?

Slowly the smell of coffee faded. Something inside me shifted, and my inner being began to flood with the identical sense of certainty I'd experienced when I had first laid eyes on the teddy bear. I felt a lightness growing from within, and my consciousness became permeated with the secure knowledge that I was moving to Arizona. I knew it as surely as if the move had already been accomplished. It was a certainty born from a trust of the deepest kind, for it went beyond faith to an absolute knowing, a timeless awareness that something already existed. It was as if the script of my life, written so long ago, had been made available at last for me to view. That script placed me in Arizona, and it only remained for me to play out my part.

So this was the reason! Without the magic I'd experienced with Ugly Teddy the night before, I would have rationalized this experience away through some convoluted thought process and doubted my own sanity. I would have dismissed this divine guidance as a product of wishful thinking or an aftereffect of the wine I'd consumed the night before. I had always doubted the promptings that I thought might be from God, but I could not deny this profound sense of certainty that I had experienced.

I quit my job the next day, and two weeks later moved to Arizona. My career never recovered from this move, but my life bloomed in more important emotional and spiritual ways. The move proved to be an important cog in the chain of events that have brought a more complete sense of fulfillment to my life.

Today Ugly Teddy sits high on a shelf overlooking the living space my husband and I share. I met my husband shortly after moving to Arizona, and together we have learned how to join with God in our love and communicate with one another in a way that heals any challenges or difficulties that arise in our lives. I am now learning to share that love and learning with others in new ways.

I look back now with great gratitude at the tapestry of my life, at how each separate event folded seamlessly into the next, and how following the guidance of divine knowingness led me exactly where I was meant to be.

Georgianne Giese works as a database programmer and has three children and eight grandchildren. Writing is her hobby. Learning to recognize the Voice of God and experience God's Presence is her passion.

God Speaks Up

I got in and slammed the car door. *Damn*, I thought, *he just won't listen! How can we possibly get along?* It was 3 o'clock on a weekday afternoon and I drove back to work, still stewing about the interaction. I had just left a counseling session with my husband, who had not heard anything I said. "I had to miss work to go to that session and I have so much work to do!" I vented. "Now I'm so angry I won't get anything done when I return."

Then I did something uncharacteristic for me. I prayed.

As a teenager, I had decided there either was no God, or, if He had made a world like this, I wanted nothing to do with Him. I saw too much pain in the world. I'd been physically, sexually, and emotionally abused, and judged what I saw around me as uncaring. Before reaching this conclusion, I had attended a Christian church with my family. God was supposed to be an all-powerful, all-loving creator. In my reasoning I couldn't see how an all-powerful, all-loving creator could create a world filled with so much pain, so if a God existed, I would not interact with Him. I was not open to prayer or hearing God's Voice.

Twenty years later I had married, had children, divorced, and remarried. This time, unknowingly, I had married an alcoholic. That discovery was a shock. I wondered what I should do now. After living with that question for four years, through serendipitous circumstances, my husband went into treatment and joined Alcoholics Anonymous. I joined Alanon, the 12-Step group for families of alcoholics.

When I came to Step 3 of the 12 steps, "Make a decision to turn our will and our lives over to the care of God as we understand Him," I had difficulty. I came up against the wall of my old conclusions about God. I talked about this with Alanon friends who said I should act as if God existed, define Him as I understood Him to be, and see what happened. I could admit that I'd made a mess of my life; maybe I was wrong about God.

I determined that if God did exist, I would pray to Him. I began praying, but at first I simply felt foolish. I thought only the four walls could hear me. But I was still willing to admit there was a chance I was wrong, and persisted. Then this day of the frustrating counseling session came.

From my heart I prayed, "Help me with this anger." Immediately I heard an authoritative, caring, and powerful Voice within my mind saying, "Think of something else."

With no awareness of making a decision, I did what the words instructed. Hours passed at work. Wow! I had accomplished so much! Instead of feeling angry, I was calm, peaceful, and happy. I felt amazed! My prayer had immediately been answered!

Gratitude flowed through me. I remembered times in the past when my anger had interfered with my life. This day, I had been given help with it. I knew I no longer had to deal with it alone. I felt there truly was a God and He listened to me and helped me when I asked Him.

This day remains a clear memory, for it was the first time I prayed and was aware of a direct response, the first time I heard God's Voice. As a result I continued praying, talking to God and expecting Him to guide me, trusting that He cared for me. More and more prayers were answered, so I increased my willingness to daily, hourly, turn my will and life over to God's care. This one incident initiated a way of living with God's Voice that has continually brought more understanding, peace, love, and joy into my experience.

Since that day, the Voice of God has lovingly communicated with me in words, images within my mind, thoughts, feelings, and external events, whatever is most effective at that moment. He has guided me and always loved me even when I was being anything but loving. I now live with the comfort and security of knowing He is always there when I need Him. I am continually blessed!

After raising a family and working in the software engineering and social assistance fields, 62-year-old Jamara Luma is now retired. She loves the natural beauty of Spokane, Washington, where she lives, and spends much of her time focusing inward on her own self-healing and growth.

Eggs, Farm Smells, and Hidden Gifts

I stifle a gag as I open the door to the chicken house. My nose instinctively slams shut as if suddenly submerged underwater; the strong scent of ammonia chokes out the unfolding freshness of early morning on the farm. I don't want to be part of this "chicken concentration camp," as I often call my farmer husband's main source of income: 35,000 laying hens. Not only does the hen house assault my nose, it is offensive to me ecologically, morally, and mentally. I don't enjoy the dirty, boring work of gathering eggs. I love my kind husband though, so saying nothing, I take my place beside him and begin stacking egg flats onto the cart beside the conveyor belt. I work quietly, while internal grumbling rises in tidal wave proportions.

During a lull in the egg flow, I look out the door and marvel at the beauty of the morning. Late March snow covers the fields, mist hugs the land, the rising sun turns the whole scene into rosy softness despite the bitter cold. The metal hand railing on the tiny porch outside the door glitters with delicate frost crystals. Horses munch hay, their hairy backs sprinkled with crisp, icy snow. Steamy breath wafts around their heads, adding to the gentle morning mist.

Egg flats ram into each other at the end of the conveyor. I leap into action, grabbing and stacking, before the flats can buckle or up-end to explode into gooey, snotty, drippy messes of crumpled shells, yolks, and whites. As I stack egg flats, I gripe about not being able to open the door for extra ventilation. I grumble about my crappy lot in life being stuck here morning and evening doing a job I hate. Ranting on silently, I work on the dirty job before me while longing for a walk in the beautiful countryside. I often waffle between being wholly present and escaping the present monotony by daydreaming or otherwise distracting myself.

Tiring of my peevishness, I begin bringing my attention to what my hands touch—the smooth, warm eggs and stiff plastic flats. The switch to the conveyor belt is firm, cool as my fingers flip it on and off; running my hand over the belt I'm amazed as it feels smoother than eggshells. I carefully nestle five flats of eggs on top of each other, then lift the pile up on the egg cart, noticing the heaviness of the stack. Suddenly, I feel enveloped in a gentle mist of profound gratitude. I am grateful for my body, its ability to touch, to move and breathe; for my mind and the freedom to believe differently than my husband; for our deep love, despite our differences. Gratitude and love moves me from within, then radiates outward. I think about the farm cats, foxes, and scavenger birds that eat the discarded raw eggs, about the people whose hands will also touch these eggs: the processors and packers, the truck drivers, store clerks, the cooks, and all the neighbors, friends, and family who use our eggs. I reverently bless each precious life.

I smile, remembering my grimace at the stink of this place. I notice, with compassion, my tendency to focus on unpleasant areas of my life; the suffering of those I love, my own restlessness and boredom, my negative thoughts and emotions. There is a beautiful, spacious quality to my life when I step back from my present problems and become receptive to God's Voice of love and wisdom. When I listen with openness and gratitude, I see how rich I am with friendships and opportunities. Life is full of joy when I am present and grateful, finding the hidden gifts in each moment.

There will always be days when the chicken house fans won't run enough to dissipate bad aromas, or when personal and life situations also stink. In those moments, if I can somehow behold my whole life while living moment by moment, I can see incredible beauty. Each moment is precious. My failures and smellier moments can teach me more about myself, as do my successes, joys, creative works, and celebrations. All of life can be embraced as a gift, thus releasing the grace I need for self-knowledge, spiritual growth, and living life abundantly.

Sharon Joy Landis is a poet, writer, gardener, grandmother, former 4H leader, dog trainer, and goat dairy manager. She is also an avid reader and lover of God, life, art, color, and nature. She lives in Lititz, Pennsylvania.

Alone but Not Alone

I was 4 years old, sitting on the sunny grass in my backyard. Contented and peaceful, I was alone but not alone, feeling perfectly happy. My memory captured three such similar events during different seasons, separated by several years. Though separate occurrences, they all had one thing in common: I was outside, alone but not lonely, my surroundings were beautiful and peaceful, and I felt encircled by an intense feeling of love and joy.

For years I was haunted by the mystery of these memories because they made no rational sense. It took 25 years to discover that they were no accident. They'd been put there by God like some sort of time-release capsule, to be decoded and used when most needed in my life.

Life's dreams all seemed to be coming true for me: college, career, marriage, and a beautiful son. Then, without warning, my life's dream turned into a nightmare when my marriage failed. My life unraveled from a happy family to three suffering individuals. It didn't matter who was at fault. A failed marriage is like a war; there are no winners, just casualties. I took it extremely hard and accepted the guilt and failure along with the financial responsibility. I felt that I had not only failed my wife and son, but God as well because I had broken my marriage vows and betrayed my duty as a husband and caregiver.

The divorce reignited my uneasy relationship with God. My perception of God was long on fear, guilt, and vengeance, and short on love, acceptance, and forgiveness. My next experience changed all that.

Before long the burden of guilt about my failed marriage and estrangement from God was too much to bear. Night after night I prayed for forgiveness and for God to take away my incessant pain. I soon slipped into a deep depression, overcome by despair. There was only one way out!

In my cold, lonely apartment I sat in the dark contemplating how I was going to accomplish what had to be done. A bullet was the surest and quickest method. Sitting on my bed, I tried to bolster enough nerve to pull the trigger. I began to cry uncontrollably. My entire life played before my mind's eye, both the bad and the good times with a pause between each event.

I began to consider what my son was going to think of his father, what kind of an example this was setting. What would my death do to my parents, brothers, and friends? It was a coward's way out. My hand shook so hard I couldn't control it. I put the gun down and cried until there were no more tears. Emotionally exhausted, I drifted off to sleep.

In my dream I walked at night down a gravel country road under a cloudy autumn sky. A harvest moon darted in and out from behind the clouds. I yearned to find my home, but no longer knew who or where I was. For miles I walked without a farm in sight. If only I could find a farm house and knock on the door, I could ask someone where I belonged.

In the distance I saw a streetlamp. The moon peeked out from under a cloud to illuminate a park bench beneath it. Someone sat on the bench. Excited, I ran full speed, yelling. "Mister, mister! Can you help me? I don't know who I am and I'm so lonely. I need to go home!"

The figure stood as I approached but his face was hidden by the hood of a robe. When I asked him for help, he reached out his hands, drew me close to his breast, and embraced me. My mind flashed immediately to another time when I was alone but not alone, a time when I was surrounded by complete peace and love.

The man in the robe softly said, "My son, my son, your name is Timothy and I love you and will take you home. You will never be lonely again!"

I woke the next morning with an overwhelming feeling of faith, hope, love, forgiveness, peace, and inspiration. I knew God would never stop loving me. This was identical to the tranquil and peaceful memories I had experienced in childhood. The veil lifted and it became clear that those mysterious recollections of my youth were the latent Voice of God revealing His presence. God had deposited them into my consciousness like money in the bank for a rainy day—savings that would sustain me during the critical times.

There were other methods God used to converse with me. I was scheduled to attend a week-long national healthcare conference in Dallas, Texas. Arriving too late for Sunday dinner, I bought a book in the hotel gift shop, ordered room service, and retreated to bed with the book after dinner. Reading in bed is like taking a sleeping pill for me. After a few words I'm asleep, snoring at the top of my lungs. However, this time was an exception and I read late into the night.

After the conference ended I boarded my flight to return home. After take-off I settled in to finish my book. On the last page the point was made that we are all one with God. I sat there for a moment pondering the thought before closing the cover. As I looked up I found myself staring at a newspaper being read by a man directly across the aisle from me. On the page in huge black letters was printed "WE ARE ALL ONE!" The words jolted me like an electric shock, sending a shiver up my spine. I intuitively knew it was the Voice of God, but once again I couldn't grasp its significance.

My mind drifted back to my spiritual encounter and the dream I'd experienced. My faith and love for God and myself had been restored, but something was still missing. I wanted to deepen my personal relationship with God and to once again experience that "ONENESS" with Him, but how? I realized the only way to establish a deeper friendship with God was to somehow become better acquainted. That required a heart-to-heart discussion that went beyond prayers. God only knew how much I needed to reconcile regarding traditional beliefs.

It was in that moment I heard a little voice inside me say, "Why don't you write your questions down?" I listened and did just that. In a most peculiar way I felt an intuitive response to each question, which I also recorded. Each response begged another question, which was again followed by an intuitive response. I soon realized that when I opened my heart and mind and listened, I was tuned in to the Voice of God—a Voice that up until then I thought could only be heard in scripture. Yet all this time, from my childhood experiences to my darkest moments, God was continuing to broadcast His Voice. It was up to me to dial in the right station. I was alone but not alone. I was Home with God.

Timothy J. Adams is retired from a professional career in healthcare and lives with his wife in Woodinville, Washington. He devotes most of his time to writing and connecting with family and friends.

Becoming the Change

The list was one I never thought I would make. I stared at the book titles I had jotted down for reference; each of them looked at divorce from a different angle: how to tell your kids, how to do it amicably, how to maintain financial stability in its wake, how to heal the emotional scars. My trepidation magnified at the thought of even considering such a move after more than 30 years of marriage. But I felt I was at the end of my rope as I drifted farther and farther away from any hope of restoring the unity we had once enjoyed. Divorce seemed to be the next logical step. The question was, did I have the courage to take it? And beyond that, was such a drastic and life-altering decision really the solution?

I considered what had led to this overwhelming feeling of discontent. My husband and I had been married for 34 years. We had created many happy memories—some of the best of our lives. We had four beautiful daughters who had grown into sensible, competent, and caring adults. We had been blessed with three granddaughters whom we cherished. Our lifestyle, although not opulent, had been comfortable and secure. We had always been solid in our spiritual beliefs and experienced God's faithfulness in getting us through tough times. Through all the ups and downs, we had considered each other our best friend. So what was it now that made all of that history together insufficient enough to sustain me?

When he lost his father, I thought my husband would never recover. They had shared such a special relationship it had taken him more than a year to rise up from the emotional heap he'd been stuck in. Then a restructuring at his company occurred that forced him to take a job that brought little pleasure and a lot of heartache from a boss who belittled him.

As his wife, I thought I had been as supportive as any loving spouse would be in the same situation. I'd done everything I could think of to help him rise above his circumstances, but it never seemed enough to keep his spirits lifted. Time and again he would take a step forward into a more positive perception of the future only to take two or three back into the past where old memories dominated his thinking. He began to drink more and communicate less. As he fell further into despair, I came to resent his playing the victim and that he wouldn't, or couldn't, transcend his circumstances.

I began to see him as weak. My respect for him diminished. A barrage of negative internal chatter seized my mind daily: Why couldn't he just get over it and move on? Why did I constantly have to be the cheerleader? I'd already raised four kids, why did he have to be my fifth? Why couldn't he see he was allowing other people, and circumstances outside of his control, to dictate his future? Would I ever be able to look him in the eye again?

So here I was, faced with a decision I didn't want to make. I wanted to be happy, but the way things were going, my happiness seemed doomed. I wanted him to be happy, but nothing I tried worked. I became resentful and bitter that all I suggested or complained about fell upon deaf ears. The inner turmoil was more than I wanted to deal with. But did I have the courage to move on and endure the consequences of choosing to end a relationship that would affect so many? My head told me to surrender and move on, but my heart told me I couldn't give up yet.

Often I would surf the Internet for sites that fed my desire for spiritual growth and awareness. It was on just such an occasion that I visited one promoting beautiful art prints that highlighted quotes from great sages and masters of our time. As I clicked from print to print, one stood out, as if just waiting for me to absorb the words of wisdom blazoned across the artwork.

"You must be the change you wish to see in the world."

The quote, attributed to the Eastern mystic philosopher Mohatma Gandhi, was one I had heard before. But this day it spoke directly to *me*. Waves of goose bumps traveled throughout my body, and my heart raced as wisdom took hold. Here in bold revelation, presented in simple but astounding truth when I least expected it, was the answer I had been searching for. An amazing gift of clarity had been specially delivered to me, and the screen of self-righteousness I had been hiding behind suddenly collapsed.

I realized in that moment how wrong I had been. In trying to force my advice and philosophies on my husband, I'd been treating him like a lost child in need of parental guidance. In viewing him as such, I had lost my respect for him as a man and a husband. Now I could clearly see that it was *my perception* of his faults that had delivered me to this place, and only I could change that. I could continue to react to him as I had been, with disdain and disrespect, or respond with compassion for a man temporarily struggling to find himself. A sense of peace accompanied the undeniable certainty that I had to begin a journey inside *myself* and *become* the change I wished to see. My husband was worth it, and so was I.

Little by little, I worked on allowing my husband to "grow forward" in his own way, at his own pace. I made every effort to think before I let critical statements roll off my tongue. I made it a point to support whatever attempts he was making to overcome his own self-limiting behavior. And most importantly, I strived to stop standing in judgment of him, something I had been doing much too often of late.

In time, I began to see a change in our relationship. We were arguing less and communicating more. Our household returned to one of laughter and lightheartedness. We began enjoying each other's company again. Shared prayer, meditation, and positive thinking became a part of our lives. Though I knew that *my* change in attitude contributed, it was *his* that enabled him to move forward into action-oriented realization of his strengths. His confidence returned in exponential measure to the newly embraced efforts he was making to improve his life.

The unexpected gift in this process is that our entire family has benefited. Together my husband and I have become a team in leadership, leading by example as well as providing guidance in the spiritual principles we believe to be true. The result is that our children, as well as members of our extended family, are reaping the rewards of what our experience has taught us.

As I revisit the last year, I see with new and perfect vision, and I am overwhelmed with gratitude for everything that we have gone through to arrive exactly where we're supposed to be in this present moment. And I smile because, finally, I get it.

Vecchi Talarico has been married to her husband, Pete, for 35 years. She has four daughters and three granddaughters. A hairstylist for 25 years, Vecchi currently volunteers in the Look Good Feel Better program, where she teaches women in cancer treatment how to overcome the appearance-related side effects of their treatment through makeup, wigs, and head coverings.

Follow Me Home

In April 2002, my wife, Lynne, and I lived in Somerset, England, near Glastonbury, a place well-known in spiritual circles and layered in myth and legend. On a whim, Lynne booked us onto a trip to Germany to see an Indian mystic called Mother Meera. We knew little of her, but the itinerary included a visit to the abbey ruins at Disabodenberg where Hildegard von Bingen, the 12th-century mystic, lived part of her life. This intrigued us as we had read of her life and admired her music.

About 50 of us traveled by coach and ferry to a little village called Oberdiebach in a steep valley just off the Rhine. The group stayed at an ashram, but Lynne and I took a room at the village inn. The Rhine, the idyllic castles sitting on high hills overlooking the river, the steep vineyards, and the beautiful villages were a delight. The week passed with group meditations, communal meals, peace dances, healing sessions, and sightseeing.

The trip's main purpose was to have four silent audiences, known as darshans, with Mother Meera. *Darshan* is a Sanskrit word meaning "vision of the divine" or "epiphany." These took place over four consecutive evenings and were conducted in a large castle lounge. About 250 people attended each darshan. When you felt ready, you joined a queue of people who, sitting or kneeling, shuffled forward until it became your turn to approach Mother Meera.

The protocol was to kneel at Mother's feet with eyes downcast and place your hands on her sari-covered slippers. Mother then placed her fingers against your temples, and after a few seconds would remove them. This was the signal to raise your eyes and make eye contact, which lasted only a few seconds. Mother would then lower her eyes and darshan was over.

I didn't feel anything unusual until the third darshan. I was determined to see something deep in her eyes, but instead, for one brief moment, my vision turned inward and I saw the inside of my own head filled with crystal-clear water.

The final group meeting at the ashram was the night before my 60th birthday. Everyone in the group was invited to speak of their experiences at darshan. Many spoke of emotions, insights, experiences, or of funny and profound things. I decided to be light and funny and share some of the week's comic happenings. I also tried for a big laugh when I said that deep in my heart I had really wanted to find enlightenment before age 40, then 50, and now before I became 60. As they knew my birthday was the following day and with only two hours to go, when I looked at my watch and raised my eyebrows in mock resignation, I got my laugh.

Lynne and I returned to the inn and went to bed. Early in the night I awakened to the church clock striking. It was too dark to see a thing. The night was moonless and the vineyards rose steeply behind the inn, preventing light from filtering into the room. I lay there musing, thinking it really hadn't been in jest when I said I wanted enlightenment before 40, then 50, then 60.

Within moments of that thought, a tingling sensation started in my toes and slowly crept to my ankles, then spread into my legs. Although I thought it strange, I consciously decided not to do anything that might impair the feeling; I only observed it. The sensation crept up my body, and within five minutes everything tingled, from the top of my head to my toes. A picture formed in my mind of myself suspended within a silver cocoon. I remember thinking this was all very pleasant, but I avoided questioning it or awarding it any value. I was there, it was happening, and I was simply the observer.

Suddenly, completely out of left field, came the thought, *Is this enlightenment?* I recall immediately thinking what a stupid thought that was. Nothing was happening that could even remotely lend support to such a question. Then a voice I recognized from previous experiences spoke as if someone stood beside me: "Yes, this is enlightenment."

There was a tremendous rush of energy up through my body and out through the top of my head. Then the voice spoke again: "The path has been smoothed that you may follow Me home."

With this, I reached across the bed for my wife's hand and burst into uncontrollable tears. I cried hard and loudly for what seemed like ages. I couldn't speak or explain what was happening. Lynne hugged me and comforted me, saying "It's okay, everything's alright." A flood of emotion laden with years and years of pain and distress flowed out of me. The collective grief and worry of a lifetime was gone in a moment, and I felt such incredible relief, as if a great burden had been lifted from me. The emotions were so strong that even as I write this, six years later, tears start in my eyes and my skin tingles.

After what seemed like an hour, my crying turned to silent tears and we returned to bed. I couldn't sleep. My mind was in a whirl of joy such as I had never known, an outpouring of love I could never have guessed at. Everything was joy, everything was love, and the silent tears flowed on.

The following morning we arose early to meet the coach for our return journey. I avoided conversation with anyone and sat looking out of the window. For long periods I meditated, and or pretended to meditate, just to avoid conversations. I remained so emotional that even when Lynne spoke to me, I could only respond with monosyllabic answers or short sentences. It was four days before I could blurt out words of explanation to Lynne.

I had been born to a new world. Even the familiar was new. I was seeing with new, clear eyes that made everything bright and clean. Each brimmed with the most ridiculous joy, every minute full of love, every instant holy. When I finally sobbed out my story, Lynne asked me what enlightenment was like. I surprised myself by answering, "It's no big deal."

I realized then that although it was the most dramatic event of my life, I had described it as "no big deal" because the feelings were so comfortable and natural. Even with their unexpected arrival, extraordinary impact, and cleansing purge, they suddenly seemed normal. Yet there continued the complete and overwhelming experience of unconditional love and the presence of an almost wild joyfulness which filled me. My mind experienced itself as existing fully in the present moment, no longer in the grip of past emotions, traumatic events, or fears. I remembered the past, and certainly knew it had happened, but its importance had vanished, and with it had gone all sense of guilt.

I've pondered why this experience had occurred. Was it due to Mother Meera? I don't know for sure, but my heart tells me it was the voice of Jesus that set me free, and that the dramatic changes were possibly due to it being the first time in my life when I had made no judgment. There had been no valuing, no preconception of what was happening. In this state of innocence my mind had been opened to Truth.

A native Englishman, John Wilcox is married and has one son, Matthew. Residing in New Zealand since 1974, he works in construction and property maintenance and enjoys writing poetry.

I Do it for You

My minivan was bursting with excited teenage girls fresh from their early evening softball win. I drove in a cacophony of blaring music, loud voices, and squeals of laughter. I might have joined in the celebration had I not been so immersed in my own dark thoughts.

Earlier that day, two young soldiers, their dead bodies mutilated in unspeakable ways, had been recovered in Iraq. My heart had felt broken as I viewed pictures of the soldiers on the news when they were alive. My God, they were just babies—beautiful, fresh-faced young men, so full of life and promise! So brave! Killed at the time in their lives when they should have been falling in love, forging careers, and beginning their lives as young adults. Their lives had instead been cut short. They had not died quickly in battle, but in an exceedingly slow and cruel way while being tortured by monsters who cared nothing for their youth, their promise, or their humanity.

Inside my head I screamed my heartbreak at God. *How could You let this happen? Where were You? Why them? I know I shouldn't blame You, but it's so hard not to, God. They were babies. Scared, away from home, away from the families they loved. Did You help them? Could they feel You there with them?*

I was becoming too upset to drive rationally. As I slowed for a broken traffic light ahead, something unexpected happened: My normal perception of reality suddenly shifted. Everything around me slid into slow motion—all the girls laughing in the back of the van; an older lady riding a bicycle on the sidewalk; the people in the car to my left, arguing; and to my right, a man eating french fries in his car.

As I looked past him I could see the sun had lowered beyond the western horizon. The sky was painted with hot reds and oranges, and strokes of purple and lavender, almost as if the sky were both bruised and on fire at the same time. The sky, awash in its vibrant glory, contrasted with the slow-motion urban scene of reality that oozed around me.

Instead of lifting my spirits and brightening my mood, I felt even sadder and more despondent. The sunset only enhanced my frustration and the sense of futility I felt at being in a world that had obviously gone so wrong. I couldn't bear the thought that those poor lifeless soldiers would not see any more sunsets like this one or grow old with their families. The world would be poorer because of their loss.

Tears fell from my eyes as I stared at the sunset. *Why, God? Why do You do it? Why do You even bother? Look around. Nobody cares. No one is paying attention to all the beauty you deliver. Everyone is too busy— hopelessly caught up and distracted by all the issues and dramas that come with life.*

Without warning I felt a warmth growing inside my chest, spreading through my whole body. It erased every trace of the emotional pain I felt. My skewed perception of time completely stopped. It felt as if I were floating in a warm womb of pure love. Gently, this warmth became a voice speaking from inside me and all around me. I could hear it in my head. I could feel it on every pore of my skin as a tactile vibration or hum. It brought the same blissful ecstasy as a cool breeze, soft and fragrant, that whispers over your cheeks and through your hair when you stand in a meadow with closed eyes and your face turned up to the sun. The voice was as gentle as the loving way a mother gazes at her sleeping newborn, yet as powerful and intense as lightning in a summer storm.

The voice said, "I do it for you."

A profound understanding of the word *you* accompanied those words. It was me, it was everyone—humanity as a whole. The words carried only the healing intention of love, and I knew at that moment God saw and cared deeply for each individual, and for all people everywhere. That knowledge gave me great peace, and in that moment I was changed forever. Whether my needs were monumental or inconsequential, God was there with his sustaining love every minute. In the midst of my tremendous sorrow, I felt truly blessed.

Yolanda Tims moved to the United States from Spain when she was 12 years old. Blessed with three wonderful daughters and a rowdy pack of four doggies, she and her husband, Christopher, own a home repair business and hope to move to rural Kentucky to be closer to nature and allow their four dogs to run free.

Healing for a Wounded Heart

As my husband and I traveled near the town of Junction City, Kansas, on our way to a military reunion in Nevada, we saw a signpost that said "Vietnam Veterans' Memorial." We often stop to pay our respects to his "fallen brothers" at such sites when traveling. My husband, who served with the 4th Infantry Division in Vietnam in 1967 and 1968, pulled off the road, telling me he was going to look for it.

We entered the town, home of Fort Riley Military Post, and found the memorial site in a downtown park. It was a beautiful site made of granite and bronze, honoring fallen heroes from the State of Kansas. My attention was drawn to a small, beautifully arranged flower bed, in whose center sprung a myriad of small white crosses. Upon closer inspection, I saw names and pictures of young men and women on each one. The signage told me it was dedicated to those "Fallen Heroes" of Iraq and Afghanistan who had deployed from Fort Riley. Suddenly, I came upon a very familiar name, Jonathan Melchora.

I have been active in a project called "Marine Comfort Quilts," making quilt squares and sewing quilts together to be sent to families who have lost a son or daughter in Afghanistan or Iraq. The quilts are a way for people to show the love they feel for families who have suffered this tragic loss. Squares are sent from many states and locations with messages of love and sympathy, to be sewn into these quilts. It is our hope that the quilts will convey to each family the deep love, caring, and gratitude of our nation, and our recognition of the ultimate sacrifice given by their loved one. The loving and powerful energy incorporated into these works of art is indescribable.

I stared at the little white cross before me. Jonathan Melchora was one of the soldiers for whom I made a Marine Comfort Quilt in honor of his memory. Tears blurred my eyes as I snapped a picture of the scene for the album I keep with photos of the quilts and information about each person they honor.

Eighteen months later, in October 2006, I was asked to give a talk about the Marine Comfort Quilt Project to a group of Prime Timers Senior Citizens in a town near my home. Because the story of the quilts is much more real and effective when people can actually touch a quilt and see the picture of the person it honors, I brought a quilt I had just sewn along with the picture of the small flower bed at Fort Riley with the white crosses. My audience was very receptive to what I had to tell them. A few of the women had even made squares for the quilts and displayed some of them.

Next on our schedule was a trip to Fort Leonard Wood in Missouri where we would help cook and serve food for a Welcome Home Celebration for the 5th Engineer Battalion. It would be a huge celebration for returning soldiers and their families.

Upon our arrival, I was "stationed" at a table inside the recreation center to pass out brochures to returning soldiers, inviting them to join an association of fellow veterans. We were expecting a crowd of around 1,500 people, and the men were outside manning huge grills.

Taking a break, I walked toward the lobby, where my attention was suddenly drawn to a large man sitting by the doorway holding strings from two brightly colored balloons. On any other day I would barely have noticed him—perhaps even walked by without seeing him. But the sensation I felt could not be ignored. God's Voice spoke emphatically to my heart, saying, "See the balloons."

Instead of walking on by, I greeted him and mentioned how good he looked holding such colorful balloons. I could see he was a command sergeant major, and as I passed in front of him, my attention was drawn to his name tag. I walked on, suddenly realizing his was a familiar name—an unusual name, but one I had seen before. I returned and told him his name seemed familiar to me.

"Is it possible you had a relative who died in Iraq?" I asked.

To my astonishment, he replied, "Yes. My son!"

"Was his name Jonathan?"

He looked shocked at my question. "Yes," he said. "How do you know that?"

"Did you receive a Comfort Quilt in honor of your son?" I said softly. I could feel my heart beat faster.

The man's eyes rounded, "Yes! But how did you know that?"

My answer astonished him, "Because I am the woman who made that quilt."

If ever I had doubted God speaks to me and guides my day, there was no longer any doubt. Tears flowed freely as CSM Melchora and I embraced and held one another for the longest time. I took the opportunity to tell him how very sorry I was for the loss of his beloved son, and how honored I was to have been the one to sew and finish his quilt. I remembered I had made one of the squares in the quilt also. CSM Melchora told me that he had read every word on the quilt many times and had hung it in his living room under a picture of his son.

I felt a strong sensation of Jonathan's presence as we embraced, and could almost hear him telling his dad that indeed he was alright and it was time his father let go of the tremendous pain he carried. The time for healing had begun. His father had been in Iraq with the unit when Jonathan was killed. How painful that must have been for him. The pain had been internalized as he went about finishing the job he had to do. Now, it suddenly broke open to be healed in that split second we held each other. Jonathan was finally free to move on, knowing his father would now find peace.

What elaborate plans God must have undertaken in order to facilitate our meeting on that day. What an honor for me to be included in that process. Never will I forget that special moment and the gift I received of being a part of the process. I still cannot tell this story without tears coming to my eyes. But, they are tears of gratitude for being so blessed by Spirit.

Sue Gass celebrated her 70th birthday shortly before the trip to Fort Leonard Wood, Missouri. She has worked with the Marine Comfort Quilt Project for three years now and has completed the construction of 40 quilts.

The Auction

Two and a half years ago my life's direction was not clear, focused, or intentional. I had dreams to truly wake up and be happy, prosperous, and deliberately create my life moment to moment. Unfortunately, I was about as far from my ideal as I could get. Searching for answers through seminars, books, and conversations, I made some progress and my life began to improve, yet I still struggled. A piece of the puzzle was still missing. I realized the logical side of my brain could take me only so far, and if I was going to have something different, I needed to be thinking and doing something different.

Soon afterward, my sister sent me a Website she thought I'd be interested in. She knew better than anyone of my ongoing search to figure out how life works. I was beginning to trust and act on my thoughts and intuition, yet there were too many moments when I panicked and trust fled. I experienced little peace along the way. My sister knew I was searching for more confidence, clarity, and faith.

Immediately, the Website's 30-day program for hearing God's Voice intrigued me. On Day 15 I heard one of the most powerful messages I'd ever heard. The instructor said that the reason he didn't hear God's Voice as a separate voice was because hearing it that way would cause even more separation inside him. I was floored, and completely related to that. I had just come to terms with how huge my ego had been in my life, and to hear that message was life-changing.

I've had lots of ideas come and go while sitting quietly. Even when the thoughts were kind, loving, encouraging, or suggesting that I change certain old habits that no longer served me, I thought they were my own ideas. As a result, I paid little attention to them. For some reason, I didn't make the connection that my loving thoughts were God's thoughts.

After that revelation, I started hearing God's Voice in my life for what seemed like the first time. I was expecting a separate, even booming voice to really get my attention, and all the while, every kind, loving, and inspiring thought I had ever had was God inside me.

For months, my fiancé, Patrick, and I had been seriously looking into real-estate investing. Opportunities came and went, offers fell through, our timing was off—and then, as if on cue, something new and different began to happen.

We had been throwing away a free newspaper deposited on our doorstep every Wednesday without our even looking at it. This time "something" inspired me to read those papers. Inside there were real-estate auction ads that stood out as if they were the only writing on the page. I read every detail. Some ads were for huge farms out of our range and interest. But there was one ad for a house just three blocks from our own home, of a family selling the family estate by auction, and it was to take place in four days, on Sunday.

Our strategy session began immediately. Knowing the neighborhood and the values, we estimated the house was worth approximately $255,000. We set our maximum bid at $196,000 including any fees or commissions.

Sunday came quickly. I grabbed my checkbook and headed for the auction. Once there, I took a quick walk through the house and confirmed it was a sound investment. As I read the rules posted on site, my plan came to an unexpected halt with the simple sentence, "Make your check payable to...." I felt myself panicking. The reality of the situation became clear. Every fearful thought lying dormant inside me about buying a house at auction came rushing to the surface. I had never done anything like this before, and my ego went into high gear. My ego's voice roared inside my head: "You can't do that! You don't know what you're doing! You've never ever written a check that big!"

I grabbed a chair and tried to keep my shaking knees from buckling. Doing my best to calm down, I heard a quieter voice in my head that sounded like my own thoughts. It said, "You don't have to bid. You can keep your mouth shut. Just fill out the check, register your name, and get to the next step."

God had met me right where I was. He knew my logical side. He knew my practical side. He knew just what to say and how to say it.

I thought, *I can do that. That makes sense. All I want to do is keep my option open to bid, and if I don't write the check, the game is over.*

My brief moment of panic quickly calmed with logical thinking. I would get my deposit back at the end of the auction if I was not the successful bidder. To me, that was safe enough.

The auction was about to begin. With my numbered card ready, I nervously took my place where the auctioneer could see me. I was prepared to play if I felt it was right.

The opening bid was $300,000. No takers.

It dropped to $250,000. From there it sank by $20,000 increments to $150,000.

The bidding started. I kept quiet until the initial flurry of bids slowed down. I jumped in at $175,000. Then someone else bid $180,000. I went to $185,000.

The bidding stalled.

The auctioneer said he was going inside to talk to the family members to see what they wanted to do. They had reserved the right to reject all bids if the price didn't go high enough. I realized in that moment the auctioneer had walked into the house with MY BID! I called Patrick at work to tell him we were in the game.

The auctioneer came back out and said, "The family wants to see if we can go higher." He started the bidding again and the price jumped another $5,000 to $190,000. The auctioneer looked right at me to see if I would go to $195,000. I shook my head no. My inner voice was telling me, "No, be quiet." The auctioneer tried and tried to go to $195,000. No one budged. He went back inside with someone else's bid of $190,000. I found myself surprisingly calm with the possibility that I was about to lose the house.

The auctioneer came out with a message from the family. "The family has decided to sell today. Do I have $195,000?"

Again, no one budged. "Okay, how about $191,000?" As if on its own accord, my hand went up. Something inside me said, "Bid." At that very same moment, Patrick and his son arrived just in time to see me raise the bidding card.

The auctioneer searched the audience for a higher bid. "$192,000. Do I hear $192,000?"

Nothing. It was one of those moments when time stands still.

Again he said, "$192,000. Do I hear $192,000?" He searched the faces of the crowd, hoping for another bid. "Okay, $192,000. Going once. $192,000. Going twice. Sold to the woman for $191,000."

I stood there stunned. $191,000 plus 2.5 percent commission equals $195,775. My final bid was $225 under our original cap of $196,000.

Within moments of the gavel hitting the lectern, I was approached by a tall, distinguished, elderly gentleman who shook my hand and said, "You just got a great deal. Congratulations! This is a beautiful piece of property."

It was as if God had sent a messenger to say "Well done." As quickly as the man appeared, he was gone.

Days later, we discovered that our value estimate on the property was low and we would have approximately $80,000 in equity in this house—$25,000 more than we projected. I'm going to listen to the Voice of God within to guide me all the way to closing.

Jennifer Monahan enjoys traveling and writing. She lives in rural Pennsylvania with her husband, three step-sons, and two very cool cats.

Finding Peace Amidst Despair

"Mrs. Laferty, do you have a daughter named Sarah?"

The call came at 7:00 a.m. from the local police department. Instantly, every gut-wrenching fear I'd ever felt for my child whispered its foreboding terror in my heart.

"Yes, yes I do. What's wrong? Where is she? Why are you calling me?" My heart hammered inside my chest. Had the worst finally happened?

The officer calmly explained Sarah had been arrested for drug possession. She had told the police she was actually Sarah's cousin who lived in Iowa and was just using my daughter's identification. Sarah has no cousins in Iowa. This was the beginning of a painfully long road into the world of drug addiction, but it was also how I came to find peace and the voice of Spirit.

By the time I received that phone call, Sarah had been addicted to heroin for several years. In hindsight, I could see something was wrong. There had been a change in her behavior so gradual that it was easy to excuse it as Sarah just having a bad day or even a bad week. Whenever I inquired about her health or demeanor, it was easy to accept her excuse that she didn't feel well or hadn't gotten enough sleep. Sarah didn't live at home and had done some traveling, so I didn't have daily contact with her. She assured me she was fine, and I eagerly convinced myself that she was telling the truth.

Now I could no longer look away or pretend everything was fine. There was a part of me that wanted to blame someone—anyone—for what was happening to my daughter. I felt overcome with guilt, anger, and fear that I had somehow failed Sarah, though I realized on some level that this wasn't my fault. Still, I had trouble laying the blame at Sarah's feet. Who had done this to my beloved child? What could I have done to stop this spiral into madness?

Sometimes I felt in danger of losing my mind with no means to stop it. I couldn't eat or sleep, and spent hours pacing, trying to fit the pieces together to make sense out of the knowledge my child was in serious trouble. I blamed her boyfriend, who was also addicted, for not protecting her. How could he have let this happen to my Sarah? I tried not to imagine how Sarah's choices and actions would impact her health and her future, and I cried for what I thought I'd lost. Frustrated with my ignorance and my inability to stop her from using a drug that could so easily end her life, I felt helpless and alone. Though I had to keep living, working, and putting one foot ahead of the other to get from one day to the next, I thought of myself as the walking dead. The pain was that profound, that deep, and it became a permanent part of my everyday life.

There were some fleeting moments when Sarah seemed to be getting better, but then she would call from jail and my hope would plummet. She always apologized for putting me though the pain, and begged me to forgive her. Every time she entered a treatment program, she smuggled in any drugs she could. She even fed her habit by frequenting various hospitals, describing phony symptoms and manufacturing painful ailments for which doctors prescribed narcotics. I thought I'd reached the end of my rope and had nowhere else to turn. It seemed I had hit bottom before Sarah did. It was then I started to spend time in meditation, reaching for a source inside myself for the first time.

For several years I had tried meditation, and although I found it mildly comforting, I failed to experience the wonderful communications others reportedly received from Spirit. They spoke about the beautiful places they saw and the feelings of boundless joy they experienced. This wasn't happening to me, and though I felt a sense of calmness and serenity, my inability to reach states of joy or enlightenment left me feeling sad and unfulfilled. I even entertained the thought that God chose to whom He wished to communicate, and He didn't want to talk to me. I slipped into a deep and painful despair, an overwhelming sense of loss and isolation.

Morning after morning I sat in quiet anticipation of finding an answer that would help me withstand the pain in my life. Then one day, in the quiet of my meditation, it suddenly felt as if time had stopped. My body felt light, without form or shape, as if I were floating on a vast cloud of peace while a sense of infinite expanse seemed to fill my mind. In that moment, I experienced a profound knowing that Spirit wasn't just *with* me, but was *who I am*. I felt a deep connection to everyone and everything, the warmth of a vast, all-encompassing love. In that moment of profound union, I let go of my pain, frustration, and fear because I realized that I *was* the divine and infinite extension of God's love. Tears flowed freely from my eyes as intense awe and gratitude filled me and a perfect peace flowed within me. That loving peace infused in me the will to go on in the knowledge that my daughter, my child, would be fine no matter what. I didn't need to worry any longer because she was a part of that same changeless, limitless power of Spirit. I had taken the hand of Spirit to lead me to that place of perfect peace within me and had opened a space for Sarah to grow in Spirit when she was ready. This has become all the answer I will ever need.

My daughter has had many ups and downs in the past few years and has even spent time in prison. Often I thought I couldn't survive if the "worst" happened, but I've learned to let go and rely on the peace of my inner Spirit, and that has given me the serenity I longed for. I know now that regardless of what happens in the world, the same source of Spirit cares for Sarah. When the time is right, she, too, will find peace. There are days when the world seems so unsure, but what I found that day during my meditation sustains me through the hardest days. I am aware I can help and care for my daughter, and can now love her without limitations.

Sarah has now finished her first drug treatment program and is living with us while going to school. I am so grateful to her because it was through her that I was able to find guidance and the voice of Spirit. The changeless love of God has shown me that I can forgive her, and that knowledge has given me love, peace, and joy. She is my perfect Child of God.

Marie Lafferty—loving wife, mother of two daughters, and grandmother of four—takes delight in participating in all phases of her growing family. A former hairdresser, water aerobics instructor, and pool manager, she now enjoys managing a small psychology office.

Fall in Love With Yourself

On September 11, 2001, I sat in my living room with my builder and watched the Twin Towers come crashing down. I had no idea that image would become a metaphor for my own life. Weeks later, two days from signing a loan for an extensive home remodel, my world collapsed. My husband phoned to say he was on his way home for good; he and his team had been let go when new management took over after a reorganization.

I felt as if someone had punched me in the stomach. The luxuries an executive lifestyle and paycheck had provided were suddenly a thing of the past. In my despair, I had no way of knowing this was the beginning of a long journey to self-discovery that turned out to be far more rewarding than a new home or a large paycheck.

After the initial shock, I convinced myself everything would be fine; one or both of us would find work at the perfect time. It was easy to feel secure because all the facets of my external life felt secure. We had plenty of money to survive for a while, and decided we'd take some time to enjoy being home together.

This optimism slowly disintegrated in the next three years as the money ran out, the debts piled up, and no work was found. My mood spiraled downward until I began to lose faith in my beliefs—that simply by having faith, everything would turn out okay. Time was proving me wrong. What had seemed to be an opportunity for something positive and new morphed into a burden, a scary place, full of questions with no answers.

I used credit cards to pay for food and clothes. Spending money made me feel sick inside. I began talking to my Higher Self, to God, asking questions about how to change what appeared to be an ever-worsening situation.

As my mounting fears became harder to hide, I avoided family and friends. It was more comforting to be alone, praying and meditating; I found it helped me stay in the moment, and kept me from thinking about anything else. When I wasn't alone, I would fall apart on the inside while pretending nothing was wrong. Though I asked God for help, I wasn't hearing the answers.

In spite of appearances, I felt if we stayed true to ourselves we would be okay. I wasn't exactly sure what that meant, but it gave me a shred of hope. Everyone told us to go get a job—any job—but something felt very wrong with that plan. Confused, I still didn't know what to do. Sometimes, when alone in my car, I screamed and cried in agony, yelling at God, demanding an answer. My brain scanned constantly for someone to call, someone to ask for help, but there was no one. No one but me.

One night, after a day when everything had gone wrong, my dishwasher broke. We didn't have the money to fix it. We didn't have the money to fix anything, and my life felt as broken and unfixable as the dishwasher. I fell into a heap on the couch feeling utterly hopeless. My body wouldn't move. No tears would come. Feeling alone in the Universe, I started to talk out loud to God. My deepest fear was coming true—that everything would be gone and my family and I would be living on the street. I told God I didn't care anymore, that I just couldn't control any of this, that I was tired, and was leaving it up to Him to show me what to do.

When I finished speaking, I suddenly became aware of a faint, thought-like voice speaking to me in my mind. The whispered words were so subtle I could barely make them out, but their meaning washed over me full force: To change my life, I needed to change the way I thought and talked about it. When I asked how to do that, I heard very clearly within my mind, "Fall in love with yourself."

I rose from the couch and went to bed feeling as if I had truly connected to God, that there was an answer for me, and that I was supported and loved. For the first time since 9/11, I felt hope.

The next day I received a powerful sign. Several e-mails arrived, all announcing a new book written by Immaculée Ilibagiza, the Rwandan woman who had spent three months in a tiny bathroom with several other women, surviving the holocaust in her country.

After reading her story, I couldn't feel sorry for myself any longer. I began to consciously appreciate the abundance in my life, from the grass and trees to the availability of credit to help me with my bills. I continued my mental dialogue with God, asking for guidance and expressing gratitude for the love and support I received. Each day I asked how to move from fear to trust by mentally posing the question to God or by writing in my journal at night.

The following day I would read or hear words from someone that directly addressed my question. It was as if a little light would go on; I would experience a sudden knowing that those words were meant for me, that they had been sent because I had asked for them. They came in the form of conversations, e-mails, a line in a song or movie, a bumper sticker, even a stranger in the grocery store. Sometimes when I wasn't sure, I'd get the answer in two or three different forms in one day. God gave me direct signs by introducing me to uplifting stories, wise people, and opportunities daily, opening me up to a whole new experience of life. Every signal I received strengthened my faith. Every day, I began to feel a little less scared, a little more hopeful.

One day I realized that by following God's loving guidance, I had, indeed, fallen in love with myself. This shift in me caused a shift in my entire family and our lives finally started to turn around.

Now I know what it means to hear God's Voice, to accept the guidance He offers continuously, to be connected to Source energy, and to express and receive love. Daily I journal my ongoing letter to God about all I'm grateful for in my life. I'm constantly tuned in to the abundance all around me and take every opportunity to appreciate God's grace. I continue to be guided toward inspired thoughts, words, and actions. My recovery began with surrender. I gave up control and began to listen, to trust, and to deliberately re-create my life by allowing God to assist me in shifting my energy to a positive place. I learned to love what is and to trust myself and God. My life will never be the same again.

Shannon Oakley is an artist, wife, and mother. She lives in New Jersey with her husband and two young sons. She enjoys tennis, traveling, and playing board games with her family.

Third Time's the Charm

I always assumed life would continue in the same familiar patterns. Perhaps I'd experience a few surprises here and there, but hopefully nothing earth-shattering or traumatic. Like so many people, I loved my family, worked through my challenges, and celebrated my successes. Life continued to go on. And then I discovered a tiny lump in my breast in 1983. It was cancer. You never know how you'll respond to a life-threatening event until it's upon you. After the tears in the doctor's office, I said, "Well, if I have only six weeks to live, they'll be the best six weeks of my life."

I let go of my fear of dying that moment. When I went home to tell my husband and son, I'd even recovered enough to be humorous by saying, "Well, the thing is, they were a matched set." I was trying to make light of it to help them so they wouldn't worry so much.

I had a lumpectomy, radiation, and got back to "normal" with follow-up scans and checkups. Six years later, the same tiny lump appeared again. This time I had only a lumpectomy, but no radiation. I was a strong, healthy woman who had love, faith, and trust in God, plus the love of my dear family. I exercised, ate healthy foods, had a positive outlook on life, and loved uplifting books and music. I just had one tiny spot that was a problem. The rest of me was just fine.

All my life, whenever something serious came up, I would turn to God and Jesus with my tears and ask for help. That is where I again turned. I felt it would only worry my family or friends if I shared my problems with them, and besides, I placed my life in God's hands anyway. I also had the attitude that if I went around thinking every time I had a pain or got a little sick that maybe the cancer was back, I might as well die right then and get it over with. That wasn't living to me. That attitude served me well, and I enjoyed my life tremendously.

In 1991 another lump was found in the same breast. This was my third bout with cancer, and I can't describe the terror I felt at the thought of the surgery, the pain, the needles, and the uncertainty all over again. It wasn't fear of dying, it was the fear of lingering with horrible pain before I died that I just couldn't handle**.** My family was so supportive and loving, but again I couldn't burden them with my feelings, so I turned to my only source of hope—God.

About a week before the surgery I totally surrendered from the bottom of my heart and soul to God. I slept peacefully all week, confident that God was in charge and He would take care of me. I had no idea what a remarkable, awesome event lay ahead.

I woke in the recovery room horribly sick from the anesthetic. Alone and groggy, my mind was blank as I heard a clear inner voice saying, "Don't look at the blood, the needles, all the tubes and machines. Think about vacations and positive things."

I obeyed, fell back asleep, and wasn't sick. When I awoke the voice was back. I was confused, because I couldn't remember hearing a voice like this the other times I had surgery. It seemed to come from inside me, outside me, everywhere in the room. As I came out of the anesthetic, amazing thoughts and feelings swirled inside me. I experienced a profound sense of peace unlike ever before. I felt love for God that far exceeded what I felt for my family. I bubbled over with joy that had nothing to do with my surroundings. All of this came from inside me. Then Bible phrases filled my mind: "Your Father knows what you need before you ask," and "You will seek me and find me when you seek me with all your heart." Also, "Ask and you shall receive. Seek and you shall find. Knock and the door will be opened." Love songs sounded like songs about God, instead of my husband or family.

I realized I had been seeking God my whole life, and God had been right here inside me all this time. He had been patiently waiting for just the right moment to make His Presence known. I felt as if I had no needs and should wear a sign that said, "I found it. I found it!" A sense of "knowing" also came of a God who was not an angry, vengeful, wrathful God, but an all-loving one. I believe that my "letting go" had been the key to this experience, along with the simple faith and trust in God I'd always had.

There was a time when I used to feel negative things such as jealousy, anger, and especially fear. They were all gone now. There were no regrets from my past. Even though I didn't attend church every week, or read the Bible every day, or have any exposure to spiritual knowledge or special religious training, I realized that just being myself had been enough for this awesome event to have happened to me. The wonder of it has never left me after 19 years.

I walked around the hospital after the surgery feeling euphoric, babbling to everyone about the peace, love, and joy I had found. I told family, nurses, the doctor, other patients, anyone who crossed my path, wanting to share my experience with them. The cancer was totally irrelevant. My family and friends were confused and having a difficult time dealing with this "new" person who was constantly talking about peace, love, and joy as she recuperated from breast cancer.

Today life is back to "normal," with family, friends, concerts, vacations, and work, but the peace, love, and joy inside me never leaves. Because of this, I view every event that happens in my life as a lesson for my highest good. I've also come to realize that God's Voice has been with me my whole life in one form or another, whether through intuition, thoughts, or a distinct inner voice, though I never recognized it at the time as God.

Patricia Ann Cahill is a wife, mother, grandmother, and senior citizen who loves life. She has three children, eight grandchildren, and enjoys traveling, concerts with rock and blues bands, and especially spending time with her family.

Coins From the Heart

For a long time I've struggled with the idea—and the reality—of prayer. I've never had a clear belief about God, though I feel certain there is a force greater than myself in the universe. After trying many different paths to prayer throughout the years, in recent months I've participated in public prayer at our synagogue mainly by meditating, rather than reading and following the prayers in our prayer books. A few months ago, during a period of silent prayer, I gazed out a large window, looking at the sky and the trees swaying in the breeze, and opened my mind and heart fully without having any particular thoughts. Suddenly, I heard a clear, distinct voice in my head. It wasn't my voice, nor was it a voice I recognized. It was deep and firm. It said: "Go to the bank and get $100 in silver dollars, and give them away. It will change your life."

The voice repeated itself once. I didn't know where the voice—or the idea—came from, because I'd never had such a thought before. Once, years ago, I'd had another experience of hearing a voice, clearly not my own, speaking loudly in my head, directing me to do a particular thing. But then, as now, I wasn't certain what the source was. Both times I sensed it was from a place "outside" myself, and that it was something I could trust. I felt I was being guided by a power or wisdom greater than myself, and that it was important to listen and do what I was being instructed to do. As I'd done before, after hearing the instruction repeated, I thought, *All right. I'll do it.*

The next week I went to our bank and asked to buy $100 in silver dollars. The teller said they had no silver dollars and I would need to order a minimum of $1,000 in coins. Momentarily I was flummoxed, but then the teller explained they had other kinds of dollar coins, some silver and some gold. I figured other kinds of dollar coins would still fit within my instructions, so I bought all they had—$74 worth—saying I would come back in a few weeks to get the rest.

Since then, I never leave home without carrying several dollar coins. Whenever I see someone in need, I give that person a coin, often mentioning it's a dollar so the person doesn't confuse it with a quarter. Because I live in San Francisco whose homeless population is large, it's quite rare for me to come home with all my coins. Nearly always, the person receiving the money is very appreciative. Sometimes there's even a moment of real connection between us.

Throughout the years, I've had mixed feelings about the poor people on the streets and their pleas—sometimes demands—for spare change. For a long time, I've wrestled with conflicting ideas and feelings about giving. My heart tells me the person before me is a fellow human being in need, however they spend the money, and my religion tells me not to turn away from those who come to me for help. Yet some people say giving money only encourages panhandling, that it's better to give to agencies or organizations that help the poor. For the most part, I've looked away—trying to avoid eye contact, pretending not to hear—or have given a quick smile and a "Sorry." I have often told myself that it wouldn't really help anyway, that there is no way I can respond to everyone who approaches me. At the same time, my heart always felt the pain of turning away from another human being.

Since my "instruction" to give out silver dollars, I am no longer concerned with the rightness or wrongness of giving to a person on the street. I'm simply responding to a fellow human being without judgment. Whatever the recipient's reaction, mine is joy in the giving. I know it's not a lot of money, but I see that it does make a difference to the people receiving it. I stop, meet the person's eyes, and say a few words. The caring human contact means as much as the coin to most, and I am no longer rejecting them or the urges of my own heart. My husband, who used to hate it when such people approached us, often responding with impatience or anger at the intrusion, now will point out someone I'm about to pass when my attention is elsewhere. And the one time when I'd given out all my coins, he reached into his own wallet for a dollar bill, something he'd never done before.

I know this is a small thing, but in some significant way it *has* changed my life, just as the voice said it would. Every time I give someone a coin and speak to that person for a few moments, my heart opens. And although my sense of the divine is no more certain or clear than it was before, I do feel a presence in my heart, and I know that I will do this for the rest of my life.

Judith McCullough is an editor and lover of classical music who lives with her husband in San Francisco. Her principal teachers in life have been her family, especially her twin daughters. Judith feels blessed to share her life with her husband of 20 years, her daughters and sons-in-law, her two beautiful grandchildren, and wonderful friends.

Advice From a Dear Friend

My church was hosting a workshop by a husband-and-wife team on hearing God's Voice. Though I had decided to take part in the class, God didn't wait for me to get instruction. Perhaps because I felt so open and eager to hear His Voice, He jumped in to talk with me the weekend before the workshop was scheduled to begin—something I later learned is quite common when someone makes a deep decision to hear God's Voice.

At the time, I had been participating in an online dating site. I had contacted a man whose profile interested me, but his response had been somewhat brusque. I felt a bit hurt that he didn't return my interest, and my reaction was to send an angry and accusatory reply to him.

When I related my response to my friend, Diane, she admonished me.

"Julie, why do you do that?" she asked. "Why do you get so angry and act so nasty when someone does something like that?"

At first I was taken aback, but on thinking it over, I realized Diane was right. This particular behavior pattern had been such an integral part of my social skill set that I didn't know its origins, nor could I figure a way to stop the pattern. Finally, I prayed to the Holy Spirit for an answer to why this negative, knee-jerk pattern had such control over me.

For several days, I received no answer. Then, while running errands, I heard a distinct Voice say, "Beloved, do you not realize that you and this man are playing the same game?"

The Voice was so gentle and loving. Though it seemed audible inside my head, I knew it was not my normal voice. I have never addressed myself as "Beloved." Shocked, I replied, "Excuse me?"

228

The Voice continued in its gentle way. "Beloved, this man was afraid that you were not really interested in him, and his response was to back away. When you felt him back away, you then perceived he was not interested in you, and so you attacked him. You were both playing the same game, just in different ways."

The same game? What game would that be? I did not understand, so the Voice provided an example.

"Do you remember playing Monopoly with your mother?"

I began to laugh, immediately understanding what I was being told. My mother had taught me to play a very aggressive game of Monopoly. It was a take-no-prisoners version. As a result, people who ordinarily loved the game often refused to play with me. My aggressive style of play sucked all enjoyment out of the game for them. The Voice was pointing out that this man I had met online was playing the same game as I was. We were just playing it differently.

God's Voice spoke again: "And where do you think you got this pattern of attacking someone when you perceive they have withdrawn their energy from you, as this man seemed to do?"

I was stunned to realize that I had also learned this from my mother. That revelation amazed me. It explained a long-standing behavior pattern I had never understood nor had any clue how to fix. God had led me to a whole new way of looking at a situation that had brought me pain in the past.

God's Voice was gentle, loving, and completely non-judgmental. It was not critical, just explaining something in much the same way a very dear friend would. With this new knowledge, I slowly began to heal. I no longer felt the need to attack others as I had before. When the urge to "attack" surfaced, I was able to step back, analyze my default reaction, and modify my behavior before it could hurt someone else.

This experience opened the door to allow God's Voice to be an integral part of my life. I may have sometimes been shown a piece of myself I'd never seen clearly before, and have sometimes had to face aspects of myself that weren't serving me, but my life is now enriched by the presence of God's Voice on a continual basis. I feel blessed to know this source of Love and guiding compassion accompanies me on every step of my path through life, and is ready to offer gentle advice whenever I want it. I need only ask.

Julie E. Bradshaw lives in South Carolina with her husband and two much-loved, spoiled-rotten cats. She loves to read and is an avid hiker.

Life-Changing Birthday Gift

The high-end suburb in which I lived among upper-middle-class professionals with their shiny new SUVs and neat, manicured lawns seemed every mother's dream. I ran a small sculpting business from home and worked long hours late into the night. My days were sprinkled with trips to scout meetings, gymnastics, dancing, and music lessons. But the idyllic façade of my life was a sham.

Pressures and stress robbed me of sleep. Severe back pain or excruciating migraine headaches that lasted several days increased my tension, but my schedule didn't allow for time out. At times my mind drifted to my children, plaguing me with fearful, anxious thoughts about their safety. I once awoke from a dream, drenched with sweat, crying uncontrollably because I had accidentally microwaved one of them. Even vacations brought no relief. I developed a terror of flying that even two shots of bourbon couldn't drown, and felt both ashamed and afraid. Something was out of whack but I couldn't figure out what it was.

I was feeling run-down and unsupported, both emotionally and financially. My husband had been out of work for several years and was depressed and despondent. Communication between us had died—him not wanting to hear my angry complaints, and I turning away from his deafening silence. More weight rested on my shoulders. I masked the guilt, and a hole of sheer emptiness that dwarfed the Grand Canyon opened within me. It grew deeper and deeper, twisting and gnawing in my gut.

My 44th birthday was fast approaching. I thought my life would be a cakewalk at this point in my physical journey. Far from it! I was besieged daily with other people's schedules, work deadlines thrust upon me by clients, schoolbus rendezvous for my children, and running a small business with several employees. I was the family's breadwinner living a supposedly happy life, while deep within me I was tumbling out of control.

In spite of everything, I continued. The weekend for my birthday arrived. As always, this meant inviting my family over for my party and running around frantically the night before. It meant shopping for groceries, ordering a cake, and getting candles, paper hats, blowers, plates, cups, and a large colorful tablecloth. Rising early in the morning on the day of the party, I prepared everything for lunch. With the kids showered and dressed, I threw on a dress and finished up the last-minute preparations. The party unfolded as it usually did with screaming, laughing children scooting to and fro and all the grownup relatives munching and chatting.

I served endless cups of tea and coffee to my elderly parents, and when all had had their fill and were chatting comfortably, it was time to light the candles on the birthday cake. Though it was the middle of the afternoon, we turned off the kitchen lights. Even the kids knew: "Oooooooooh! It's time for the cake." In the midst of all the chatter and pushing and shoving on the part of the little ones to get a good look at the center of attraction, the oddest thing happened.

I was listening to them singing "Happy Birthday to You" when suddenly it was as if somebody pulled out the microphone cord on the loudspeaker. There was complete silence. Lips and faces continued smiling and moving in space. As if on command, I leaned forward in slow motion to begin blowing out the candles, when in front of me, just to the left of my forehead, a resounding voice penetrated my very being. It said, "You have now reached the halfway point."

In that holy instant, time stopped. A bolt of electricity coursed through my body. A dense, loving energy overcame me. Immediately I felt my connection to a reality greater than my own, and knew this Voice was part of it. A sense of all-knowing truth flooded my awareness, and I *knew* that a glorious kingdom was somehow layered beneath and that I was part of it, destined to go on forever though my years on earth might be numbered.

This was HUGE! Something outside of reality had inserted itself into my world. No one standing around me at the party knew what was going on within me. The whole experience lasted for only a moment, from standing to bending forward to blow out the candles, but it stretched out so much longer in my experience. I was stunned. Quite suddenly the roar of the party clicked back on, and I blurted out, "Did anyone hear that voice?"

Not one person understood why I was asking such an odd question.

I blew the candles out on the cake, wrapped the party up as usual, and life continued on its way as it had before. I could never have guessed it would take years to fully incorporate the true meaning of this event.

Not long after the party a coworker noticed a red spot on my lower eyelid. I sauntered over to a bathroom mirror and realized it was blood. After a doctor's visit, I was diagnosed with cancer. My eyes were a necessity in my sculpting work, and the thought of losing my sight terrified me. The lower section of my eyelid was removed.

Then an MRI revealed a tumor the size of a film canister in my neck. Unsure if it was malignant or not, the doctor warned that surgery might cause the loss of my voice. I was filled with terror imagining the cancer had returned and that I could die and never see my kids again. But as I lay quaking with fear on a stretcher just before being rolled in for surgery, I remembered that Voice saying, "You have reached the halfway point." Peace immediately enveloped me. I knew the operation would be a success and my life would continue on with my family. The Voice had given me a precious gift—a foreknowledge of the future.

But it gave me so much more. In my hunger to explore the source of that magnificent Voice that had penetrated my heart and mind like no other, I came to experience that I am an eternal being who is profoundly loved and has always been connected to God. I even participated in a program that taught a specific process for accessing this Voice quite deliberately, consciously, and "at will" any time.

As I have allowed this connection to be a part of my everyday life, the more elegant, serene, and simple it has become. I look exactly the same on the outside, but the past aching emptiness waiting to be filled with food, money, things, and endless drama has been filled with Godself.

Sure, all the stuff of life still goes on—flat tires, sick parents, mortgage payments, broken cell phones—but I can now pull the plug on the noise of the world at any moment and join with that loving, all-knowing Voice within me. Even in the midst of intensity, I am able to be still, quiet, and connected. I simply remember that Voice and its message.

I was transformed by God's Voice that day. I was gradually liberated from the chains of a confusing existence into a beautiful world that I now see all around me, and now I know that I am held in great loving arms forever.

Sandra Bilotto is a mother of two grown children and three poodles. After working in prosthetics and orthotics for several years, she now specializes in sculpting toys and dolls.

He Was There All Along

Go peacefully amid the
noise and haste and remember
What peace there may be in silence.

—Desiderata

It could be so easy, I thought as I began to pass the semi truck. Tired from an exhausting evening of work that I despised, and saddened by a rejection letter received earlier in the day from a job I had recently applied for, my feelings of despair overwhelmed me. *Just a quick turn of the wheel to the right. Just one minute to lose control of the car,* I thought, *and I could cease my constant struggle with depression forever.*

Depression had always been a constant in my life, a shadow accompanying my struggles with the many challenges I have faced. When I buried my infant daughter, the pain was too intense to understand, so I buried the pain as well and walked in deepening melancholy. When my son became seriously ill with spinal meningitis, and then throughout his recovery, I stuffed the hurt and intensified my relationship with depression. When my marriage crumbled, and then throughout the challenging years of single-parenting four young children, I continued to walk in depression. Tonight this depression was almost too intense to bear.

I grasped the steering wheel, and the darkness of the night and of my soul seemed to welcome this idea. It would be deemed an accident. So simple. I looked up into the starry sky, and for a moment, the chains of depression lifted as the moon rolled out from behind a cloud and lit up the darkness.

After arriving at home, I went to my bookshelf to search for wisdom that might end this constant heartache. There on those shelves were all the answers I thought I needed: the Bible, and a

234

wide variety of prayer, healing, and self-help books. I had been able to acquire this incredible amount of knowledge, but could not feel it in my heart. The simple message of "Jesus loves me this I know, for the Bible tells me so" gets lost somewhere between my head and my heart.

I grabbed my journal and began to write, whining about how unfair life had been to me, ranting about the chaos in which I felt my life tumbling, demanding that the burden of depression be lifted from me. When I had expressed all my anger and frustration, I paused in my writing. Then I wrote, "Hush, be still and know that you are a child of God."

I dropped my pen and stared at what I had just written. An overwhelming sense of peace washed over me as I reread what I had written. I quickly flipped the pages of my journal back to where I had written a similar angry entry, and found at the end: "Be gentle with yourself. Walk in trust." I then dug out other journals I had kept through the years and began to read through them. A pattern emerged. Almost all the entries with the greatest pain and sadness ended with a loving, affirming message.

God had been speaking to me throughout the years, amidst all my struggles, through my journaling process. I had just not been listening. I placed in my lap my journal, closed my eyes, and rested in the stillness of the early morning.

Of all the books on my shelf, the most significant ones for me have become my journals, for within them lies the Voice of God. If only I listen.

Connie Killgallon's life has been focused on the raising of her four children. As the children leave to begin lives of their own and her home empties, she plans to continue her education. The world is open to her explorations.

IN CONCLUSION

I hope you enjoyed these stories as much as I did.

When we share with one another our personal experiences of connecting with God, something magical happens. In our moment of remembering, our awareness of that connection is brought back to life within us, and when we share that experience with another, our awareness becomes a catalyst that helps another become aware of their connection as well. More than likely, you have had your own experience connecting with God—perhaps even while reading this book.

Now you may be asking yourself, "But how can I experience my connection with God all the time, in every area of my life?"

That indeed is the question.

After reading these stories numerous times, I discovered that these diverse and personal experiences of hearing God's Voice were like pieces of a giant puzzle that, when fit together, painted a picture of the dynamics behind our capability for hearing God's Voice in the world.

There are hundreds of inspiring messages and insights layered within these personal accounts of hearing God's Voice, but there are a few key traits I would like to share that seem to bind these experiences together. These traits may indeed help you to hear God's Voice more fully and consistently in your life.

Perhaps the most important of them is the unconditionally loving nature of God. Not a single person experienced a judgmental, angry, or vengeful God. In fact, the depth of unconditional love, peace, and joy that every single person experienced in one form or another was so unlike anything they had ever experienced in the world that their lives were forever changed.

Dear friends, let us love one another, for love comes from God.
Everyone who loves has been born of God and knows God.
Whoever does not love does not know God, because God is love.
—1 John 4:7-8 (Today's New International Version)

For most, their moment of hearing God's Voice came as a result of tremendous hardship or pain. Of the many different forms of hearing God's Voice that were described, every case resulted in a dramatic shift in perception or awareness *away* from fear, judgment, and other painful thoughts and emotions, *to* one or more aspects or qualities of God, such as love, compassion, understanding, joy, and union.

What happened within them to spark such a powerful opening to God's Voice?

Whether they were in the throes of despair just prior to hearing God's Voice or in a quiet and peaceful state of mind, each person exhibited a similar set of mental and emotional qualities in their actual moment of hearing. These common qualities included, among others, desire, willingness, surrender, and not knowing—four key traits that helped to open each one to an experience of God.

To one degree or another, each person who experienced hearing God's Voice possessed the desire to do so. For some, this desire was latent, long ago buried beneath years of guilt, fear, or unworthiness, just waiting to burst forth at a time when their pain had became too great to bear. For most, however, this desire was not hidden away, but was instead at the forefront of their awareness. They openly prayed and talked to God about their wants and needs. They were sincere and wholehearted in their seeking, and they never gave up on their desires for God's help, understanding, and support. They truly wanted to hear God's Voice. They intended to hear God's Voice. And they sought to hear God's Voice in whatever ways they knew how.

For everyone who asks receives; those who seek find;
and to those who knock, the door will be opened.
—Matthew 7:8 (Today's New International Version)

Willingness was another common trait. Although many fought to the very end to hold on to that which they were afraid of losing, in their moment of hearing God's Voice each one had courageously opened their heart and mind to something greater. They were for a brief moment willing to be willing, and it was this small act of willingness that proved powerful enough to open the door.

> *For if the willingness is there, the gift is acceptable according*
> *to what one has, not according to what one does not have.*
> —2 Corinthians 8:12 (Today's New International Version)

In addition to willingness, surrender also played an important role in opening the door to God. Each person's circumstances was unique, but in their moment of opening to God's Voice each one surrendered to something greater. They let go of their attachments and agendas. They released their expectations and painful desires. They surrendered to what is. They surrendered to the Will of God. As with willingness, most experienced tremendous pain leading up to their moment of surrender. Many felt the despair that comes from hitting bottom before finally giving up everything they held in resistance to God, yet as soon as they did, God's Comforter was there to help them.

> *Or suppose a king is about to go to war against another*
> *king. Won't he first sit down and consider whether he is able*
> *with ten thousand men to oppose the one coming against*
> *him with twenty thousand? If he is not able, he will send*
> *a delegation while the other is still a long way off and will*
> *ask for terms of peace. In the same way, those of you who do*
> *not give up everything you have cannot be my disciples.*
> —Luke 14:31–33 (Today's New International Version)

Finally, each person also experienced a moment of not knowing, some moment of recognition that perhaps they did not know the truth, they did not know how to proceed or what was best for them, or that perhaps there might be a better way. By being open to the possibility of a greater truth or a wiser, more loving, and graceful approach to their challenge or situation, they became open to receiving the wisdom and guidance of the Holy Spirit instead. It was through their willingness to not know, that they finally were able to open the door for greater knowledge to be given them.

> *But the Advocate, the Holy Spirit, whom the Father*
> *will send in my name, will teach you all things and*
> *will remind you of everything I have said to you.*
> —John 14:26 (Today's New International Version)

Desire, willingness, surrender, and not knowing—these four qualities can be found in nearly every experience of hearing God's Voice. They are the characteristics that release our fearful and ignorant limitations and open us to the love and wisdom of God. What's more, these four qualities of heart and mind are not hidden away, shrouded in mystery, or too lofty to attain. They are simple and available to everyone.

If you desire to join with God and hear His wise and loving Voice in your life,

- feel your desire for this with all your heart
- be willing to open your heart and mind to God
- surrender and release your fears, attachments, judgments, and all that would keep you from your awareness of God, and
- let go of what you think you know in the world so you can open yourself evermore to the truth that God would give you

These four qualities—desire, willingness, surrender, and not knowing—work hand in hand to open the door to God. Be patient and steadfast in your pursuit, and it will be done.

> *And I will ask the Father, and he will give you another advocate*
> *to help you and be with you forever—the Spirit of truth. The*
> *world cannot accept him, because it neither sees him nor knows*
> *him. But you know him, for he lives with you and will be in you.*
> —John 14:16–17 (Today's New International Version)

Know in your heart that it is God's Will for you to hear His Voice. The voice of Spirit was given to you by God to restore your awareness to Him, to bring you comfort and peace in times of despair, love and reassurance when you are afraid, and guidance and wisdom when you feel confused and uncertain. This Voice and Advocate for God is part of you. You are worthy of hearing His Voice. You are capable of hearing His Voice. And you will hear His Voice. All that is required is the desire and willingness to do so. If the desire and willingness are there, the outcome is assured.

SUBMIT YOUR STORY

God speaks to all of us. If you have ever received guidance, inspiration, healing, or communication from God in the form of an inner dialogue, emotional and physical feelings, intuition, signs, visions, dreams, journaling, speaking, a deep inner knowing, an audible voice, or one of the many other ways God speaks to us, we would love to receive your story.

To submit your inspiring story for consideration in one of our next *When God Spoke to Me* books, please visit *www.thevoiceforlove.com* for our submission guidelines. Possible book topics include, *When God Spoke to Me…*

- For Spouses.
- For Parents.
- For Teens.
- For Children.
- For Christians.
- About Addiction.
- About Healing.
- About Forgiveness.
- About Achieving My Dreams.
- About Finding My Life Partner.

Your story does not need to fit one of these possible categories to be considered.

For more information, please contact:

The Voice for Love

P.O. Box 3125

Ashland, OR 97520

www.thevoiceforlove.com

INDEX

A

Adams, Timothy J., 199
Advice From a Dear Friend, 228-230
Alone but Not Alone, 196-199
Angel, My, 107-108
Auction, The, 212-216
Autism, Overcoming My, 174-177
Avalon, Raena, 60
Awakening, 184-188

B

Backyard, In My Own, 104-107
Banister, Katie Rodriquez, 81
Baty, Diannia, 39
Beginning, New, 76-78
Bilotto, Sandra, 233
Birdhouse, Mom and the, 132-133
Birthday Gift, Life-Changing, 230-233
Book by its Cover, Don't Judge a, 162-165
Bradshaw, Judith, E., 230
Breath at a Time, One, 140-144
Bridges, Linda, 118
Brook, Sharon, 144

Brooks, Alan, 94
Brothers and Sisters, 125-128
Buick That Changed My Life, The, 36-39
Bush, Amy Christine, 101

C

Cahill, Patricia Ann, 225
Caldarano, Sharon, 162
Calledare, Janet, 159
Carel, Jill, 121
Carlson, Rita, 18
Castle, Kare, 188
Change, Becoming the, 200-203
Charm, Third Time's the, 222-225
Clarity, 122-123
Club, Polar Bear, 22
Coins From the Heart, 225-227
Cutting Through the Fog of Uncertainty, 134-136

D

Day I Got a New Name, The, 108-111
Days, Four Glorious, 91-94

Death, Succumbing to an
   Unlikely, 98-101

DeCorleto, Lisa, 125

Despair, Finding Peace Amid,
   216-219

Doyle, DavidPaul, 149

Dreams, The Whisper in My,
   23-25

Drive South, 81-85

Dyer, Kenneth, 91

E

Eggs, Farm Smells, and Hidden
   Gifts, 194-196

Ellames, Elizabeth, 49

Emissary, From Monster to, 66-69

F

Faith, Twist of, 152-156

Falling in Love, 156-159

Farm Smells, 194-196

Finding Peace Amid Despair,
   216-219

Fog of Uncertainty, Cutting
   Through the, 134-136

Follow Me Home, 203-206

Form, Love in its Purest, 159-162

Foster, Valerie J., 88

Four Glorious Days, 91-94

Fowler, Marilyn, 97

Free at Last, 116-118

Freeman, Colleen, 75

Friend, Advice From a Dear,
   228-230

G

Gass, Sue, 212

Giese, Georgianne, 191

Gift of Grace, The, 57-60

Gift, Life-Changing Birthday,
   230-233

Gifts, Hidden, 194-196

Gleason, Nicole, 62

God, Finding a Personal,
   119-121

God, Healing With, 129-132

God's Voice,
   Expressing, 144-149
   Journeying to, 137-139

Goose Bumps From Heaven,
   30-33

Grace, The Gift of, 57-60

Grimm, Anita, 56

H

Halter, Tom, 123

Healing
   for a Wounded Heart, 209-212
   With God, 129-132

Heart,
   Coins From the, 225-227
   Healing for a Wounded,
     209-212
Heaven, Goosebumps From,
   30-33
Hellenberg, Kathleen, 73
Hidden Gifts, 194-196
Hill, Russell, 156
Hindu Prayer for Peace, 70
Home, Follow Me, 203-206
Homeless Man, A, 181-183

I

Initiation, 74-75

J

Journeying to God's Voice,
   137-139
Joy, Sharon, 196
Junk-Wright, Vicki, 172, 173

K

Killgallon, Connie, 235
King. Jr., Martin Luther, 125

L

Laferty, Marie, 219
Lanoie, Paul, 103

Lelekatch, Gayle, 36
Lewis, Tonya, 78
Life,
   the Buick That Changed My,
     36-39
   the Subway Train That Saved
     My, 19-22
Listener, The, 70-73
Loan, On, 85-88
Lord Stay With Me, 34-36
Love in its Purest Form, 159-162
Love,
   Falling in, 156-159
   Lukie's, 62-66
Luma, Jamara, 194

M

MacDonald, Myra s., 139
Man Who Hears the Voice, The,
   43-47
Man, a Homeless, 181-183
McClintock, Tara, 177
McClung, Rosalie, 152
McCullough, Judith, 227
McDonald, Jodi, 53
McIntosh, Caroline, 165
Milam, Debbie, 27
Miller, Theresa, 181
Moldovan, Donna, 136
Mom and the Birdhouse,
   132-133
Monahan, Jennifer, 216

Monster to Emissary, From, 66-69

Moon, Snake Around the, 94

Mouth of a Stranger, Through the, 98-91

Mulrooney, John, 133

Mummy Murder, The, 94

N

Name, The Day I Got a New, 108-111

Nelson, Terri, 33

O

Oakley, Shannon, 222

Oneness, Remembering, 60-62

P

Peace Amid Despair, Finding, 216-219

Peace, Hindu Prayer for, 70

Polar Bear Club, 22

Power, Christine, 66

Prayer for Peace, 70

Prayers, Tiny, 54-56

Prisoner's Experience, A, 28-30

R

Remembering Oneness, 60-62

Robertson, Leonard, 22

Romano, Ariadne, 29

Ross, Grace, 183

Ruiz, Stephen, 69

S

Sapsford, Marilyn, 115

Saved My Life, The subway Train That, 19-22

Schock, David, 85

Sensation, A New, 149-152

Sermon, The Surrogate, 50-53

Shade, The, 79-81

She is Mine, 15-18

Silbermann, Susana, 169

Sisters, Brothers and, 125-128

Smith, Jamie McNiven, 128

South, Drive, 81-85

Speaks Up, God, 192-194

Stranger, Through the Mouth of a, 89-91

Subway Train That Saved My Life, The, 19-22

Succumbing to an Unlikely Death, 98-101

Surrogate Sermon, The, 50-53

Synchronicity, Simple, 169-173

T

Talarico, Vecchi, 203

Tap, Tap, Tap, 178-181

Tattooed Angel, The Lesson From the, 25-27

Teddy, Ugly, 188-191

There All Along, He Was, 234-235

Thing, The Simplest, 123-125

Third Time's the Charm, 222-225

Three Words, 95-97

Time,
Just in, 111-115
One Breath at a, 140-144

Tims, Yolanda, 209

Tiny Prayers, 54-56

Tracking the Divine, 94

Twin Towers Fell, The Day the, 48-49

Twist of Faith, 152-156

U

Uebersetzig, Janice, 25

Ugly Teddy, 188-191

Upanishads, the, 70

V

Voice,
Expressing God's, 144-149
Journeying to God's, 137-139
The Man Who Hears the, 43-47

W

Whisper in my Dreams, The, 23-25

Whispers, God's, 166-169

Wilcox, John, 206

Wolfe, Joseph, 30

Words, Three, 95-97

Wounded Heart, Healing for a, 209-212

Y

Yellow Just Like Me, Throw-Up, 40-43

Yourself, Fall in Love With, 219-222

Z

Zimman, Rebecca, 107

ABOUT THE AUTHOR

In 1989 at the age of 21, DavidPaul Doyle knew the direction he had plotted for his life. From the 8th grade, his passion had focused on his becoming a fighter pilot, an astronaut, and eventually running for the United States Senate. Having studied in Russia and worked in the American Embassy in Moscow, and with his third year at the Air Force Academy only two weeks away, his life's goals were unexpectedly turned upside down by an extraordinary event. While riding in a car, listening to his favorite sax musician, he was suddenly enveloped by a powerful wave of overwhelming love. It was unlike anything he'd ever experienced or had even known existed. Out of this incredible infusion of love, a question formed in his mind: "If I was an old man on my deathbed, what would I have done in my life to have had absolutely no regrets?"

The question was answered as a bright light materialized in his mind. Rays from the light reached out to touch other lights, and a vivid vision of his future and true purpose became clear. It predicted he would write books that would impact people's lives throughout the world.

The thought of becoming an author had never occurred to him. Though he had no clear knowledge what form this prediction would take nor what sort of books these might be, DavidPaul was transformed by this unexplained phenomenon. He turned his back on his dreams of becoming a pilot and made an instant decision to leave the Air Force Academy. Finishing his education at UC Berkeley, he threw himself into the single-minded aspiration of understanding and experiencing the source of this profound love and truth that had so changed his life.

After years of devoted study and commitment to a spiritual path, DavidPaul has dedicated his life to helping others open themselves to God's Voice and to discovering their own true natures. He has traveled worldwide conducting seminars and workshops to enthusi-astic crowds on how to hear God's Voice, has coauthored *The Voice for Love: Accessing Your Inner Voice to Fulfill Your Life Purpose*, and has con-ducted tele-classes, year-long certification and teachers' programs, delivered free daily inspirational messages online, and produced the 30-day course, *How to Hear the Voice of God*.

DavidPaul's heart lies in teaching. His passion is to reach as many people as possible with the gift of spiritual discovery, and hopes this book of collected stories from people around the world who have experienced communication with God will inspire readers to want to learn more about hearing God's Voice and to recognize the many ways they already hear this Voice in their lives.

For more information, visit *www.thevoiceforlove.com*.